EYEWITNESS COMPANIONS

Religions

PHILIP WILKINSON

"KNOWING THE GOD... ONE IS FREED FROM ALL BONDS."

Svetasvatara Upanishad, V

LONDON, NEW YORK,
MUNICH, MELBOURNE, DELHI

Managing Editor   Debra Wolter
Managing Art Editor   Karen Self
Americanization Editor   Jenny Siklos
Production Controller   Sophie Argyris
Production Editor   Tony Phipps
Art Director   Bryn Walls
Publisher   Jonathan Metcalf

Produced for Dorling Kindersley by

cobaltid

The Stables, Wood Farm, Deopham Road,
Attleborough, Norfolk NR17 1AJ
www.cobaltid.co.uk

Editors

Marek Walisiewicz, Kati Dye,
Jamie Dickson, Louise Abbott

Art Editors

Paul Reid, Darren Bland,
Claire Dale

First American Edition, 2008

Published in the United States by
DK Publishing
375 Hudson Street
New York, New York 10014

08 09 10 11   10 9 8 7 6 5 4 3 2 1

ED614   August 2008

Copyright © 2008 Dorling Kindersley Limited
Text copyright © 2008 Philip Wilkinson
All rights reserved

Published in Great Britain by Dorling Kindersley Limited.

A catalog record for this book is available from the
Library of Congress.

ISBN 978-0-7566-3348-6

DK books are available at special discounts when purchased in bulk for sales
promotions, premiums, fund-raising, or educational use. For details, contact:
DK Publishing Special Markets, 375 Hudson Street, New York, New York 10014
or SpecialSales@dk.com.

Color reproduction by Media Development Printing Limited.
Printed and bound in China by Leo Paper Products Limited.

Discover more at

www.dk.com

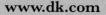

CONTENTS

RELIGION PLAYS A MAJOR PART IN THE LIVES OF
MILLIONS OF PEOPLE AROUND THE WORLD. BELIEF
IN GOD OR THE GODS GIVES COUNTLESS PEOPLE
A SENSE OF PURPOSE AND MEANING. BELIEFS,
DOCTRINES, AND SACRED TEXTS GIVE PEOPLE
MORAL GUIDANCE. RELIGIOUS LEADERS OFFER
INSTRUCTION AND MAY BECOME ROLE MODELS.

Religions provide a sense of moral purpose and a focus for spiritual expression, but the world's belief systems have many "incidental" results too.

The world's faiths organize and carry out all kinds of charitable and aid work, helping the poor, healing the sick, and campaigning on behalf of the disadvantaged. Religion has inspired some of the planet's greatest paintings, sculptures, and music. Many of the most remarkable buildings in the world are churches, mosques, or temples.

A crucifix from medieval Europe, where images of Christ replaced local gods as objects of worship.

Religion often occupies the center of the world stage in politics, diplomacy, and even war. More positively, temples, churches, and mosques are often the centers of their communities, participating in education, welfare, and social services for those who need them most. Despite the changing nature of our times, religion is still at the heart of our lives.

COMMON ROOTS

The faiths of the world are very diverse. They range from ancient primal or tribal religions to new religious movements; from those, like Islam, that believe in one God to those, such as Hinduism, that honor many deities. This book begins with a chapter called "What is religion?" that looks at the things religions have in common—features such as doctrines, stories of God or the gods, systems of ethics,

patterns of worship and ritual, and sacred objects or places. Looking at these shared areas, one can begin to see the similarities between the varieties of our religious experience.

GUIDE TO THE FAITHS

The main body of this book explores in turn the religions that have the most adherents and have had the most influence through history. After the primal religions comes the group of monotheistic faiths (Judaism, Islam, Christianity, and Zoroastrianism) that first flourished in the Middle East before spreading far and wide across the globe. These are followed by the four key Indian religions (Hinduism, Buddhism, Jainism, and Sikhism) and a trio of Eastern belief systems (Confucianism, Daoism, and Shinto).

Next comes a selection of the numerous new religious movements that have taken hold over the last hundred or so years, and which continue to demonstrate humanity's amazing capacity to explore the meaning of life and belief.

The book ends with a "who's who" of religious figures and a reference section that enables the reader to look up key figures (deities, prophets, and others) quickly, and notable facts and statistics about religions.

Borobudur, a 9th-century Buddhist monument in Java, central Indonesia, is impressive evidence of the faith's ancient heritage.

WHAT IS RELIGION?

O RIGINATING FROM almost every corner of the globe, the world's religions are as diverse as its cultures. This makes religion difficult to define, especially as it deals with intangible concepts: God, the purpose of life, the afterlife, and so on. Nevertheless there are several threads common to all faiths the world over that make religion what it is.

Virtually every culture that we know of has some kind of religion. In fact, worship of God or the gods is so common that archaeologists, when they come upon some ancient object or structure that they do not understand, usually ascribe to it ritual or religious purpose. Not only is religion almost universal, it has also had a huge impact on human culture. For example, many of the world's greatest buildings, from medieval cathedrals to Mayan temples, are religious. And a great deal of literature, from Dante's *Divine Comedy* to the works of the great Sufi poet Rumi, not to mention the sacred scriptures of the world's great faiths, is religious in inspiration.

A medieval chalice, designed to contain the wine in the Roman Catholic rite of Mass.

ENDURING RELEVANCE

Religion, because it deals with the big issues in life—good and evil, first causes and last things—is important to people. Believers cling to their faith and some have even been prepared to die for it. In cultures where the state has tried to wipe out religion or to discourage it—for example, under the communist regimes that flourished in the 20th century—people carried on worshipping, even if they risked falling foul of a ruthless state. Even today, when, for many, science offers a more rigorous and hopeful set of answers to life's problems, people persist in their faith. Many of the major religions, including Christianity in the developing world and Islam worldwide—are

expanding and winning more converts. Religion is playing as prominent a role in life today as it has ever done.

RELIGIOUS DIVERSITY

For centuries, people have looked at the phenomenon of faith and tried to answer the question "What is religion?" They have come up with a striking variety of answers. The 19th-century English writer Matthew Arnold described religion as "morality touched with emotion." Around the same time, German theologian Friedrich Schleiermacher called it "a feeling of absolute dependence;" while the English cardinal John Henry Newman found its essence in "authority and obedience." English anthropologist Sir James Frazer, who was most famous for his text on comparative religion, *The Golden Bough* (1890), spoke of it as a way to appease the powers that "control the course of nature or of human life." The 19th-century German social and political theorist Karl Marx was suspicious of religion, quoting British writer Charles Kingsley when he called it "the opium of the people," but he also saw something positive in it when he called it "the heart of the heartless world."

In many cultures, the essence of religion is the relationship between humanity and one or more gods. But not all of the belief systems that we call religions have gods. Many Buddhists do not worship a deity, and Jainism (an

A Daoist priest prays to banish evil spirits from a commercial precinct in Taipei, while worshippers look on.

important and influential Indian religion) does not have a God. Another common thread in much religion is morality: teaching people to be good. But some religions, such as that of the Ancient Greeks, are centered on amoral deities, and other faiths, such as many primal religions, place more emphasis on honoring the gods in the right way than on living a moral life. Most religions have authority figures or ritual leaders who provide guidance and instruction. But some groups, including certain Protestant Christians such as the Quakers, reject the idea of the priesthood and insist that all believers can have access to the divine.

On close inspection, though, the world's religions are sometimes less dissimilar than they at first seem. There appears to be a sharp division between the monotheistic faiths (Christianity, Islam, and Judaism especially) and those, like Hinduism, that recognize many gods. But Hindus see their multitude of gods as aspects of one supreme reality, and even the Chinese have a supreme deity, the Jade Emperor or ruler of Heaven. Even so, it is difficult to generalize about belief systems. To understand why, we need only compare Shinto, with its countless spirits or *kami*, and Judaism, with its one

Muslim women at prayer in a mosque in East Timor, during the 'Id al-Fitr celebrations that follow the month of fasting, Ramadan (*see pp.138–141*).

A statue of Mary on the Hill of Crosses in Šiauliai, Lithuania. The site is a center for Christian pilgrimage in the Baltic region of northern Europe.

God; or Islam, with its proscription of images of God, and Hinduism, with its use of deity images for worship.

THE COMMON THEMES

Rather than settle on one phrase that tries to sum up all religions, students of religion today try for a more broadly descriptive approach. They speak of religions as belief systems that display seven or eight key features that are combined in each faith. The seven elements in this book are based on the key features listed by the British philosopher and theologian Ninian Smart in books such as *The Religious Experience of Mankind* (1969). The first feature is doctrine, a body of basic principles and

A brightly colored mask once used by shamans of the Tsimshian tribe of Alaska.

teachings. The second, mythology, comprises the stories about the gods and the history of the religion. Next comes the concept of religious experience, the way in which humans can encounter the divine, often in heightened states of consciousness. The fourth feature is the religious institution, which can be a vast global organization such as the Catholic Church or a small but organized body such as a Buddhist monastery. The next feature is the ethical content of the religion—the set of practical instructions that tell followers how to live their lives—which covers both Matthew Arnold's emotional dimension to religion and broader guidance about the correct way to do things. The sixth feature is ritual, the gamut of ceremony from solemn sacrifice to the joyous outpouring of religious festivals. Finally come the sacred objects and places: inanimate items, buildings, or natural settings that have some spiritual significance. Together, these seven features describe what is common to the varied religions of the world.

BIG QUESTIONS

Through its various common elements, religion addresses some of humanity's biggest questions. These issues are big in the cosmic sense, encompassing the creation of the world, the meaning of life, the significance of suffering and pain, and the realm of the supernatural. They are also big in the sense that they affect everyone, dealing with behavior and ethics. The beliefs of followers of primal religions touch day-to-day life and survival—worshipping the gods may be said to help the crops grow, or lead to success in the hunt. Highly developed belief systems, with their scriptures and sophisticated theological arguments, may seem remote from these primal faiths, but they are not. Every faith looks to the absolute in the hope of making life better on Earth.

RELIGIOUS COMMUNITIES

All faiths are also, in one way or another, both individual and collective. The believer may pray or worship at

Laksmi, the Hindu goddess of wealth, fortune, love, and fertility, in a typically colorful portrait that depicts her showering coins upon the world.

regular opportunities for followers to join together and many pay special attention to the notion of the religious community. Terms such as "church" or "synagogue" refer as much to groups of worshippers as they do to the buildings in which they worship. Religious people acting collectively have often been a powerful force for good in the world,

"WITH GOD ALL THINGS ARE POSSIBLE."

Matthew 19:26

home, or may take part in solitary meditation. For the Buddhist, solitary meditation may be the most important of all religious activities, and some Christians see private prayer as the activity that brings them closest to God. But there is usually also a coming-together—in collective worship, religious instruction, or work for the community—which allows people to share their faith. Most religions offer

helping the sick and the needy, taking part in education, and providing community services that, even today, are not provided by governments in many parts of the world. The collective aspects of religion are particularly emphasized at key times in the year, such as major calendar festivals, or at key times of life—for example, at birth, coming of age, marriage, and, when the time comes, death.

THE SPREAD OF FAITHS

The faiths that have had the most widespread influence began in various parts of Asia before spreading around the world. Western Asia, the Indian subcontinent, China, and Japan have all been fertile seed-grounds for major religions. Each of these areas has produced faiths with distinctive themes, from the emphasis on monotheism in western Asia to the development of the concept of *karma* in India.

A number of different factors led to the foundation of the major world religions. One was the presence of a rich indigenous religious tradition that was able to develop beyond the tribe or area where it first evolved. Hinduism, for example, traces its roots back to concepts that evolved thousands of years ago in what is now Pakistan—for example, belief in a number of different gods, and practices centering on the use of water for ritual cleansing. Elaborated and combined with other Indian

deities and ideas, these grew into the sophisticated belief system known today as Hinduism.

ROOTS IN ANTIQUITY

China also had an ancient polytheistic system that eventually influenced Daoism, Buddhism, and Chinese popular religion. And in Japan, Shinto had its roots in traditional beliefs in a multitude of spirits. Another early factor that allowed religions to develop was the emergence of religious leaders,

This map shows the geographical regions where the major world religions began, along with the approximate dates of their foundation or early revelation.

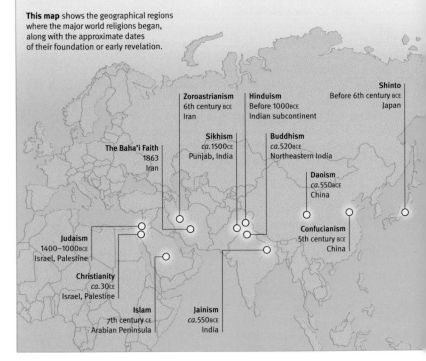

Shinto
Before 6th century BCE
Japan

Zoroastrianism
6th century BCE
Iran

Hinduism
Before 1000BCE
Indian subcontinent

Sikhism
*ca.*1500CE
Punjab, India

Buddhism
*ca.*520BCE
Northeastern India

The Baha'i Faith
1863
Iran

Daoism
*ca.*550BCE
China

Judaism
1400–1000BCE
Israel, Palestine

Confucianism
5th century BCE
China

Christianity
*ca.*30CE
Israel, Palestine

Islam
7th century CE
Arabian Peninsula

Jainism
*ca.*550BCE
India

The Alhambra in Granada is the 13th-century palace of southern Spain's Muslim rulers. Christians reconquered the area in 1492.

prophets, and teachers who became revered as mouthpieces of the words of God or interpreters of sacred texts and ideas. The teachings of Jesus Christ, or the words of God as revealed to the prophet Muhammad, inspired followers in western Asia and the Arabian peninsula.

THE WRITTEN WORD

A final factor was the growth of literacy, because once ideas and doctrines could be written down, a religion was no longer reliant on one group for leadership or teaching, but could spread as sacred texts were carried and distributed by travelers. The followers of the founding fathers of the world's religions soon began converting others in their own regions and beyond. Religious ideas

The Japanese goddess Kannon evolved from the Indian male *bodhisattva* Avalokitesvara as Buddhism spread east.

could also be spread by missionaries, migrants, teachers, soldiers, or merchants. The spread of religious teachings was further encouraged by educational developments, by political conquests, and by the growth of global trade. All of these carried Christianity and Islam far beyond the places where they first took hold. Trade routes also helped to spread Buddhism. Other faiths, such as Judaism and Sikhism, have been spread not by missionary work, but by the often forced migrations of persecuted peoples. The process continues to this day. In our modern era of mass communication, the spread of religious ideas and the creation of networks of faith has a new impetus.

RELIGION AND DOCTRINE

The basic principles of any religion are known as doctrines, which believers are taught to understand and accept. However, because they deal in concepts that are often hard to grasp, doctrines are also open to interpretation, which in itself leads faiths to change and diversify.

SOURCES OF DOCTRINE

Religious doctrines derive both from scripture, the sacred texts of each faith, and from the continual process of reading and interpreting these texts. Doctrines are therefore inseparable from the mythological context of religion. A religion's mythology (*see pp.22–23*), which we find written in the scriptures, provides a body of stories about God or the gods. The descriptions of the divine beings and the moral and ethical ideas that these beings put forward in the scriptures are themselves doctrinal. For example, Muslims found their belief in the One God of the Qur'an.

Sikh doctrine is laid down in the Adi Granth, which contains the teachings of Guru Nanak and nine other Sikh gurus.

exposition of the doctrine of *dharma*—the spiritual law that governs each person's conduct (*see pp.172–173*).

However, there are additional doctrines that do not come directly from the scriptures themselves, but from the way that later priests, scholars, and others have interpreted the sacred texts. These doctrines organize the stories in scripture and give them an intellectual framework. A body of religious narratives often provides a sweeping, frequently inspiring, set of stories, but it also leaves philosophical loose ends and begs many questions. Doctrinal thought addresses these loose ends, and tries to explain them and tidy

"TAKE THE BEST POSSIBLE HUMAN DOCTRINE."

Plato, *Phaedo*

This book, which Muslims believe is made up of God's own words, therefore contains a body of ethical and moral instruction that, according to Islam, comes directly from God himself. Another example is Hinduism, in which believers read one of their most important sacred texts, the Bhagavad Gita, both for its account of Krisna (an incarnation of the god Visnu often worshipped in his own right) and for its

them up, with the result of making religion more rigorous, more focused, and more structured for its followers.

INTERPRETING DOCTRINE

The monotheistic religions have a long history of doctrinal debate, and huge literatures that record the ways in which rabbis (in Judaism), priests (in Christianity), and imams (in Islam) have read, explained, or interpreted scripture. Many of their writings are concerned with guiding believers in the minutiae of life, but they also address the big doctrinal questions. For example, in a monotheistic belief system, there is an omnipotent God. This fact begs the question: if God is all-powerful, why does he allow evil into the world? This question has generated lengthy debates about free will, with Christian theologians concluding, for example, that God gives us the freedom to act so that we are able to make moral choices. Obviously doctrinal conclusions such as this have themselves to work within the framework of scripture, which for many believers comes directly from God. So specific groups of divinely guided people are often responsible for the formation of doctrine. Shi'i Muslims, for example, look to imams for doctrinal advice communicated directly from God. Catholic Christians heed the moral guidance of their leader, the pope; Jews respect the scholarly and doctrinal pronouncements of the early rabbis.

UNITY AND DIVISION

Doctrines are designed to bring the faithful together and to give believers a coherent set of beliefs to focus on. But, as we have seen, forming doctrines requires the debate and interpretation of scripture and this can lead to religious differences opening up. Disagreements and divisions may raise challenges and cause problems within a faith, but they also nurture in it an endless process of development and renewal. As a result, new varieties of religion and religious movements evolve all the time to take up the challenge of doctrine and to give believers new perspectives on life and faith.

Buddhist monks at the Angkor Wat temple complex in Cambodia, which has been an important religious center since the 12th century.

RELIGION AND MYTHOLOGY

A mythology is a collection of stories about God or the gods, covering particularly the origins of the cosmos and humanity, and the roles of the divine. A religion's mythology underpins its beliefs, explains the way the world is, and provides moral lessons to guide followers.

THE ORAL TRADITION

The mythologies of primal religions have been passed down orally for probably thousands of years. In general they show that cultures with an oral tradition have lived a life close to nature. Primal deities often take animal form and sacred places tend to be natural sites, such as rocks and springs, particularly in belief systems that need to explain certain features of the landscape. In addition, many primal deities exist to embody phenomena, such as the sun or the rain, on which humanity depend for food and survival. Although today many of these ancient, oral narratives have been written down, they stay alive most vitally in the mouths of those who recite them from memory, perhaps altering them slightly in the retelling, so that the living tradition of their faith continues to evolve.

Padmapani is one of hundreds of *bhodisattvas* that guide Mahayana Buddhists toward enlightenment.

In the primal religion of the Aztecs, the wind god Quetzalcoatl was instrumental in separating the Earth and heavens and creating the first humans.

MYTHS OF MANY GODS

The world religions, by contrast, record their mythologies in their sacred texts, the narratives, hymns, poems, epics, and other writings that define and diffuse their faith. Although a relatively "young" faith, such as Sikhism, might have a fairly small and well-defined body of sacred writings, most religions have a whole library of holy texts, many of them telling stories of God or the gods. Hinduism is an outstanding example, with many of its myths enshrined in two of the longest epic poems in the history of literature, the Ramayana and the Mahabharata. Chinese religion, which has countless deities, has also built up a vast body of myths. Even belief systems that are not necessarily "God-centered," such as Buddhism, may have a huge body of mythology. Buddhist texts tell the stories of the Buddha himself, and of the countless *bodhisattvas*, the saintly figures who help others along the road to enlightenment. These complex mythologies help to explain something about many Eastern religions—their ability to diversify constantly, to take new forms while also preserving something of the original.

STORIES OF ONE GOD

The monotheistic religions also have rich storytelling traditions. The stories of the early Jewish kings and prophets, for example, both provide the history through which the Jews developed their nationhood and identity, and offer a wide range of guidance on ethics, morality, and law. Both Christianity and Islam drew on these early narratives, while developing their own distinctive monotheistic belief systems. And they tell stories of their own, too. Islamic tradition tells many stories of the prophet Muhammad's life and deeds, giving moral insights that complement those in the Qur'an, which Muslims believe to be the word of God himself. In a similar way, tales of the early Christians supplement the words of Jesus. The accounts found in St. Paul's letters, for example, address pressing moral questions, such as the value of the bonds of love and of marriage, and show how the embattled early Christian church could survive in tough conditions and eventually flourish.

The Greek goddess
Athena was associated with heroism and chastity.

RELIGIOUS EXPERIENCE

Common to all religions is the idea that worshippers, in some way or another, can experience the absolute, or God. This experience is most obviously recognizable as a kind of heightened state of being—ecstasy, trance, exaltation, or calm—that reaches beyond the everyday.

FOUNDERS, PROPHETS, AND HEROES

Some mystical revelation or vision stands at the inauguration of many of the world's religions. The Buddha, meditating under a tree, reached a transcendent state that enabled him to see his solution to the problem of suffering in the world. The prophet Muhammad had the religion of Islam revealed to him when he received the words of God that are now collected in the Qur'an. The prophets of the Old Testament reported

A Buddhist yogi, like the Buddha himself, can enter a trance, which may afford deep spiritual insight.

direct and life-changing experiences of God, experiences that still inform the religion of the Jews. The blinding light of Krisna overwhelms the Hindu hero Arjuna in the Bhagavad Gita, filling him with amazement and devotion. Events such as these seem to throw inspiring light on God and accompany new perceptions about reality, and thus they open up new directions of thought and belief.

LEADERS AND VISIONARIES

Religious experiences are not solely the preserve of the founders and founding prophets of the world's

Pentecostal Christians build their faith around religious experience, including speaking in tongues and spiritual healing.

religions. Many faiths are rich with stories about how religious experience affected a belief system's first followers too. There is a famous example in the early history of Christianity. The Book of Acts relates how, after Jesus's crucifixion, the Holy Spirit visited the apostles in what is known as the first Pentecost. The apostles heard a sound like a strong wind, and then tongues of flame rested on each of them; then, "filled with the Holy Spirit," the apostles began to speak in unfamiliar languages. Foreigners of several different nationalities were gathered nearby. Amazingly, each listener heard the apostles speak his or her own language. Jesus's followers interpreted this remarkable event as a sign from God of the spiritual renewal—the birth of a Christian church, separate from Judaism—made possible by the Holy Spirit.

Similar experiences, apparently inexplicable except in terms of divine intervention, occur in the histories of other faiths around the world. They represent renewals of faith, instances of prophecy, and tangible confirmation of the benevolent work of God, or of many gods, in the mortal world.

Joan of Arc took guidance from the saints when she fought for France in the 15th century.

FOLLOWERS AND WORSHIPPERS

The world of prophets, saints, and historical figures can seem remote, but experience of an inspired or heightened state is familiar to many religious people today, too. In primal religions, the rhythmic beating of drums and continuous dancing can bring about a state in which participants can experience or even see the deity that they are worshipping. Taking part in any religious service that involves intense music, incense, dancing, or similar elements, can find worshippers in a state of religious experience, contemplating the absolute or drawing close to God. Such perceptions are not limited to ritual that involves aesthetic elements. Worshippers in more down-to-earth Evangelical Christian services sometimes experience "speaking in tongues," in a similar phenomenon to the first Pentecost described in Acts. And a practitioner of yoga or a meditating Buddhist can undergo a trancelike spiritual transformation that resembles a perception of the absolute. But religious experience is not limited to dramatic moments such as these. The deeply felt belief of Christians that the act of prayer enables them to communicate with God, or the quiet but meaningful glance exchanged between the image of the deity and the devotee in Hinduism, and similar moments during worship in other religions, all bring the ordinary believer close to the ultimate reality that they seek in their faith.

RELIGIOUS INSTITUTIONS

Religious institutions are the groups of people who come together to lead a faith. A religion may have a single, central leader, who presides over a highly organized administration; or it may have a less formal governance, or consist of several churches with local leaders.

PRIESTS AND TEACHERS

The roles of religious leaders vary from one faith to another. Some are scholars, people who study the sacred texts and help others to read and interpret them; some are teachers or gurus, who attract followers and inspire and instruct them in the faith; others perform a priestly function, presiding over sacraments and rituals. In many religions, the leaders may also play the role of spiritual guide, counsellor, or even healer; or do several of these jobs at once. Jewish rabbis are teachers and spiritual leaders, but, although ordained, are not priests. Christian priests and ministers teach and celebrate rituals and sacraments, as well as performing all kinds of pastoral duties, from providing spiritual advice to visiting the sick. Indian religions have produced many notable gurus, but may also have priests, such as the members of the Hindu brahmin class.

In many religions faith is centered upon instruction from a specific guru, who in Buddhism, for example, may be a teacher, the head of a monastery, or someone with extraordinary charisma or spiritual insight.

TYPES OF ORGANIZATION

The priests, shamans, teachers, counsellors, and other leaders of the world's religions operate within a wide variety of different organizational frameworks. Some, such as the Catholic Church, have a highly

structured, top-down organization, with a defined hierarchy of pope, cardinals, bishops, and priests (*see p.104*). Others, such as Orthodox Christianity, are made up of a number of independent churches, each with its own unique hierarchy. Other faiths are more loosely organized. Hinduism, for example, has no unifying creed and no overall hierarchy; however in countries outside India it does have umbrella institutions, such as Britain's National Council of Hindu Temples, which brings congregations together, works for the Hindu community, and provides information about the religion to non-Hindus. Other religions, notably some of the reformed Protestant churches, stress local organization.

The "new" religious movements that have multiplied over the last hundred years often have a highly centralized organization. This is because many of them began with the vision of a particular founder. This vision was translated over time into spiritual and moral leadership, which persisted after the founder's death. Those religious movements that have grown through missionary work are often highly institutionalized, with branches around the world reporting to a central headquarters. Publications can be key to their success, and faiths such as Christian Science and the Jehovah's Witnesses have put newspapers and other media at the heart of their highly successful missions.

This Baha'i House of Worship in Illinois in the US is a public symbol of faith as an institution.

Pope Benedict XVI (*left*) is the supreme head of the Catholic Church, while the Ecumenical Patriarch Bartholomew I (*right*) leads Eastern Orthodoxy.

ETHICS

Common to all the world's religions is the idea that we should try to live better lives. Sacred texts and later teachings brim with the moral instructions of early leaders, of prophets, and of God himself. The result is a rich framework of ethical values for all followers to live by.

THE EASTERN RELIGIONS

Moral instruction lies at the very heart of Eastern religions. Confucius, for example, was interested above all in teaching people how to live, and the writings and sayings attributed to him are full of moral guidance.

A church collection box from 1684 is carved with text promoting the Christian ethic of charitable conduct.

Values such as goodness are central to his thought, and he tells his followers how to base their relationships on those of an ideal, harmonious family.

Other Eastern religions describe very clearly the ethics that devotees should follow. One of the meanings of the term Dao (see p.251) is "the moral path." The Noble Eightfold Path (see pp.190–191) of Buddhism instructs people to cultivate the correct kind of behavior in the areas of understanding, thought, speech, action, livelihood, effort, mindfulness, and concentration. This Path and its ethical goals covers everything from one's everyday occupation to the sacred rites, from the best kind of job to have to the best way in which to meditate. Underpinning several of the Eastern religions (particularly Buddhism, Hinduism, Sikhism, and Jainism) is the concept of *karma*. This is the notion of moral cause and effect, that good actions in one life can have positive benefits—and so a better rebirth—in the next life. *Karma* underpins a host of ethical principles, from the Sikh commitment to the community to the Jain philosophy of non-violence. Such precepts show that even an exacting faith like Jainism (see p.224–233), with relatively few followers, has much to teach others, whatever their beliefs.

THE MONOTHEISTIC RELIGIONS

In the monotheistic religions of Judaism, Christianity, and Islam, moral precepts come from God. Jews aim to follow God's law as laid out in the Torah, as well as according to the interpretations of the Torah by later scholars and rabbis. Muslims follow the ethical instructions laid out in the Qur'an, which they see as the word of God as revealed to the prophet Muhammad. Christians

A Bangladeshi Muslim prays during 'Id celebrations. 'Id marks the end of Ramadan, a month of fasting and special emphasis on charity (see pp.138–141).

Both Jews and Christians adhere to the ethical and moral teachings that God laid down to the prophet Moses as the Ten Commandments.

follow the teachings of Jesus Christ, as recorded in the Gospels. Because Jesus saw himself and his ethics as in some way coming after and fulfilling the words and commandments of the Torah (which comprises the first five books of the Old Testament), Christians also pay heed to the ethical guidance found in the Jewish text.

teaches worshippers to obey the commandments of the Torah precisely and rigorously, but Reform Judaism (a movement that began in the 19th century and aimed to modernize the Jewish faith) interprets the laws of the Torah in a way that responds to the realities of modern life and lays strong emphasis on individual moral choice.

"THOU SHALT LOVE THY NEIGHBOR AS THYSELF."

Mark 12:31

All these sacred texts provide very specific instructions on how to live an ethical, moral life, and modern believers face the challenge of reading the ancient texts in a way that makes them relevant for today. This challenge has led, especially in Judaism and Christianity, to a variety of different branches of the religion, each offering a slightly different view of ethics and belief. For example, Orthodox Judaism

THE COMMON CAUSE

In all religions, there is heavy stress on both understanding the ethical teachings and acting upon them. People who live their lives fully in accordance with their faith command great respect. Across the variety of ethical viewpoints, two precepts stand out. The first is the notion of reverence for the absolute and respect for the moral insights this can bring. The second is the ethical "golden rule," common to all faiths—that is, that you should treat others as you would wish to be treated yourself.

RITUAL

A common theme runs through the practice of rituals in all the world's religions: rituals that resonate with the regular pulse of human life give believers chances to connect with the absolute—at specific stages of development, at particular times of year, or as part of regular worship.

RITES OF PASSAGE

Throughout most of the world, religion presides over the life-cycle rituals that mark the key transitions in a person's life—birth, coming of age, marriage, and death. Belgian anthropologist Arnold van Gennep was the first to describe these rituals scientifically, and his book *Rites of Passage*, published in 1909, gave such rituals the name by which we know them today. Rites of passage usually link important personal milestones to religious transformation.

Incense is burned in Catholic ritual—the smoke represents prayers rising toward heaven.

The ceremony involved helps both to mark the transitional point in the person's life, and to cement their attachment to their faith. For example, birth rituals, such as infant baptism, often involve either a naming ceremony or a rite that signals the child's admission into the religious community—and often both together. Coming-of-age rituals commonly celebrate the person's "rebirth" into the adult religious community—a 13-year-old Jewish boy, for example, becomes *bar mitzvah* or "son of the commandment" at a special ceremony held only for this purpose.

In many faiths further rituals mark other important events, including the appointment or ordination of a priest; and specific milestones in a person's religious life, regardless of age or life-stage, such as the Christian rite of confirmation.

CALENDAR FESTIVALS

Every calendar year includes certain religious festivals. Calendar festivals may mark key moments in the history of the religion, such as the birth of a god or prophet (for example, Christians celebrate Christ's birth on December 25). They may mark the end of a period of fasting, such as 'Id al-Fitr, which celebrates the end of Ramadan in the Muslim year, or the start of a new year. They are sometimes solemn events that remember martyrs or tragic times, but there may also be joyous feasts, such as the Jewish feast of Passover, which bring whole communities together.

REGULAR WORSHIP

The regular rituals of worship enable the worshipper to have a formalized connection with God or with the

A Jewish scholar cradles a Torah scroll as he reads holy texts. Judaism is rich in rituals that demonstrate the sincerity and commitment of devout believers.

absolute. Regular religious observances, usually performed in a set way, at certain times, and often at a specific sacred place, can involve prayer, singing, meditation, or other rituals. By worshipping in these prescribed ways, the believer not only engages in a kind of conversation with God; he or she also demonstrates a commitment to God. Faiths such as Judaism, Islam, and Sikhism emphasize this commitment because in these religions there is actually a divine commandment to worship or pray regularly.

The actual form the worship takes illustrates how seriously it is viewed within the faith and the depth of commitment on the part of the believer. For example, worship may take place frequently—Muslims pray five times a day and observant Jews three times. It can also often have an aesthetic quality—there might be beautiful music or eloquent prayers, and the person leading the worship might dress in elaborate robes or vestments.

For Catholic or Orthodox Christians, such elements are a key part of worship, of making their observance as worthy of God as possible. However, some faiths take an almost opposite view. A Quaker meeting can occur in a plain room in virtual silence, and a Buddhist might empty his mind completely while meditating.

Statues of Ganesh, Hinduism's elephant-headed god of wisdom and success, are ritually immersed in the sea every year to mark the god's birthday.

SACRED PLACES AND OBJECTS

Held in special reverence, sacred places and objects are often linked with specific deities, religious leaders, or specific times in a faith's history. Places may be marked with grand temples or monuments, but even a wayside shrine used for spiritual contemplation can be sacred.

NATURAL SITES

In many religions, holy places are natural sites that are remarkable in some way—tall mountains, wide or fast-flowing rivers, or large rocks. Such impressive natural features seem to stand out, and over time become associated with particular deities or religious stories. For the Ancient Greeks, for example, the gods lived on top of Mount Olympus. There are also sacred hill-top sites in Buddhism, Shinto, and Chinese popular religion. Rivers, especially the great Ganges River, are important in Hinduism. Many Hindus hope that they will die near the Ganges, so that when they are cremated, their ashes can be scattered on its waters.

HISTORICAL SITES

Other sacred sites mark places central to the history of a particular religion. The city of Jerusalem played host to important events in the stories of Judaism, Christianity, and Islam, and is sacred to all three faiths. Worshippers usually hold the birthplaces of religious leaders and prophets in special

The Horn of St. Hubert, patron saint of hunting, illustrates how traditional elements of people's lives are bound to religion.

reverence, too—from the birthplace of Jesus at Bethlehem to that of the Buddha at Lumbini, in modern-day Nepal, they are among the most revered of all sites.

Whether or not they have a specific association, churches, temples, and other places of worship are made sacred both by some formal ritual of consecration and by their continued use by the faithful. A place where people have worshipped for hundreds or even thousands of years is likely to attract still others. And whether it is a place designed with the utmost simplicity, like a Buddhist monastery in rural Thailand, or somewhere that has accumulated rich adornments, like a spectacular Catholic cathedral, it is likely to exemplify the faith of those who have worshipped there over the years.

PILGRIMAGE

Visiting sacred places is an activity that is common to most faiths—and is central to some. All Muslims hope to make the pilgrimage to the holy city of Mecca (in western Saudi Arabia) at least once in their lifetimes. In fact, this pilgrimage, known as the Hajj, is one of the five major tenets or Pillars of Islam—essential duties

The first stupas (bell-shaped sacred structures) are thought to have housed the ashes of the Buddha.

Mount Tai in Shandong province, China, is one of the five sacred mountains identified in the Daoist faith. Its spirits are believed to govern the fate of humans.

that every Muslim must perform (*see pp.134–137*). Buddhism, Hinduism, and Christianity also have strong traditions of pilgrimage. In most cases the pilgrimage has a certain set code or manner to which the devotee must adhere. For example, a pilgrim may have to dress in a specific way or perform particular rituals. Making the pilgrimage in the right way stresses the holiness of the enterprise and makes clear how much the pilgrim has in common with the countless others who have gone before. Whether a solitary expedition to a Buddhist shrine or part of a huge collective pilgrimage, such as the Hajj, the pilgrim's journey is often deeply moving or even life-changing, so powerful is the combination of place and spirituality.

HOLY OBJECTS

Objects can be sacred too. They can make real or tangible the believer's connection with a guru, prophet, or god. An object associated with a person or deity who might otherwise seem remote from our own lives and everyday experience can bring the owner's reality into focus and lend it substance, helping us to understand something of that being's character.

It is well known that relics of holy men and saints are revered by Christians, especially Catholics—the Shroud of Turin (the cloth in which Christ was said to have been buried) is the perfect example of this. But relics are also important in other belief systems. For example, the Temple of the Tooth at Kandy, Sri Lanka, houses what is said to be the tooth of the Buddha, making it a popular place of Buddhist pilgrimage. And for some, a simple object, such as a cross once owned by a religious leader or teacher may be said to have a sacred power.

DISTRIBUTION OF FAITHS TODAY

The long history of the world's major religions, combined with the upheavals of the past two centuries, have created complex patterns of distribution. Today, many Westerners follow "Eastern" religions; faiths such as Islam and Christianity have made rapid inroads in the developing world; primal religions still attract followers in advanced industrial societies; and some people follow no faith at all.

The Americas were transformed by colonialism and the subsequent creation of new nations over the past 500 years. North America is today dominated by Protestant Christianity, with significant Catholic populations in areas such as Mexico and tribal beliefs still strong in parts of the far north.

South and Central America remain largely true to the influence of Spain and Portugal, and so are strongholds of Catholic Christianity, with primal religions surviving in the Amazon basin and beyond.

KEY

- Roman Catholic
- Protestant
- Eastern Orthodox
- Sunni
- Shi'i
- Hinduism
- Judaism
- Buddhism
- Chinese Religions
- Shinto and Buddhism
- Primal
- Primal and Christian
- Primal, Christian, and Muslim
- Mormons

Europe has a strong Christian heritage (Protestant in the north, Catholic in southern and central Europe, Orthodox in the east), with emerging minorities of other faiths, from Islam to Hinduism.

CULTURES IN MOTION

Northern Africa, most of western Asia aside from Israel, and much of Central Asia are Muslim, while the changing cultures of sub-Saharan Africa are now host to countless new Christian churches and Muslim mosques, alongside traditional faiths.

India remains predominantly Hindu, but there are sizeable groups of adherents to other faiths, such as the Sikhs in the Punjab. Southeast Asia is a patchwork of faiths—for example, Buddhism in Thailand and Laos, and Islam in Indonesia. Buddhism is still dominant among many Chinese communities, while Shinto, Buddhism, and many local new religions flourish in Japan. All of these patterns of distribution are in a state of dynamic change. In spite of the fact that religion deals with absolutes, the map of world faiths is as fluid as ever.

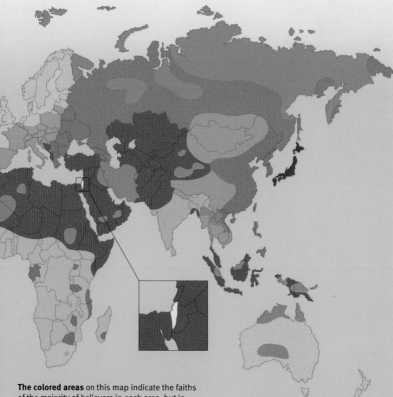

The colored areas on this map indicate the faiths of the majority of believers in each area, but in most parts of the world there are also significant minorities following other religions.

PRIMAL RELIGIONS

S OME OF THE WORLD'S most distinctive religions belong to those people who live traditional "tribal" lifestyles in different parts of the world. There is no universally accepted term for these religions—many tribal societies do not even have their own word for religion—but writers widely use the term "primal religions" for faiths that are rooted in indigenous culture.

The phrase "primal religions" means "belief systems that came into being before the great worldwide religions." These religions developed before their adherents were literate, so their beliefs and traditions have been handed down by word of mouth, in some cases over thousands of years or scores of generations. There are still followers of primal religions among the indigenous peoples of parts of North and South America (especially in northern Canada and the Amazon Basin), in sub-Saharan Africa, in Australia, and in parts of northern and eastern Asia. These religions may be some of the oldest faiths practiced today. But this great age, and the tribal lifestyles lived by many of their followers, does not mean that the faiths are unsophisticated. On the contrary, primal religions have evolved into complex belief systems, tailored to the needs of their adherents.

COMMON IDEAS

The religions followed by people as diverse as the Inuit of North America and the Australian aboriginals are

"LOOK FOR THE GODS WHEREVER WIND BLOWS."

Aztec poem

varied, but they do have some broad similarities. Adherents often live isolated lives away from modern conveniences. They come face to face with extremes of climate, food shortages, and natural disasters, such as floods and earthquakes. Primal religions provide a focus to help indigenous peoples to cope with these problems. These religions have thousands of spirits or deities that help to explain the powerful natural forces of the cosmos, and offer a way to live in harmony with these forces. Much of their religious practice is concerned with the proper worship or pleasing of these spirits, to prevent disasters or to elicit help or mercy when problems occur.

Another common theme among primal religions is that the spirits shape the lives and destinies of individuals. Spirits are present in ceremonies that mark key stages in life, from birth, through coming of age, to death. Presiding over such ceremonies are those most skilled in religious practice— either shamans who can make

Primal religions make use of artefacts, such as this fertility doll from Angola in Africa, to solicit the aid of spirits in their followers' lives.

"journeys" to the spirit world, or elders who are steeped in the ways of the gods. These experts keep much of their knowledge a closely guarded secret.

A SECURED FUTURE

As the European powers began to colonize much of the world between the 16th and 19th centuries, primal religions came under threat. But in the post-colonial era, indigenous peoples have kept hold of their identities and their religions. There are still between 200 and 300 million people living tribal lifestyles all over the world. Many of these people see their beliefs as vital, not just to the survival of traditional cultures, but to the very life of those who live in places populated by the spirits of their ancestors and by the deities whom, they believe, brought that land into existence.

The ruined city and temple complex at Palenque in Mexico was a center for Maya culture and religious belief from the 4th to the 8th century CE.

ORIGINS AND HISTORY

The origins of primal religions are so remote that it is impossible to pinpoint them exactly. Archaeologists interpret many ancient remains, such as cave paintings, menhirs, and stone circles, as religious in origin, but no one knows for sure what beliefs inspired their creation.

There have been many ideas about the early histories of primal religions. However, these beginnings occurred so far back in time, among people who have left no written records, that the theories are impossible to prove. The writer Sir James Frazer (1854–1941), in his book *The Golden Bough*, traced a development from the use of magic to proper religion, in which devotees used rituals to appease or propitiate the

An elaborate Maori carving of a Polynesian creator god, from Whakarewarewa in New Zealand.

gods. Other anthropologists argued that beliefs began with the idea of an impersonal spiritual power before people developed the notion of personal gods or spirits. Others, such as the psychoanalyst Sigmund Freud (1856–1939), looked to beliefs such as totemism (a set of beliefs linked to sacred beings or objects associated with

a kinship group) to explain primal religions. Still others, intent on finding links with later monotheistic faiths, especially with Christianity, insisted on the presence of a high God behind the myriad traditional spirits.

Theories such as these mostly tell us more about the theorists than about the origins of religion. Little can be said for sure about the first religions except that early peoples had a rich material culture—from rock art to stone circles—which was probably used for religious purposes, and that early cultures showed a deep interest in the natural world, the heavens, and ritual.

A LONG PREHISTORY

It is tempting to see the religions of ancient tribal societies as unchanged for millennia. The lack of written records seems to reinforce this view, but the truth is that tribal religion is likely to have been much more fluid and complex. For example, in West Africa, different tribes gained and lost power with the rise and fall of kingships, such as the Asante kingship of Ghana. Powerful kings sometimes adapted religions to provide a way to bolster their power—but opponents could also use rival cults as a means to express dissent. In a similar way, in Central Africa religious prophets sometimes attacked the actions of political leaders who abused their power. Religion could

---

ANCESTORS

Many of the most ancient religions incorporate beliefs about ancestors. Previous generations play a major role in traditional African, American, and Australian beliefs. In some cases, such as in Australian aboriginal religion, the ancestors are seen as creators at the center of the beliefs of each tribe and are essential to the people's identity. In other tribes, such as those of Africa, ancestor cults have had a huge effect on daily life because, in defining lineages, they influence key aspects of existence, such as whom a person may marry or what goods or land they may inherit.

adapt, and defining influences change, even though concrete evidence for this process remains sparse.

THE COLONIAL ERA TO MODERN TIMES

Traditional religions came under attack when European colonizers took power in much of Africa, Australia, and the Americas. In Central and South America, Catholic missionaries followed the 16th- and 17th-century conquerors from Spain and Portugal. The attack on primal beliefs in Africa and Australia became especially active from the 18th century, as European countries, from Britain to Belgium, developed colonies there. Colonial leaders encouraged Christian missionaries to convert people to their religion, while Western politicians took over land that contained sacred spaces. These conquests put primal belief under vast pressure.

Since then, the spread of scientific ideas and the adoption of modern technology has tended to marginalize traditional beliefs about how the gods help the crops to grow or how devotees should perform rituals before the hunt. The rise of new Christian churches, especially in Africa (*see pp.122–123*), has also been a major agent for change. But, against the odds, traditional religions have survived in many places. The network of relationships between humans and the natural world that is embodied in African religion is as relevant today as it ever was. And the concern of the Australian aboriginal religion with sacred places has helped native peoples to define their right to the land. Primal religions still have a powerful resonance today.

Totem poles, some dating back 185 years, stand on display at Totem Heritage Center and Nature Park in Ketchikan, Alaska.

CORE BELIEFS

At the core of most primal belief systems lie myriad spirits or deities, believed to be enormously influential over life on Earth. These spirits live everywhere, and are especially associated with nature, signaling the close link between tribal peoples and the land that they inhabit.

Certain notions are common to many of the world's primal religions—a belief that we are not alone on Earth, there is a close relationship with the land and the natural world, and a feeling that humans often need some help or guidance from higher powers. These notions are fostered by the idea, in the primal religions of every continent, that the cosmos is populated by countless spirits. These kinds of spirit-based religions are sometimes known in the West as "animism" (a term that derives from the Latin word for "spirit").

A CROWDED PANTHEON

The many spirits or deities are diverse beings, both in their overall role and in their relationships with humans. Some are similar to the gods of other religions —their roles are to control one or more specific aspects of the cosmos. Ogun, for example, is the deity of metalwork in the religion of the Yoruba in Nigeria; the Hawaiian god of war is called Kukailimoku. Other spirits are less powerful or less specific in their power, but still have significant influence over human life; many are benevolent, but some are evil or mischievous spirits whom devotees have to appease with prayers and offerings. In addition, some cultures have a high god or a creator spirit. Such deities, although clearly important in the world view of believers, are often distant, remote

Tikis at Pu'uhonua O Honaunau (Place of Refuge) National Park, Hawaii. These large, humanoid sculptures mark sacred places in Hawaiian culture.

A Vodun fetish ceremony in Benin takes place while a crowd looks on. Vodun beliefs later spread to the New World and inspired the Voodoo religion of Haiti.

complex and varied. A single culture may recognize thousands of spirits, and no one person will know about them all.

ENCOUNTERS WITH THE SPIRITS

Many people encounter the spirits when they are told their myths by a shaman or story-teller. But contact with the world of the spirits can often be more personal, and sometimes more frightening, than this. The spirits are everywhere—every rock or large tree may have its spirit, every spring or waterfall. So there are many opportunities for the spirit world to make its presence felt.

People often attribute their dreams to the spirits, and may visit a wise man or woman to have their dreams interpreted. Many primal religions also have rituals that encourage heightened or ecstatic states, during which people may have visions or speak in the language of the spirits—which again requires interpretation. Possession by a spirit may be something that needs the help of a shaman or other practitioner. In all these ways, believers may meet with spirits, and each meeting with them reinforces the overarching belief in primal religions that humanity is not the only inhabitant of Earth.

figures, who communicate with humans through the religion's many other spirits rather than by direct contact.

THE WORLD OF MYTH

The beliefs of traditional cultures about the way in which the spirits created the world, their various powers, and their relations with humanity are mostly laid down in myths. These stories, handed down orally from one generation to the next, are often long and complex. As well as recounting key events such as the creation, they also relate how people acquired the skills they needed to survive, many of which are believed to be the gifts of the spirits. The skills of hunting or of using fire, and the techniques of pottery or house-building, may be held to have come from the spirits. The myths that tell of these gifts are therefore hugely important in defining the identity of a people. Although these stories have been preserved carefully by word of mouth, they are amazingly

"THOSE WHO ARE DEAD ARE NEVER GONE."

Leopold Senghor, *Chants d'ombre*

The Dogon people of Mali, West Africa, have a complex religion involving ancestor-worship. Members of a group called the Awa society are charged with carrying out many Dogon rituals, often wearing masks. The meanings of these masks are known only to the society's initiates.

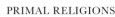

PRACTICES AND FESTIVALS

Ritual plays a major part in primal religions, with ceremonies used both to please or propitiate the spirits and to enlist their help in all kinds of human activity, from agriculture to warfare. Rites of passage, especially to mark the beginning of adult life, are also popular.

Many rituals and other religious practices bind a tribe or society together. For example, in many tribal groups, if one person is sick, the whole group may come together to take part in healing dances or chants, with the aim of releasing a spirit that has possessed the sick person. If a cure is not forthcoming and the patient dies, there are further rituals that have to take place to make sure that the whole tribe maintains a positive relationship with the spirit world. A priest or shaman (*see pp.48–49*) may perform such rituals, but in many places the rest of the community participates in them, too.

Rituals may also accompany key events in life or important times of year. In traditional island societies, as in Melanesia in Oceania, there may be rituals to perform before undertaking a sea journey or welcoming a visiting

> **RITUAL MASKS**
>
> In the ritual practices of many tribal peoples, such as the Yoruba of western Nigeria, masks play a central part. The mask is much more than a piece of ceremonial costume. Made with great care—sometimes in secret—by a skilled craft worker, and looked after with reverence, it is the item that enables the wearer to "become" the spirit invoked in the ritual. The Yoruba Epa mask (*left*) named after the wood-carver god Epa is carved from a single piece of wood and can be up to 5 ft (1.5 m) tall.

Observances such as these help to nurture the complex web of relationships, between one person and another, individual and tribe, and tribe and the spirits, on which society depends.

KINDS OF RITUAL

Making an offering to the spirits or gods of something valuable to the people—a sacrifice—is common to many primal

"THE GOD LOVED MUSIC, OR AT LEAST NOISE."

E. E. Kellet, *A Short History of Religions*

trader. Among farming peoples there will be rites associated with planting and harvest. Hunter-gatherers, such as the Australian aboriginals, celebrate "increase rituals" to make sure they will find plentiful food that season. Most peoples have religious rituals for the initiation of a new ruler.

religions. In some cultures, such as those in ancient Mexico or the Kui of Orissa in India, there are records of human sacrifice—especially of prisoners taken during warfare—which devotees once offered to the gods. In New Zealand, although the Maori did not generally practice this kind of ritual sacrifice, followers offered the heart of the first person to be killed in a battle to the war god Tumatuaenga.

Other kinds of primal rituals involve shamans, who become possessed by a spirit and enter a heightened state during which they are said to be able to perform healings or other services to society (*see pp.48–49*). Some of these rituals are carried out in response to a specific problem—an illness or a drought, for example. Sometimes they are practiced as part of regular religious observance—for example, to mark the passing of the seasons or to welcome the arrival of the New Year.

In addition, adherents hold many religious rites in secret, carefully guarding them from outsiders. Many traditional societies have a prevailing sense of the sacred, which they have

A young Xhosa man wears face paint to take part in a ceremony that will initiate him into manhood.

to protect from "pollution" by members of other tribes or peoples.

COMING OF AGE

As well as celebrating key events such as births, marriages, and deaths, rites of passage play a key role in the transition from childhood to adulthood in primal religions. In many groups, the youths of the tribe undergo a lengthy ritual when they come of age. This usually involves them spending some time in isolation from the rest of their society, while tribal elders visit them to teach them about their adult responsibilities and may reveal to them secrets about their religion. Once the teaching is complete, the youths undergo a ritual of reintroduction into society. Such rites of passage form a pivotal event in the lives of the participants and ensure that religion continues to lie at the heart of a culture, assisting each new generation by passing along the values and traditions of the past to them.

Australian aboriginal men perform traditional dances during a meeting of tribal elders on Groote Eylandt in the Gulf of Carpenteria, Australia.

THE SHAMAN

Inspired by the gods, a shaman is a person who is able to make spiritual journeys to Heaven and Hell, and to control or incarnate spirits. Shamans use their powers to effect healings and other protective acts, to settle disputes, and to defeat enemies. Shamanism pervades the traditional belief systems of many peoples, especially those in northern Asia, but also in North and South America.

In the primal belief systems of Siberia and North and South America, the cosmos is populated by myriad spirits. These may be nature deities who reside inside such things as animals or trees, or they may be the souls of human ancestors.

An Inuit shaman mask. The mask is said to help the shaman "become" the spirit during ritual.

Some spirits are benevolent, some evil, but all can exert a powerful influence on human life. Shamans often have a special relationship with a specific spirit, who helps him or her and who is sometimes said to "marry" the shaman. By summoning and controlling the spirits, shamans aim to help their fellow humans in their daily lives.

Because of the help they can give through their contact with the spirit world, shamans are often seen as the most important people of their communities. Becoming a shaman usually involves a long period of training and a complex

A Shaman striking a drum during a ritual in Tuva, Siberia. The drum represents the universe, according to the belief system of the region.

A Mongolian shaman makes burned offerings to the spirit world in a forest glade.

initiation. A trainee shaman will probably spend a long time isolated from the rest of the community. He or she may fast and avoid sexual contact during this period. Experienced shamans will teach the novice about the rites and duties of the shaman, as well as the music or chants that will summon the spirits, and the spirits' likes and dislikes.

TOOLS OF THE SHAMAN

Shamans use a variety of special rituals and techniques to reach spiritually heightened or inspired states. Ceremonies involving music are especially common. Percussion instruments, such as rattles and, in particular, drums, play a central role in shamanic music. For many shamans, the drum is their most vital piece of equipment, because beating out a rhythm on the drum is said to summon the spirits. In Siberia, shamans see the drum as the mount —a reindeer or horse—that they ride on their journeys to other worlds. The shamanic drum, which is often shallow and round, may also be seen as a shield with which the user can fend off the weapons of the malevolent spirits that they may meet in the Underworld.

Another important piece of shamanic equipment is the mask. Wearing a costume or mask of the right type—that is, one that the shaman has made with the appropriate care and rituals— is a way to attract a spirit and, in some cultures, enables the shaman to "become" the spirit, or to become possessed by it. Peoples of shamanistic cultures treat both masks and drums with great respect and awe. They also hold hallucinogenic substances such as magic mushrooms (*see p.288*) in high regard, because people have used these and other hallucinogenic plants for centuries to induce trancelike states. Shamans often see these kinds of substances as teachers that instruct the user in ways to reach the spirits.

PRIMAL RELIGIONS

Traditional, primal belief is an important part of the identity of native peoples in North and South America, Africa, Asia, and Oceania—even in places where colonization has meant that traditional lifestyles have long been left behind.

THE AMERICAS

Various   Prehistoric   Less than 100,000

In spite of invasion and colonization by many different peoples from Europe, primal religions survive in parts of both North and South America.

NORTH AMERICA

The traditional religions of North America are as varied as the continent's scenery and climate. Over the centuries, religion has played so vital a part of all human life there that the native peoples of North America do not even have to distinguish it by its own term—they have no word that means "religion."

Everything, from animals and birds to the trees and the land, is part of the all-pervading religious vision.

In most North American cultures there is a supreme god who presides over the cosmos, but he or she is usually remote and adherents interact with the sacred through more accessible deities. The best known of these is a figure who combines the roles of trickster and shape-changer with that of culture hero —the creature who brings humankind the key tools of life, from fire to water. In some places he is known as Raven; in others, Hare; in still others, Coyote. Some cultures, especially those on the Plains who once relied on hunting, have an important deity called the Master or Mistress of the Animals. Many respect the Thunderbird, who brings storms. Others recognize the Hero Twins, who in some tribes are gods of war.

Even closer to humans are the guardian spirits. To contact their guardian spirits, people participate in a ritual called a vision quest. This often takes place at puberty, when a person fasts and prays until he or she has a

A Peruvian shaman conducts a ritual with coca leaves near the city of Cuzco. Shamans in Peru use the leaves to induce a trancelike state.

vision of the spirit who will protect them for life. Some people have especially powerful guardian spirits, sometimes giving them the ability to cure others of disease. These people usually become shamans (*see pp.48–49*) and take part in healing rituals, which sometimes involve the removal of objects from the bodies of the sick—objects that have allegedly been placed there by malevolent spirits. Another means to contact the supernatural world is through beings known as *kachinas*, who are said by the Hopi to bring life-giving rain and other benefits to those who believe in them.

A Raven rattle used by shamans of the Haida tribe in North America. Raven was seen as a trickster god.

SOUTH AND CENTRAL AMERICA

In South and Central America, a number of different civilizations have followed traditional religions that recognized many different gods. In most of these religions, three principal gods were key.

They are best known by their Aztec names: Quetzalcoatl (the feathered serpent who was the creator god), Huitzilopochtli (god of war and the rising sun), and Tlaloc (god of rain and agriculture). The Aztecs made human sacrifices to Huitzilopochtli, which they believed would give them success in war and ensure that the sun would continue to rise on their civilization. The Incas of Peru also worshipped many gods, with the sun god playing a vital role for them, too.

When the Spanish and Portuguese conquered South and Central America, they imposed Catholic Christianity, replacing a faith of many gods with one that revered many saints and worshipped one God. Catholicism also replaced the blood sacrifice of the Aztecs with the symbolic sacrifice of the Mass.

An Apache girl at her Sunrise Dance, or formal initiation into adulthood.

AFRICA

Various   Prehistoric   63 million

Africa's primal religions usually include a creator and many lesser deities, some of whom act as agents of the creator, while some are independent.

KEY THEMES

African traditions have many stories to explain how disease and death began. They often center around the disruption of a "golden age" of order and happiness. For example, a myth from Zaire tells how the supreme god and the humans lived together in the same heavenly village. But the humans quarreled and God exiled them to Earth. Here they built a tall tower to try to reach Heaven. When they did so, they held a noisy party on top of the tower to celebrate, but God did not like the noise, and cut down the tower, making permanent the split between Heaven and Earth.

Trickster figures also feature widely. These help humankind to cope with the hardships of life. In West Africa the trickster is a spider, who brings water; among the San Bushmen, the praying mantis steals fire from the gods.

All traditional African cultures see it as vital to observe the correct rituals to please the gods. Among the most common are animal sacrifice (often of chickens, sheep, goats, or other domesticated creatures) and the use of music (for healing, to encourage fertility, or for celebration). As well as the common life-cycle rituals, such as marriage and funerary rites, some of the most important ceremonies in many African cultures are the initiation rites that mark the transition a person makes from childhood to adulthood. Acts of making scars or bodily marks, or circumcision, are used to represent the taking-on of adult responsibilities.

Red Figure made from natural materials, used by the Nte'va people to ward off illness.

South African Sangomas are healers and ritual leaders who are supposedly chosen by their ancestors to follow a traditional training.

ASIA

📖 Various   ☸ Prehistoric   ⚰ Not known

Although Asia is the home of many influential organized faiths, such as Sikhism in India (*see pp.208–223*) and Confucianism in China (*see pp.238–249*), its peoples have preserved the knowledge of their countries' primal religions, too. We can glimpse the spirits of these primal faiths both in later belief systems such as Shinto (*see pp.262–271*) and in the shamanism practices of northern and central Asia.

ANCIENT BELIEFS

In many parts of Asia, the primal religions have been absorbed into the rich traditions of the later faiths that originated in the continent. In India, for example, early deities were absorbed into the vast pantheon of Hindu gods and goddesses; whereas in China, the host of traditional spirits, ancestors, and gods eventually combined with the ideas promoted in Confucianism and Daoism to create a vibrant polytheistic religion, known as Chinese popular religion, that still flourishes in Chinese communities around the world (*see pp.256–257*). The Japanese faith of Shinto incorporates beliefs in a multitude of spirits, or *kami*, who have played a part in Japanese religion for centuries—long before Shinto became a religion in itself.

SHAMANISM

Until recent times primal beliefs have survived in their own right in isolated communities in central and northern

The Naxi shamans come mainly from Yunnan and Sichuan provinces, China. Their religion is called Dongba.

Asia. Countries such as Mongolia and particularly Siberia are the homeland of shamanism, where the shaman, the divinely inspired person who can contact or visit the spirit world (*see pp.48–49*), lies at the heart of religion.

In some places, the spirit world of shamanism is seen as a high mountain. Shamans can travel either upward to the peak, where the gods are said to dwell; or journey downward from the base of the mountain, to enter the underworld, the home of the souls of the dead.

In the harsh conditions of central and northern Asia, the experience and vision of the shaman are thought to be vital for a successful life. The regions' climate and topography can make food hard to find—but a shaman can use his or her contact with the spirit world to locate the best places to hunt or fish. Shamans also use their spiritual powers to heal the sick, and to help to ease the journeys of those who are dying, taking them from this world to the realm of the spirits.

Some shamanic peoples of northern Asia believe that the world is carried on the back of a giant animal, which is variously described as a turtle, a bull, or a fish. Earthquakes are said to be the result of the animal shifting its position. In the center of the Earth is a Cosmic Tree, stretching up to the realm of the gods. For those who still adhere to these ancient beliefs, religion reaches to the very heart of the cosmos.

OCEANIA AND AUSTRALIA

📖 Various   ⚐ Prehistoric   ⛫ Less than 9,000 (Australia and New Zealand)

The scattered islands and peoples of Oceania, from Micronesia to New Zealand, and the Australian aboriginals, have a great variety of traditional religions. The belief systems of the islanders tend to be focussed on the sea, while those of indigenous Australian groups are in general more concerned with the interplay of people, deities, and the land.

POLYNESIA

Traditional religion in Polynesia is dominated by deities who preside over different aspects of life. Weather phenomena such as rain and thunder are especially important to islanders, who travel by the sea, making the gods

Huli warriors from the highlands of Papua New Guinea wearing traditional costumes while performing ritual dances at a tribal gathering.

who control these forces prominent. The gods dwell in a heavenly world, but are frequent visitors to Earth, and many religious practices, such as making sacred enclosures, are designed to encourage them to do so. Statues and masks are especially important, because people believe that the gods will be attracted to likenesses of themselves. Rituals, from sacrifices to chanting, are designed to attract the gods, please them, and send them back to Heaven. Devotees hold such ceremonies on various occasions, particularly before setting out on sea or fishing expeditions.

Among the gods, the most important are the creator Ta'aroa, and the trickster and culture hero Maui, who stole fire so that humans could cook their food, slowed down the sun to give people a long day, and fished up many

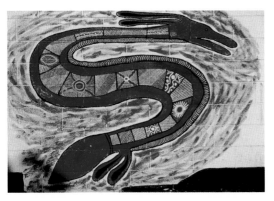

The Rainbow Snake of Australian aboriginal myth is associated with fertility, although in some tribes it is also regarded as the creator of the landscape.

of the Polynesian islands with his fish-hook. Some believe that he is the ancestor of all humanity.

MELANESIA

The many islands of Melanesia share a widespread belief in gods and spirits, the latter including both ghosts and the souls of ancestors. Treating the dead correctly is important in Melanesian culture, with funeral rites that can include lengthy mourning, disposal of the dead on a platform, and bone-collecting. Once the community has performed these and other rites, the deceased is still not always completely departed, and may reappear as a ghost or be revered at an ancestral shrine.

Masks play a major role in many Melanesian ceremonies. These often elaborate constructions of bark, leaves, and feathers are usually made ritually and in secret, and special rites attract a spirit to the mask and conduct it away when the ceremony is over.

AUSTRALIA

Each Australian aboriginal tribe has its own mythology, much of it concerned with explaining how the deities of the former time (known to outsiders as the Dreamtime or the Dreaming) gave form to the land. Some of these myths are local to the

Some Pacific cultures credited European artefacts, brought by explorers, with divine powers.

home of a specific people, but many overlap in a mythological web that extends over much of Australia.

This web exists in a spiritual dimension, too, with deities of the Dreamtime, ancestor spirits, and the people of today all interconnected both by religious rituals and by their links with the land. During the Dreamtime, powerful deities moved across the land, creating its distinctive features such as rocks, mountains, hills, rivers, springs, and lakes. Often quite complex stories explain how this happened, and the places named in the narratives have sacred significance. For example, one story explains how a primal fish created the bends of the Murray River, and the nearby swamps, by swishing its tail back and forth as the deity Ngurunderi chased it. Once he caught the fish, Ngurunderi sliced it up and distributed the bits in the various lakes around the mouth of the Murray, to become the different species of fish that live there and provide food.

Other myths describe how a creature, such as the Rainbow Snake, the Kangaroo, or the Lizard, created the landscape. Deities such as these are also said to have laid down social and religious customs, and they are reactivated during religious rituals. They also defined the organization of clans, and brought to Earth life's necessities, from food to fire. In these ways, as well as pervading the natural landscape that embodies them, deities are present in every aspect of life.

MONOTHEISTIC
RELIGIONS

T HE FAITHS centered on a single God have spread all over the world from their roots in the Middle East. In spite of the domination of science and rational thought in modern life, the beliefs, ethics, morality, and general outlook of monotheistic faiths endures. Judaism, Christianity, and Islam remain hugely influential, from the US to Africa.

Many of the world's oldest religions, such as Hinduism, Chinese popular religion, and primal religions from all over the world, envisage a cosmos with many deities. Different gods and goddesses perform different functions and often each has responsibility for a specific part of the universe, from the sun to the storms; from love to warfare. But throughout history, a number of cultures have perceived limitations with this kind of belief system. If there are countless gods, where is the ultimate authority or reality? The answer, for many people, is a monotheistic faith, in other words one in which there is just one true God, who is the source of the cosmos, reality, goodness, and truth.

Although they are not the only religions based on belief in a single God, three great monotheistic faiths, Judaism, Christianity, and Islam, have had a special influence all over the world.

HEARTLAND OF RELIGION
The three great monotheisms have several things in common. All have their roots in the Middle East. In figures such as Abraham (*see p.295*) and Moses (*see p.297*), they share a number of important patriarchs and prophets. They all emphasize the importance of prayer. They are all founded on a specific and different revelation from God. And they are all organized religions that also value the individual believer's experience of faith and God. Of the three,

The *kiddush* cup is used as part of a traditional Jewish blessing made over wine or grape juice.

Judaism was revealed to its followers first—Jews believe that the teaching of their faith, laid down in the Torah (*see pp.68–69*), was revealed to Moses by God on Mount Sinai more than 3,000 years ago. Although Judaism has no formal creed, this work forms the essence of the faith, and readings and interpretations of the Torah have guided Jews through their lives ever since.

Christianity appeared 2,000 years ago in the Jewish world. It is based on the teachings of Jesus and on the Christian Bible, which is made up of the Jewish sacred texts plus the New Testament, which

The biblical story of Jonah and the whale has been depicted many times through the ages. This painting comes from Europe's medieval era.

different, share a tradition. For this reason, adherents to them are sometimes called "people of the book."

GLOBAL INFLUENCE

The monotheisms have been hugely influential on human history. Even today, in an increasingly secularized world, their influence is widespread. Christianity, having spread to much of the Western world, formed and dominated the ethics and outlook of Europe and North America. It still has a huge influence there as well as in many other areas of the globe, such as Africa.

describes Jesus's mission and the work of his followers. Islam was revealed to the Prophet Muhammad in the 7th century CE, when the Prophet recited God's words, which were later written down as the Qur'an. The Qur'an is the heart of Islam, but Muslims also respect the earlier Jewish religious leaders, from Abraham to Jesus, whom they see as prophets. So the three faiths, although distinct and

Islam pervades the way of life in most of the Middle East, from devoutly Muslim countries, such as Saudi Arabia, to essentially secular states with a Muslim majority, such as Turkey.

Judaism, though numerically much smaller, also has a broad influence on life and thought worldwide—not least in the US. In their different ways, all three of the monotheistic faiths are exhibiting remarkable strength.

Hagia Sophia in Istanbul is 1,500 years old. Originally a church, it later became a mosque and is now a museum.

JUDAISM

Judaism is the religion of the Jewish people. For much of their history, the Jews were forced to live in exile from their homeland, making lives for themselves elsewhere in the world and taking their faith with them. As a result, today there are followers of Judaism in countries that stretch far beyond the Jewish state of Israel.

The oldest of the three great monotheistic religions with origins in the Middle East (the others being Christianity and Islam), Judaism has a history dating back to the patriarchs, such as Abraham, who are thought to have have lived around 2000BCE. One of these was Moses, who led the Jews out of exile in Egypt back to the "Promised Land" and received the tablets of the law from God on Mount Sinai. According to Moses and his followers, the Jews were specially chosen by God to receive his guidance in the form of the Torah ("teaching"), a term that can refer either to the Pentateuch (the first five books of the Hebrew Bible) or to all the Jewish laws. From these earliest beginnings, the Jews believed in one all-powerful, all-knowing God, and that the Torah is God's immutable revelation to Moses.

In the ensuing millennia, the Jews have undergone many setbacks and disasters: attacks from empires such as Babylon and Rome; exile and diaspora in the Middle Ages and later; massacres in the 19th century; and the disaster of the Holocaust in the 20th. But there have also been successes, from the development of Jewish philosophy and faith by the early rabbis to the foundation of the modern state of Israel in May 1948. The faith's long history has seen Judaism diversify, but all observant Jews believe in one God, pray regularly, and worship at a synagogue. They also share a host of customs— from observing dietary laws to holding ceremonies, such as bar and bat mitzvahs, when a boy or girl reaches puberty. These practices unite the Jews in a single community. Above all, Jews believe in the primacy of the Torah, which extols Judaism's central values: the sanctity of life, the importance of justice, the ideal of generosity, and the need for education.

This Jewish man blows a *shofar*, an instrument usually made from the horn of a ram and used during some important Jewish rituals.

ORIGINS AND HISTORY

The story of Judaism begins long ago, at the start of the vast timespan covered by the Hebrew Bible. The faith is defined by its early history and the work of the early scholars and rabbis, but has been shaped by the more recent problems and tragedies faced by the Jewish people.

BEGINNINGS

No one knows for sure exactly how or when Judaism evolved, but the Bible tells of two significant figures who were crucial to its beginnings. The first of these was Abraham (*see p.295*), the founding father or patriarch of the Jews, who migrated from Mesopotamia (modern Iraq) to the land of Canaan in the eastern Mediterranean. Famine drove Abraham's descendants from there to Egypt, where they lived as slaves, but their leader, Moses (*see p.297*), later led them back to Canaan, which God had promised the Jews during Abraham's time. On the way, Moses received the tablets of the law from God on Mount Sinai. This event, which is thought to have taken place in the 13th century BCE, marked the beginning of the covenant, or special relationship with God, that lies at the heart of Judaism.

This ancient stone tablet shows an Israelite man cutting corn using a simple hand-held sickle.

FOREIGN RULERS

After a period of self-rule under kings such as David and Solomon, in 586BCE the Jewish kingdom of Judah, in southern Canaan, was conquered by the Babylonians, under their king Nebuchadnezzar. The Babylonians destroyed the Temple in Jerusalem, and took many Jews into exile in Babylon. Here, some began to write the early books of the Bible to preserve their history and traditions.

The centuries following the Babylonian period saw the Jewish people dominated by a series of foreign rulers. In 538BCE, the Persians, who had conquered Babylon, allowed those Jews who wanted to, to return home. Under

STAR OF DAVID

In the 18th century, the Jews adopted the Star of David, a six-pointed star made up of two intersecting triangles, as a means of identification. Its origins are obscure. Some say that its shape represents the shield carried by David, the second king of Israel; others that its triangles refer to the Hebrew letter *daleth*, the first letter of David's name. A common interpretation is that the six outer triangles represent the days of the working week, while the inner hexagon symbolizes the Sabbath, the day of rest.

The Jordan River was crossed by the Israelites following Joshua, and today forms a natural border between modern Israel, Syria, and Jordan.

officials to rule the province of Judea, the Jews rebelled again, only to see their forces crushed and the Second Temple destroyed in 70CE. The Jews turned increasingly away from political ambition toward learning, with groups such as the Pharisees producing many notable scholars, including the famous rivals Hillel, a Jewish liberal, and Shammai, who interpreted Jewish law in its strictest sense.

JEWISH PERSECUTION IN CHRISTIAN EUROPE

In 392CE Christianity became the state religion of the Roman Empire. For many centuries thereafter, the Jews were widely persecuted by the Christian communities. They were expelled from many countries, forced to convert to Christianity, and excluded from the most well-paid jobs. Many lived in closed communities (called ghettos) and became merchants and moneylenders, the two jobs that they could take

the Greeks in the 2nd century BCE, the Jews, led by Judas Maccabeus, staged a successful rebellion, which led to the rededication of the Second Temple in Jerusalem and the establishment of a new Jewish ruling dynasty. However, in 63BCE this was overthrown by the Romans, who began by ruling through Jewish client kings, including Herod the Great (37–4BCE). Herod rebuilt the Second Temple in lavish style, but when the Romans installed their own

The Second Temple in Jerusalem was completed in 516BCE, but later destroyed by the Romans.

with impunity. Others remained in poverty, but became notable scholars. One such scholar was Maimonides (1135–1204), a philosopher and physician whose powerfully logical writings on Jewish law, philosophy, and medicine had an influence far beyond the Jewish world.

Two distinct groups of Jews developed on the fringes of European society. The Ashkenazi lived mainly in Germany, Poland, and Russia. The Sephardi lived in Spain, but were expelled in 1492, after which they

Auschwitz, in Poland, is the site of the infamous concentration camp where thousands of Jewish men and women were murdered by the Nazis.

diplomacy. They had other spheres of influence, too. Jews expelled from Spain carried both their own scholarship and their Arabic knowledge to Italy, helping to stimulate the Renaissance.

RELIEF AND REFORM
The 18th and 19th centuries brought better times for many Jews. Many European states, under the influence of the more open-minded thinking of the

"LET MY PEOPLE GO, THAT THEY MAY SERVE ME."

Exodus 9:1

settled in North Africa, Italy, the Ottoman Empire, and the Netherlands. For the entire Middle Ages, the Jews in Christian Europe withstood a life of persecution, although many grew rich through trade and benefitted because their life of travel and exile enabled them to take part in international

Enlightenment movement, gave them back some of their rights, although some Jews were still forced to convert to Christianity. Among those who remained steadfast to their faith were some major Jewish scholars and thinkers, some of whom, such as the German rabbi Abraham Geiger, spearheaded the Reform movement, updating Jewish liturgy and fitting the faith more responsively to the modern world. Reform Jews wanted to live more peacefully with their gentile neighbors, and they abandoned laws that hindered this; they also played down the importance of a hoped-for return to the Jewish homeland. There were various reactions to this movement. Some Jews rejected Reform, going back to the traditional values of Orthodox Judaism. Others followed the route of Conservative Judaism (*see p.83*). And in the 19th century, a very focused movement began to campaign for a return to the Jewish homeland. Known as Zionism, after the Biblical name for Jerusalem, it dominated the thoughts and hopes of many Jews throughout the late 19th and 20th centuries.

Tel Aviv is a thriving coastal city that represents the modern, rather than historical face of the Israeli state.

ANTI-SEMITISM

Although the 18th and 19th centuries brought more freedom to the Jews than they had enjoyed for centuries, a new horror was beginning. In the late 19th century, the prejudice against the Jews turned away from their religion and targeted their race—anti-Semites condemned all Jews, regardless of the branch of Judaism they followed or the part of the world they inhabited. This turned to tragedy with the rise of Nazism, the Holocaust, and the torture of millions of Jews in Europe. More than 60 years after the end of World War II, Jews and non-Jews alike are still trying to come to terms with what happened during that terrible period of history.

FOUNDING THE STATE OF ISRAEL

In 1948, the state of Israel was founded to allow Jews to return to their homeland at last. Many rejoiced that in Israel they would be able to build a just and fair society, where they could worship God in the homeland that he had promised them millennia before. From a tough beginning, settling on difficult terrain with hostile neighbors looking on, the Jews built a strong nation. But in spite of the benefits, there continue to be problems, challenges, and tragedies, especially in the relations between Israel and its Arab neighbors.

THEODOR HERZL

In 1894, the trial in Paris of Alfred Dreyfus, a Jewish French-army captain who was wrongly accused of treason, revealed the depth of anti-Semitism in Europe. Having reported on the case, in 1896 the Hungarian Jewish journalist Theodor Herzl (1860–1904) produced a pamphlet, *The Jewish State*, in which he argued for the creation of a Jewish state in Palestine. This work, and the first Zionist Congress the following year, led to the creation of a Zionist movement.

Theodor Herzl did much diplomatic work that laid the foundations for the eventual creation of the state of Israel after World War II.

CORE BELIEFS

The essence of Judaism is that a covenant, or agreement, exists between God and his followers. This covenant lays down certain instructions that Jews must follow. Judaism, therefore, is as much about how people live their lives as it is about concepts of the supernatural.

THE ONE GOD

For the Jews there is one God, who is the source of all goodness and morality. He is so holy that even his name, traditionally represented by the four Hebrew letters YHWH, was thought to be too sacred to utter. Instead, Jewish writers and rabbis used phrases such as ha-Shem ("the Name") and Adonai ("my Lord") when referring to him, to avoid committing blasphemy.

Judaism sees God as the absolute who lies behind the whole of the cosmos and life. He is a transcendent being, who exists on another plane from life on Earth. He is therefore impossible to portray in an image or to describe in words, although it is possible to name his qualities, among the most important of which are the complementary attributes of justice and mercy. But in spite of his remoteness, God is always present to the Jews and is able to communicate with humans in various ways—especially through the law handed down to Moses and the insights granted to the Hebrew prophets.

MESSIANIC BELIEFS

The prophets and rabbis looked forward to the time when a Messiah would come to establish God's kingdom on Earth. This Messianic belief remains strong in Orthodox Judaism. Orthodox Jews believe that a Messiah will one day rule in Jerusalem and rebuild the Temple there (see p.62). Other branches of Judaism lay less stress

> ### ABRAHAM AND THE COVENANT
> One of the main characters in the Book of Genesis (the first book of the Hebrew Bible) is Abraham. Although Abraham and his wife Sarah were old and childless, God promised them numerous descendants, who would form a great nation in a land called Canaan, if Abraham and his family pledged faith in God. Miraculously, Sarah and Abraham had a son, Isaac. Abraham, Isaac, and Isaac's son Jacob are seen as the founding fathers of Judaism. Abraham, or "the friend of God," provides a role model for Jews by showing faith, courage, sacrifice, and obedience to the deity.

on Messianic belief, concentrating on the ways in which God's commandments must be obeyed.

THE COMMANDMENTS

The first five books of the Hebrew Bible (equivalent to the Christian Old Testament) set out and explain the Jewish covenant. The second book, the Book of Exodus, explains the ways in which Jews are expected to obey God. It tells how Moses led the Jews out of captivity in Egypt and toward Canaan, the "promised land". On the way, Moses received the Torah, the words of the law, from God. These were written on stone tablets and later housed in a special container called the Ark of the Covenant. By accepting these laws, the Jews entered into their agreement with God. The fifth book of the Bible, the Book of

Jewish synagogues have a decorated cupboard called the Ark, which holds their Torah scrolls.

Deuteronomy, emphasizes that the covenant applies to all Jews, everywhere. It stresses that there is one God, and that Jews must love and follow him. This is made clear in a passage in Chapter Six, which is known as the Shema, from the Hebrew for its first word, "Hear." It begins: "Hear O Israel: The Lord our God, the Lord is One; and you shall love the Lord your God with all your heart, and with all your soul, and with all your might."

A menorah, or seven-branched candelabrum, symbolizes the eternal light of the Torah.

The passage tells Jews to keep these words in their hearts, to teach them to their children, and to talk of them continuously. It also instructs them to obey the commandments and live by the values of Judaism. The instruction to teach the words to children is important in that it establishes the idea of handing down the beliefs of Judaism from one generation to the next.

Education, still valued deeply in Judaism, has always been at the heart of the faith.

LIVING THE COVENANT

The Torah contains 613 instructions, covering everything from food and clothing to rituals and festivals. Orthodox Jews follow these laws exactly, expressing their faith and devotion through the way that they live. Adherents to other branches of Judaism interpret them more flexibly, but still see them as the cornerstone of their faith. The ceremony of bar mitzvah (*see p.78*), when a Jewish boy comes of age (the equivalent for girls is a bat mitzvah), marks the point at which the individual promises to follow the commandments of God.

Children march with miniature Torah scrolls during the Jewish holiday of Shavuot, which celebrates the day when God gave the Torah to Moses.

THE HEBREW BIBLE AND THE TALMUD

The essence of Judaism is contained in its most important texts—the first five books of the Hebrew Bible, known collectively as the Torah. But Judaism has always been centered on the word of God and on scholarship, so it is not surprising that it has produced a large body of other writings, too—not just the other books of the Bible, but also a vast work of comment and interpretation called the Talmud.

THE TORAH

Torah is a Hebrew word usually translated as "law," although it can also mean "instruction." The Torah, which tells the story of the first Jews and lists God's commandments to his people, is the most sacred text of Judaism. Every synagogue has a copy of the Torah, hand-written in Hebrew on a scroll and kept in a cabinet called the Ark, which is the focal point of the synagogue (*see illustration, p.66*). Each Torah scroll is written with great care, because its text is never changed and must not be transcribed inaccurately. The text is too sacred to be touched by hand. When a person reads from a synagogue's Torah, he (or sometimes

The Dead Sea Scrolls are internationally famous as an antiquity. They include early texts from the Hebrew Bible, which is also central to Christianity.

she) uses a special pointer, or *yad*, tipped with a metal hand, to follow the words. This ensures that the text is not marked or chipped. If such damage did occur, the scroll would be declared unusable and buried in a Jewish cemetery in a clay jar.

The rest of the Hebrew Bible is made up of the writings of the prophets (known as the Navi'im) and the other collected texts (the Ketubim). The Navi'im are especially important as they are the words of the prophets who brought the Jews back to their religion when they strayed, and who helped them when they were in exile. The Ketubim include books of history, lamentation, and, importantly, the Psalms, which are used in synagogue services.

A statue of Maimonides, a 12th-century philosopher and famed interpreter of the Torah.

THE TALMUD

Since the earliest times, rabbis have discussed and interpreted the words of the Torah. Early interpretations were handed down orally, but by 170CE, the body of comment had grown so large that Jews began to write down what the rabbis had said. This record became known as the Mishnah. It, too, spawned many interpretations, and these became known as the Gemara.

Mishnah and Gemara together make up a book of commentary called the Talmud. It contains around two-and-a-half million words, covering subjects as diverse as folklore and prayers, and rituals and medicines. Around one third of this material is *halakhah*, or law; the rest is the body of history, legends, stories, and maxims known as the *aggadah*. With its huge size and enormous diversity, the Talmud has something to say about every aspect of human life.

To protect the Torah from the damage that a pointing finger might cause, readers use a pointer called a *yad* to follow the text.

Mount Sinai, in Egypt, is a place of spiritual pilgrimage for many modern Jews. It is here that, as he made his journey back to the Promised Land, Moses received the Jewish law from God. The resulting covenant between God and his people forms the cornerstone of Judaism.

ETHICS, MORALITY, AND LAW

Judaism has hundreds of commandments, but Jews do not see their faith as legalistic. The teachings of the Torah and Talmud are highly practical and cover every aspect of life, so that in everything they do Jews are aware of their religion and of their connectedness with God.

THE AVOT

One of the most familiar parts of the Talmud is a work known as the Pirkei Avot ("Chapters of the Fathers"), or commonly the Avot. This lays down some of the fundamental moral teachings of Judaism and sets out three basic requirements. First, the Torah's teachings on religion and morality lay down what God requires of the Jews as the basis for a good life. Second, God requires worship, not only through regular attendance at the synagogue, but also through actions that Jews perform in their everyday lives. Third, genuine kindness is supremely important. This should be an active kindness—all Jews should help others,

A tzedakah collection box represents the requirement for Jews to be charitable.

especially the weak, the elderly, and the sick. The principles of the Avot and the text of the Torah provide a vast body of ethical instruction. The Torah alone contains 613 commandments, comprising 248 positive instructions and 365 negative commands that begin "Thou shalt not…." Orthodox Jews try to follow these commandments as closely as possible, but in other strands of the faith, they are interpreted more flexibly. This is especially true of Reform Judaism (*see p.82*), which had strong roots in 19th-century Germany and is now widely practiced in the US. Reform Judaism leaves the moral and ethical interpretation of the laws of the Torah, including which religious practices to observe, up to each individual worshipper. Nevertheless, a number of basic values, respected by all, emerge from the teachings.

HELPING OTHERS

One fundamental value is the importance of charity. On a broad scale, there are many Jewish organizations that do charitable work throughout the world, and Jews put money in a charity box each week before the Sabbath begins. However, charity goes beyond the donation of money. Jews are encouraged to help others in all kinds of ways. God visited Abraham (seen as the founding father of the Jewish people) when he was sick.

God visits Abraham (the father of the Israelites) when he is sick—a sign to all Jews to live a charitable and compassionate life.

This act was said to be a sign to encourage humans to provide practical help to others who are in need.

As a people who have had to survive for centuries in difficult or hostile conditions, and have often had to live far from home, the Jews also hold hospitality in high regard. From Abraham onward, Jews have welcomed strangers and travelers, making guests feel at home and giving assistance to vagrants and beggars. Values such as these add up to a well-developed sense of social responsibility among the Jews, summed up in the commandment: "Love thy neighbor as thyself."

JUSTICE

Fairness and justice have always been important in Judaism. Early in their history the Jews developed a legal system in which a supreme court, called the Sanhedrin, judged disputes and interpreted the instructions in the Torah. Other courts, called Bet Din (meaning "house of judgment"), dispensed justice at a local level, and there is a huge literature made up of the judgments of the rabbis who presided over these courts.

This long legal heritage continues to this day—there is still a court called Bet Din, which decides on religious matters, such as granting divorces and deciding whether food is fit to eat (*see p.74–75*). It has reinforced the powerful sense of justice in Jewish thought and encourages Jews to deal fairly with

Young Jewish men often attend a religious study group known as a *yeshiva* to teach them to read, interpret, and understand the Torah.

others, not just in specific legal disputes or in financial or business dealings but also generally, in their daily lives.

RESPECT FOR LIFE

God made people in his own image, so Jews believe firmly that they must show respect for other human beings and treat them honorably, no matter what their race or religion. Respect for life encourages care for others and

Judaism does not set a special value on those who are celibate. Parents are expected to bring up their children well and according to the faith, teaching them their religion and its ethics.

The role and status of women varies in Judaism. The Talmud tells husbands to look upon their wives as equals, but in traditional Jewish societies women have different roles from men. The woman's sphere is usually the home,

"HE HAS SHOWED YOU, O MAN, WHAT IS GOOD."

Micah 6:8

tempers justice with moderation and mercy. This benevolence and respect extends to the rest of God's creation, too—including all animals.

THE FAMILY AND THE HOME

Jewish values are practical values, and Jews are expected to espouse them in their daily lives. This is especially clear in the case of the home and family. God commands his people to marry and have children. To have a family is therefore a blessing, and parents are regarded highly; unlike some other faiths, such as Catholic Christianity,

but the role of homemaker is never seen as inferior, for it is in the home that Jews foster and pass on their values. In Reform Judaism, women's roles are broader, and some Reform communities even have women rabbis.

FOOD

Judaism is unusual in the number and detail of its dietary laws, which are observed by Orthodox and many Conservative Jews (*see p.83*), but are not

The home is central to Jewish life—the place where families gather to observe together important days in the Jewish calender, such as Passover.

A Jewish deli in London selling kosher food, prepared in accordance with religious rules.

from God and, because each meal is prepared according to God's law, eating is akin to a religious ceremony.

EDUCATION

The Torah values knowledge highly, and having a good education has always seen as binding in Reform Judaism. Food has to be kosher, which means fit to eat according to Jewish law. Kosher foods include meat from animals that have cloven hoofs and chew the cud, such as cows, and from domesticated poultry, such as chickens. Forbidden foods include pork, shellfish, and birds of prey. It is not only the animal itself that must be kosher, but also the way in which the meat is prepared. A professional Jewish slaughterer (called a *shohet*) must be a religious, practicing Jew and kill acceptable animals only in the manner laid down by Jewish law. Jews must then prepare food according to rules—for example, they must keep meat and dairy products separate from one another.

The dietary laws remind Jews that food and eating are inextricably connected with God. Our food comes

been important in Judaism. The most fundamental reason for this is that a Jewish person needs to be able to read Hebrew in order to understand and interpret the Torah. In addition, Judaism needs well-educated rabbis to carry on the important tradition of moral debate and interpretation that has existed continuously for thousands of years. Not only this; a proper understanding of the Torah enables Jews to know how to live a good life, so education therefore becomes fundamental to morality. Jews also recognize the usefulness of education in everyday life. Many Jewish people hope that their children will gain good qualifications at school and go on to enter one of the professions. Lawyers, doctors, and, above all, scholars, are traditionally among the most respected people in Jewish society.

THE STRUCTURE OF JUDAISM

The first rabbis were unpaid, learned men who acted as spiritual teachers and moral advisers. Later they became paid local religious leaders, preaching, teaching, and giving legal judgments. Places with many Jewish communities choose a chief rabbi as their religious leader and may have a representative body, like the Board of Deputies of British Jews. Branches of Judaism have their own over-arching bodies, such as the World Union for Progressive Judaism.

Today the rabbi is seen as the spiritual leader of a local Jewish community. He leads worship, preaches, educates, and offers advice.

PRACTICES AND FESTIVALS

The Jews have one of the richest of all religious calendars. Jewish people mark days ranging from joyous festivals such as Simchat Torah to solemn holy days such as Yom Kippur, which, with its focus on atonement and repentance, is a time of fasting and prayer.

PRIVATE PRAYER

Prayer lies at the heart of Jewish practice. Observant Jews pray in the morning, afternoon, and evening, and there are extra prayers for the Sabbath and for festivals. They may say prayers in their own words or recite passages from the Jewish prayer book, the *siddur*, which contains both prayers and blessings. When they pray, male Jews cover their heads with a small skullcap called the *kippa* or *yarmulka*. They also put on a *tallit* (prayer shawl) and, for morning prayers, wear the *tefillin*. These are two small boxes containing the text of the Shema, from the Book of Deuteronomy (*see p.67*). One box is worn on the forehead, to make the

A devout worshipper wears *tefillin*—boxes containing passages of holy text—to keep the scriptures close.

THE SYNAGOGUE

At the center of Jewish life is the synagogue. The word *synagogue* originally meant "gathering," and if 10 Jewish men gathered in one place, there was said to be a synagogue, and communal prayers could take place. This quorum (minimum number) of 10 is known as a *minyan*, and there must be a *minyan* before prayers in the synagogue can begin. Orthodox synagogues still require the *minyan* to comprise 10 men, but in Reform Judaism, the *minyan* can include both men and women.

As well as a gathering, the synagogue is also a building, which is used for both worship and study. The idea of the synagogue as a place of education,

"AND ON THE SEVENTH DAY YOU SHALL REST."

Exodus 23:12

wearer think of his faith; the other is attached to the arm, bringing the faith close to the wearer's heart. The Bible tells Jews not only to attach the law to their bodies in this way, but also to write it on the doorposts of their houses. So, observant Jews attach a small case, called a *mezuzah*, to their doorposts. This case contains the Shema and it turns the home into a sacred space.

where people can learn Hebrew or discuss interpretations of the Torah, remains important in the Jewish faith.

Synagogues are usually rectangular buildings, with the Ark, which contains the Torah scrolls, at one end. They also have the *bimah* (the raised platform where the Torah is read aloud), seats for the elders who organize synagogue worship, a pulpit, and plaques containing the Ten Commandments written in Hebrew. There are no pictures or statues in the synagogue as the Torah bans "graven images."

The interior of a Russian synagogue with the sacred storage place, or Ark, for the Torah scrolls. These are taken out and read from during services.

THE SABBATH

The climax of the Jewish week is the Sabbath, which begins at sunset on Friday and ends at sunset on Saturday. At home, Jews mark the Sabbath by lighting candles and saying prayers. Outside the home, respect for the Sabbath varies from one branch of Judaism to another. Essentially, though, it is a time for rest, worship, and spending time with the family or community.

Worship at the synagogue involves a number of different activities, the precise contents varying according to whether the service is on a weekday,

the Sabbath, or a festival. The Psalms play a major part—the congregation reads them aloud from the prayer book. The cantor (who leads the singing, chanting, and reading) sings part of the Shema. All or part of the Amidah, a prayer made up of 19 benedictions, is recited. There may also be readings from the Torah. Closing prayers include the Kaddish, an ancient Aramaic prayer to praise God and gain his blessing.

CYCLE OF LIFE

Jews mark the beginning of a new life by giving a Jewish baby a Hebrew name in addition to their ordinary name.

A baby girl's name is announced in the synagogue on the

The *siddur*, or Jewish prayer book, contains occasional prayers as well as blessings for every day.

Sabbath after her birth, or at a special naming ceremony. A baby boy's name is announced at his circumcision, which takes place on the eighth day after he is born. The circumcision is a sign of the covenant between God and mankind, and is known as B'rit Milah, or seal of the covenant. Traditionally, a trained official, a *mohel*, performs the operation, although it may be done by a doctor.

When a boy reaches the age of 13 he is considered to be *bar mitzvah*, "son of the commandment." This means that he is responsible for observing all the

Jewish boys prepare carefully for their bar mitzvah. They are given a grounding in Hebrew so that during the ceremony they can read from the Torah.

At the end of life, funeral customs vary —although burial is traditional, many Jews today are cremated. There is traditionally a seven-day mourning period, during which mourners recite the Kaddish, a prayer in praise of God.

FESTIVALS AND HOLY DAYS

The Jewish year is punctuated with various festivals and solemn holy days that remember important events in

"THE LORD BLESS YOU AND KEEP YOU."

Numbers 6:24

commandments and rites of the religion and can be counted as part of the *minyan* in the synagogue. Jews hold a bar mitzvah ceremony to mark this coming of age, during which the boy is called to read from the Torah in the synagogue, and may also give a speech. Many congregations also hold bat mitzvah ceremonies for girls, who come of age when they are 12.

Jewish history, emphasize key beliefs, and bring Jews together in a round of celebration. During Rosh Hashanah (New Year), Jews remember God's creation and celebrate the renewal of God's covenant with Israel. It is marked with a special service when the *shofar* (ram's horn) is blown. Ten days into the new year is Yom Kippur, the solemn Day of Atonement. Jews fast and seek forgiveness for their sins. Pesach (Passover) remembers the time when Moses led the Jews out of captivity in Egypt. Jews eat a celebratory meal and read the story of the Exodus from a book called the Haggadah. Sukkot (the Feast of Tabernacles) commemorates the journey from Egypt to the Promised Land, when the Jews had to live in *sukkot* (temporary booths, huts, or tabernacles). Today, people build their own *sukkot* and either eat their meals in them or sleep there for seven days. Straight after Sukkot comes Simchat Torah (Rejoicing in the Torah), when the Torah scrolls are taken from the Ark and paraded around the synagogue or streets and a new cycle of Torah readings begins. Shavuot (the Festival of Weeks) is the Jewish harvest festival, held seven weeks after Pesach. Jews decorate both their homes and their synagogues, eat summer fruits, and make special readings from the Torah. Hanukkah (the Festival of Lights)

The *ketubah* is a Judaic marriage document. Jewish weddings can take place anywhere (at home, in the synagogue, or outdoors) and a rabbi officiates.

celebrates a Jewish victory over the Seleucids (rulers of Syria and its neighors) in 170BCE. Jews commemorate this event by saying blessings, singing special songs, and lighting one candle of the eight-branched *menorah* on each night of the festival until all eight candles are lit.

A pious young Jewish man examines an etrog (citron fruit) for imperfections. The fruit must be unblemished for use in religious celebrations.

BRANCHES OF JUDAISM

Persecution and hardship, especially in the 19th and 20th centuries, have led Jews to reinterpret their faith in several ways. Varieties of Judaism range from the mystical Hasidism to Reform Judaism, which attempts to adapt Jewish law to the modern world.

ORTHODOX JUDAISM

Canaan   *ca.*13th century BCE   3 million

The Orthodox Jews—who often refer to themselves as "observant Jews"—have the richest traditions of all the branches of Judaism. At the root of their faith is the belief that the Torah (*see pp.68–69*) contains the actual words of God.

PEOPLE OF THE TORAH

Orthodox Judaism was most deeply rooted in eastern Europe, especially in Poland and Russia, but repeated persecution there meant that many Jews moved to the US. Later they went to Israel, too, and Orthodox Judaism is Israel's official religion.

Orthodox Judaism emphasizes traditional practices of Judaism, including the use of prayer shawl, *shofar* (ram's horn), and *siddur* (prayer book).

Orthodox Jews look to the Torah for instructions about how to live their lives. This text affects how they dress and what they eat, their family life, and their inheritance laws. A close focus on the Torah gives Orthodox Jews the rich traditions that set them apart from other communities. This is especially true of those "Eastern Orthodox" Jews whose roots lie in eastern Europe and whose men wear black clothes and, in accordance with an instruction in the Bible's Book of Leviticus, let their sideburns and beards grow long. In past centuries in Europe, Eastern Orthodox Jews found themselves excluded from the rest of society. Today, still resistant to change, their lifestyle contrasts greatly with the lives of both non-Jews and other Jews around them, but they choose to stay separate, in order to live in a way that accords with God's law.

Orthodox Jews prepare for the Sukkot festival, which remembers the journey of the Jews from Egypt to the Promised Land when they rested in shelters.

HASIDISM

📖 Mezhbizh (now in Ukraine) ⏳ *ca.*1740 👥 4.5 million

The word *hasid* means "pious one" and Hasidic Judaism is a branch of Orthodox Judaism that stresses a mystical relationship with God. Hasidic Jews believe that the Torah is made up of words that are in some sense realignments of the name of God, YHWH. A true Hasid cuts himself off from the world, meditates, and studies the Torah to understand these realignments and become a Baal Shem ("Master of the Name"). A core belief of Hasidism is that God is both the center of the cosmos and infinite. These concepts may be difficult for outsiders to grasp, but the visceral, God-centered nature of this branch of Judaism is unmistakable. Adherents spend time meditating, they sway while praying, and their worship sometimes includes dancing. Even sexual intercourse is seen to bring people closer to God, as it allows mystical togetherness with the divine.

Children read aloud from the Talmud (*see pp.68–69*) at a religious school in a Hasidic Jewish neighborhood of New York.

NEO-ORTHODOX JUDAISM

📖 Germany ⏳ Late 19th century 👥 300,000

The Neo-Orthodox movement emerged as a result of the persecution of Jews in the West. While some Jews kept to their Orthodox communities and others renounced them and absorbed themselves in the culture of the place in which they lived, Neo-Orthodoxy provided a middle path. Adherents could follow the teachings of the Torah, while at the same time accommodating or adapting to the demands of the modern world. Followers of Neo-Orthodox Judaism see it as vital that Jews act as an example to the rest of the world, meaning that it is essential that they have some engagement with non-Jewish peoples. Some of the roots of Neo-Orthodoxy are in the Lubavitch Movement, a movement within Hasidism (*see above*) that began in Russia in the 18th century and later moved to New York. The most influential recent leader of this movement, the seventh Lubavicher Rabbi, Menahem Mendel Schneerson (1902–1994), extended its religious work throughout the worldwide Jewish community. Working fervently until his death, Schneerson established educational projects and a publishing house in an effort to convert secular Jews to observant Judaism.

REFORM JUDAISM

Pittsburgh, Pennsylvania   1885   1.1 million

Especially popular in the fast-changing societies of the West, Reform Judaism has its origins in efforts to update liturgy and worship in Europe. In the 19th century, there were various moves, especially in Germany, Britain, and the US, to reform the Jewish liturgy and to reconcile Jewish thought with new advances in philosophy and science.

After the development of Reform synagogues in western Europe, the decisive step came in 1885 in Pittsburgh, when Reform rabbis set out their agenda: that Judaism is a progressive religion that is in accordance with reason and that recognizes only those moral laws that "elevate and sanctify our lives," rejecting those that "are not adapted to the views and habits of modern civilization."

So Reform Jews take account of modern scientific discoveries and lifestyles and are generally less strict in their observances than Orthodox Jews. They are likely to see the Torah not as God's actual words, but as written by a

A Reform Judaism synagogue in Little Rock, Arkansas. Though the movement began in Europe, it took root and flourished in the US.

number of different writers who may have been inspired by God. Reform Jews have abandoned many of the old dietary laws and have adopted new traditions, such as the ordination of women rabbis. They have also dropped certain old-fashioned parts of the liturgy, such as the prayer that looks forward to the restoration of animal sacrifice in the Temple. In short, they tend to place more emphasis on individual moral choices and less on literal interpretation of the Torah.

A female rabbi lights devotional candles with a young Jewish girl. Reform Judaism promotes gender equality in religious office.

CONSERVATIVE JUDAISM

New York City   1887   900,000

When the Reform movement arose in the late 19th century (*see facing page*), many Jews felt that it went too far in rejecting the traditional tenets of their faith. So, in 1887, a number of rabbis founded the Jewish Theological Seminary in order to foster a branch of the faith that preserved the knowledge of historical Judaism as exemplified in the Bible and Talmud.

TRADITIONAL VALUES

This form of Judaism, now known as Conservative Judaism, accepts human progress, but also upholds Biblical laws. It identifies the Jewish people closely with the laws of their faith and so offers ways in which the laws can adapt, with every generation adding their views. It also offers a way of enabling Jews to keep hold of their Jewish roots while also adapting to changing Western ways, and of placing more emphasis on Biblical authority than on the individual moral choice stressed in Reform Judaism.

Many of the rulings of Conservative rabbis have been rejected by Orthodox Jews (*see p.80*), but the movement has proved popular, especially in the US, where around one-third of practicing Jews belong to Conservative synagogues.

RECONSTRUCTIONIST

New York City   1920s–1940s   120,000

The Reconstructionist movement was founded by Mordecai Kaplan (1881–1983), a Lithuanian-born American who began as an Orthodox rabbi before his views changed to those of Conservative Judaism (*see entry above*), and finally took on a newer direction.

Kaplan and his Reconstructionist followers emphasize the peoplehood of the Jews. They see the laws of the Torah as only useful if they have some clear purpose for the Jewish people or for humanity as a whole. According to Reconstructionists, therefore, the laws require continuous reinterpretation.

Some of the changes effected in Reconstructionist Judaism are quite radical. The Reconstructionist Sabbath Prayer Book, for example, includes no notion of the "chosen" nature of the Jewish people, and does not look forward to the coming of a personal Messiah. Instead of doctrines like these,

Reconstructionism tries to work for a better world and for better people. Its viewpoint has been described both as humanistic and, in its striving for progress, as particularly American.

Professor Mordecai Kaplan (*center*) was the leader of the Reconstructionist Judaism movement in the US, and founder of the Jewish Theological Seminary.

CHRISTIANITY

Once a minor sect in a small corner of the Roman Empire 2,000 years ago, Christianity has grown to become a major world religion. Hugely influential in Europe and the Americas, it is now growing rapidly in the developing world, especially in Africa, where thousands of new churches have been founded in the last few decades.

C hristians are followers of the teachings of Jesus Christ. They hold Jesus to be the Son of God, who will bring salvation and eternal life to those who repent their sins and believe in him. Jesus's message, explained in the New Testament of the Bible, especially in the four Gospels that describe his life and mission, is one of love and forgiveness. Christians are told to love their neighbor, to forgive the misdeeds of others, to help the needy, and above all to aim for the perfection displayed by God himself. Their faith is available to anyone who chooses to follow it, irrespective of their wealth, social status, or ethnic origins. They worship regularly and most take part in a series of rites or sacraments. The most important of these is the Eucharist, which ceremonially re-enacts Jesus's Last Supper with his disciples, drinking wine and eating bread that are said to represent (and by some Christians actually to become) the blood and body of Christ himself.

In its long history, Christianity has diversified, producing many different forms. These range widely in character, from the Roman Catholic Church, with its hierarchy of pope, bishops, and priests and its devotional practices and ritual, to the many different Protestant churches, which aim to be centered on the Bible and in some cases have even done away with the priesthood, asserting that all believers can have direct contact with God. This diversity can embrace the Orthodox Church, with its rich churches full of gilded icons, and the Quakers, who worship in plain but cozy buildings. Christian variety has sometimes led to arguments about doctrine, but it is also the faith's great strength, and one reason why it has set down roots all over the world. This success reflects Christ's insistence that the faith should be open to all.

Christ's birth is one of the most-depicted scenes in art. This 15th-century panel is from the St. Thomas Altar in St. John's Church, Hamburg, Germany.

ORIGINS AND HISTORY

Christianity's history spans more than 2,000 years. The message of Jesus Christ, which can be interpreted at every level from simple faith to complex theology, has enabled the religion to diversify widely, especially since the Reformation, which began in the 16th century.

THE FIRST EUCHARIST

According to the Gospels, the four books in the New Testament of the Bible that recount his life story, Jesus Christ preached with a small group of 12 followers, known as his disciples or apostles. When it was clear that his time on Earth was coming to an end, Jesus gathered these men together for the meal now known as the Last Supper. At this meal, Jesus identified the bread and wine as his body and blood. He told his followers to break and eat the bread and to drink the wine in remembrance of him. In so doing he instituted the rite of the Mass or Eucharist, which for most Christians is at the heart of their worship. From that moment onward Christianity became a religion in its own right.

The Celsus Library in Ephesus, located in modern-day Turkey, was part of a site that was key to the development of Christianity during the 1st century CE.

EARLY CHRISTIANS

The first followers of the teachings of Jesus did not call themselves Christians. They referred to themselves as "disciples" or "brethren," only becoming known as Christians, followers of Christ ("the anointed one"), a few decades later. To begin with they were few in number, were

EMPEROR CONSTANTINE

At first, the Romans viewed Christians as a threat to their rule. However, in the early 4th century, Emperor Constantine had to fight a rival for supremacy. Before the battle he had a vision that promised him victory if his forces carried a Christian standard. They did so, Constantine won, and he converted to Christianity. In 313CE Constantine granted Christians civil rights under the Edict of Milan. Thereafter, the Christian faith spread across the Roman world, becoming the core faith of Europe.

seen as a sect within Judaism, and suffered persecution at the hands of Palestine's intolerant Roman rulers.

SETTING DOWN ROOTS

Soon, under the influence of the great missionary Paul, the Christian faith began to spread into the gentile (non-Jewish) world. Paul was a Jewish scholar who had persecuted the early Christians. But, on a journey to Damascus, he had a vision of Jesus, was struck with temporary blindness, and converted to the new faith. Around the middle of the 1st century CE, Paul traveled around the Mediterranean preaching, founding Christian churches, and writing letters to the faithful. These

letters now form part of the Bible. Largely as a result of Paul's work in the early years, Christianity gradually put down strong roots in the Mediterranean world and by 313CE it was established across the vast Roman Empire.

A FAITH DIVIDED

The city of Rome became the center of what we know as the Roman Catholic Church, and the pope, who was based in Rome, became its supreme leader. The popes can trace their lineage back to the apostle Peter, and so claim a direct link with those who were closest to Jesus himself.

Christianity also spread eastward, to cities such as Constantinople (modern Istanbul in Turkey). These eastern Christian communities were led by patriarchs who did not agree with Rome on some aspects of doctrine. Gradually, their differences created a division between the eastern and western churches. This division came to a head in 1054, when the eastern churches, now known as the Orthodox Churches, split from the Roman Catholic Church. Both bodies

Christ's Last Supper, as painted by Leonardo Da Vinci, adorns the refectory wall at the church of Santa Maria delle Grazie in Milan, Italy.

THE CROSS

The cross at first seems an unlikely symbol of the Christian faith because of its links with the crucifixion and death of Jesus. However, its symbolism predates Christianity, and encompasses universality both in this world (by pointing to the four cardinal directions, north, south, east, and west) and in the spiritual realms by joining Earth and Heaven via its vertical axis. Today, the cross provides a potent symbol of the sacrifice that Jesus made to save humanity from sin—the doctrine that lies at the heart of Christian belief.

continued to be influential in their own parts of the world—the Catholic Church in western and central Europe, the Orthodox Church in parts of eastern Europe, including Greece, Turkey, and Russia, and in the countries of western Asia.

In the centuries after the split, the popes remained powerful in both religious and political spheres, often ruling extensive areas of land in Italy and beyond and asserting their power over Europe's kings and emperors.

RELIGIOUS REVOLUTION

By the 16th century, many people were unhappy with the rich Catholic Church, which often used its money to fund political activities and wars.

Many questioned the practice of selling indulgences—of promising that a person would spend less time in Purgatory (where a soul must be purified to be worthy for Heaven) if they paid money to the church. A number of churchmen, including the German monk Martin Luther, the French scholar John Calvin, and the Czech preacher Jan Hus, began a movement for change. This movement became known as the Reformation. Its supporters believed that the Bible, as the word of God, had more authority than the church; that true believers did not need a priestly hierarchy in order to come to God; and that faith, not

membership of the Catholic Church, was the route to salvation. At first, the reformers hoped to change the Catholic Church itself, but soon they were starting breakaway churches of their own. These were the first Protestant churches and they established the new reformed faith in many countries of Europe, such as the Netherlands, Germany, and Switzerland, where the practice of Protestantism continues to be strong to this day.

PROTESTANT DIVERSITY

The period after the Reformation saw several different Protestant churches founded in Europe. Many of these, such as the Baptists and Quakers, survive today. In England, the church broke free from the control of the pope, but in the 16th century remained fundamentally Catholic in its character and ritual. Those who wanted to reform it were persecuted, and some, known as the Puritans, emigrated to North America so that they could worship freely in their own way. As a result, Protestantism spread to America.

THE MODERN FAITH

The Catholic Church responded to Protestant reform by bringing in its own changes and getting more involved in missionary activity around the world. The Jesuits, a Roman Catholic order

Martin Luther (1483–1546) spearheaded the Reformation that ultimately led to two bodies of the Christian faith: Catholicism and Protestantism.

Gospel choirs originated among African-American Christians who, during the 20th century, began setting hymns to music inspired by jazz and blues.

founded by the Spaniard Ignatius Loyola in 1540, spread Catholicism to South America, and by the 17th century, the Catholic Church had regained its strength.

However, Christianity as a whole was soon challenged by developments in philosophy and science—notably the intellectual probing of the 18th-century Enlightenment movement, the scientific theories of English naturalist Charles needy with a down-to-earth Christian message. Some other new churches, such as the Mormons and Jehovah's Witnesses, see themselves as Christian, but hold beliefs so different from Christian orthodoxy that they are not accepted as such by the mainstream churches. The social challenges of the

"REJOICE, BECAUSE YOUR NAMES ARE WRITTEN IN HEAVEN."

Luke 10:20

Darwin in the 19th century, and the continued questioning of received wisdom in the 20th. Christianity has responded in various ways. In the 19th-century Evangelical Revival, a movement to spread Christianity at home and abroad, European evangelical missionaries traveled to Africa, India, and South America, often in the wake of European colonizers, teaching local people to read and write and converting them to the faith. Churches such as the Methodists and the Salvation Army did similar work at home, combining practical help for the 20th century have seen Christian churches respond in all kinds of ways. The Catholic Church, for example, has kept its ban on contraception, even in the light of the AIDS epidemic, whereas other churches have tried to adapt without losing sight of their core beliefs. Meanwhile, the thousands of new religious movements of recent decades include many with their roots in the Christian faith, from the numerous new African churches to evangelical movements in North America. In essence, Christianity remains as vibrant and diverse as ever.

CORE BELIEFS

Christians believe in one God, who is eternal, all-knowing, and good.
At the heart of the religion stands God's son Jesus Christ, who offers
believers a route away from sin and, through his teachings, provides
them with a rich body of advice and instruction.

THE HOLY TRINITY

Christianity differs from the
other monotheistic religions,
such as Islam and Judaism,
because it sees God, who is
a single substance, as a
Trinity of beings—Father,
Son, and Holy Spirit. This
difficult concept enables
Christians to come to
terms with the paradox
that God is infinite (and
therefore in some ways
cannot be perceived by
humans, who are finite
and limited), but can also
intervene in our lives in
ways that we are able to perceive and
understand. He can influence life on
Earth through the Son, Jesus Christ,
whom he sent to save humanity, and
through the Holy Spirit, which can
descend upon believers and inspire
them to action or give them the
eloquence to preach.

God chose Mary, a virgin, to carry
his son Jesus Christ, in order that
he might save humanity from sin.

ORIGINAL SIN

In Christianity, God first created the
universe, then he made humanity
in his own image. The Book
of Genesis, in the Bible's Old
Testament, tells how the first
man and woman, Adam and
Eve, lived in the Garden of
Eden. In the Garden grew
the Tree of Knowledge. God
forbade Adam and Eve to eat
the tree's fruit, but the serpent
tempted them, and they
succumbed. After this
original sin, God expelled
Adam and Eve from
paradise to live in a state
of sinfulness. This "fall" is how
Christians explain that life's horrors
stem from human sin, not from God.

THE INCARNATION

After the Fall, God gave human beings
the chance to redeem themselves by
sending his son, Jesus Christ, to save

THE FALL OF ADAM AND EVE

The story of how Adam and Eve are tempted
by the serpent to disobey God and eat the
forbidden fruit, and as a result are expelled
from the Garden of Eden, offers a clear
narrative of how sin and evil were introduced
into the world. It also begs questions,
especially the issue of why a perfect God
allowed his creations to behave in this
morally flawed way. One answer to this
question is that in order to have a
meaningful life, humans have to be able to
make moral choices for themselves, so God
gave us the free will to decide how to act.

Adam and Eve lived in paradise in the Garden of
Eden. By eating the fruit of the Tree of Knowledge
they fell from God's grace into a world of sin.

them from sin. Jesus's arrival on Earth is described in the New Testament of the Bible and begins with the Angel Gabriel visiting the Virgin Mary to say that she will become pregnant with God's son creation, which the Bible says took place in seven days, literally, although they still maintain that God created the world. Some have seen the resurrection as a literal reappearance of Jesus on

"I AM THE WAY, THE TRUTH, AND THE LIFE."

John 14:6

(an event known as the Annunciation). This miraculous birth, which enabled the Son of God to be born on Earth as a human being, is known as the Incarnation. Christians believe that it was predicted in many of the Old Testament's prophetic writings.

THE CRUCIFIXION AND THE RESURRECTION

The Gospels describe how, after a period of missionary work, Jesus was put on trial and crucified, but that, on the third day of his death, he rose from his grave and appeared once more to his disciples. Then he disappeared from Earth, apparently returning to Heaven to be reunited with God the Father. Christians believe that by following Jesus's teachings, and by repenting their own sins, they will be granted salvation—that is, that they too will enjoy everlasting life with God after the end of their earthly lives.

INTERPRETATIONS

Since the time of the first Christians, believers and theologians have interpreted the events described in the Bible in different ways. Many no longer take the account of the

Earth, others as a more spiritual phenomenon. But all Christians follow Jesus's teachings closely, perceiving that belief in him is the key to salvation. In doing so, they look for guidance from the Bible, which they believe to have been inspired by God and to contain God's essential teachings.

Jesus's Resurrection, when he rose from the grave and appeared to his disciples, is celebrated by Christians on Easter Sunday.

THE BIBLE

The Christian Bible, although usually bound as a single volume, actually contains many books written by various writers working in different periods of history. These books range in substance from poetry to historical accounts. However, in spite of this variety, Christians believe that all the Biblical writers were inspired by God, and some Christians refer to the Bible as God's Word.

THE OLD TESTAMENT

The first part of the Bible, the Old Testament, is the equivalent of the Jewish Hebrew Bible (*see p.68*). It covers the story of the people of Israel from their earliest beginnings to the point just before the time of Jesus. For Christians, the Old Testament includes important stories, such as the fall of Adam and Eve (*see p.90*). It also contains the utterances of prophets such as Elijah, Isaiah, and Jeremiah. These bring moral messages from God, and many seem also to predict the coming of Jesus.

St. Jerome translated the Bible from Greek and Hebrew into Latin in the 4th century CE. He is often depicted at work on the translation.

THE NEW TESTAMENT

The first four books of the New Testament, the Gospels of Matthew, Mark, Luke, and John, tell the story of Jesus's life and recount his work. Mark probably wrote his Gospel first, about 30 years after the Crucifixion; Matthew and Luke follow its story quite closely. These three books are collectively known as the Synoptic ("seeing together") Gospels.

John's text is very different and must have been written independently, probably at the end of the 1st century CE. Rather than concentrating on Jesus's life, John emphasizes the meaning of his acts, death, and resurrection.

In the Middle Ages, before printing, monks transcribed the Bible by hand to create beautiful, highly ornate illuminated manuscripts.

an account of a vision experienced by John where Jesus triumphs over evil.

TRANSLATING THE BIBLE

The books of the Bible were first written down in Hebrew, Aramaic, Syriac, and Greek. Beginning in the 4th century CE, scholars (most famously St. Jerome) translated them into Latin, which was used by the church throughout western Europe. Versions in mainstream European languages began to appear in the 15th century, following the invention of the printing press. Since then new translations have appeared, as scholars around the world attempt to render the meanings of the Bible's texts more precisely.

The other books of the New Testament are mainly concerned with the later history of the disciples. The Acts of the Apostles tells how the Holy Spirit visted the disciples and how they preached the Christian message. Acts is followed by a series of books in the form of epistles, or letters. These were written by leaders of the early Christian church, mainly Paul. The New Testament ends with Revelation,

ETHICS, MORALITY, AND LAW

The New Testament is full of instruction about how Christians should lead their lives in order to take their place in the kingdom of God. This instruction is in the form of stories that recount Jesus's teachings, and through the letters of Christian leaders, such as St. Paul.

The Jews of the Roman period looked forward to a time in the future when, as God had promised, a leader or Messiah would appear to guide them as they freed themselves from Roman oppression, and a virtuous kingdom of God would begin on Earth.

THE MESSIAH

Jesus's followers (who initially would have been Jewish) believed that Jesus was that Messiah, and they took heart because Jesus said that the kingdom of God was coming soon. The foundation of Christian ethics lies at the point at which Jesus told his

The Good Samaritan earns a place in God's kingdom through his act of compassion.

disciples that they should repent their sins immediately, because they would have to face the judgment of God if they did not. After the Resurrection, he called on the disciples to continue preaching this message, and to call all peoples of the world to God with the promise that by following his teaching they would find a place in God's kingdom.

From the beginning, therefore, Christianity was a missionary religion, one that would go out and seek converts. Jesus was not putting himself forward as the kind of Messiah

expected by the Jews—a political or military leader who would defeat the Romans by force—but as a peaceful preacher of his faith. Despite this, the Roman authorities, fearful of a challenge to their governance, saw him as a troublemaker who could cause political instability.

EXACTING STANDARDS

The Gospel of Matthew contains a summary of Jesus's teachings collected in the form of a continuous sermon, known as the Sermon on the Mount because Jesus delivers it on a mountain. (A shorter version in the Gospel of Luke is called the Sermon on the Plain.) The sermon outlines Jesus's view on Jewish law, setting higher standards for his followers than those previously imposed by the law, and stressing that any follower of God should try to emulate God's perfection in order to enter his kingdom. Among other things, followers of Christianity should put God before money or possessions; never

The Missionaries of Charity in Calcutta, India, continue the work of their founder Mother Teresa, caring for the poor and needy in God's name.

be overly critical and never discriminate; and pray simply and sincerely, with an open heart.

MEMBERS OF THE KINGDOM

Many of Jesus's teachings take the form of parables, stories that begin with the phrase: "The kingdom of God is like…." Jesus makes it clear that the kingdom is not restricted to people of a particular race or class, but open to anyone whose behavior merits it, such as the good Samaritan, who belonged to a race that was an enemy of the Jews, but nevertheless helped an injured man whom others had ignored. Jesus himself associated with people who seemed beyond the pale—tax collectors (seen as collaborators with the Romans), lepers, and sinners. Jesus was always the first to see the potential for good in people, and taught that all are welcome in God's kingdom if they heed his message.

THE BEATITUDES

So, it was not always obviously pious or good people who would enter God's kingdom. Belief in God should offer hope and consolation to those who were poor, deprived, humble, and oppressed,

The Sermon on the Mount probably began as a series of separate sayings that Matthew, the Gospel-writer, linked to make a continuous discourse.

WHAT MAKES A SAINT?

From the times of the earliest Christian churches, some followers of Jesus have stood out for their special holiness. These Christian saints include men and women who have withstood extreme difficulty or even been killed for their faith, who have suffered in order to live a good life, or who have special spiritual insight. Some Christians believe that saints can perform miracles after their death, that their relics are associated with healing, and that they have the power to help those on Earth.

St. Andrew was sanctified as one of Jesus's disciples. All saints are commemorated on special feast days. St. Andrew's feast day is November 30.

and believers should welcome those who come in peace rather than those who use violence. Jesus expressed this philosophy most clearly and most beautifully in a series of verses in the Gospels of Matthew and Luke known as the Beatitudes. These verses, which begin: "Blessed are the poor in spirit, for theirs is the kingdom of Heaven", show that belief in God can bring rewards to those who have lived well

expectations were always high. His listeners were familiar with the old commandment, "Thou shalt not kill," but Jesus said this was not enough: they should renounce hatred as well. They knew that they should not commit adultery—but they should not even entertain lustful thoughts. They should exercise forgiveness, even when that seemed difficult. To illustrate this, Jesus told the parable of the prodigal son,

"BE PERFECT, AS YOUR HEAVENLY FATHER..."

Matthew 5:48

and compensation for those whose time on Earth has been spent in poverty, suffering, or other difficulties. The bereaved, the meek, those who thirst for righteousness, those who show mercy or purity of heart, those who are persecuted, and those who make peace between enemies—all are promised in the Beatitudes a reversal of fortunes and the reward of a place in the kingdom of God.

CHRISTIAN CONDUCT

Jesus spent a lot of time teaching his followers how they should behave and, as in the Sermon on the Mount, his

who had gone away and squandered his inheritance, but who was welcomed back unconditionally by his father. Perhaps most demanding of all, rather than repaying a violent assault with violence, followers should "turn the other cheek." Jesus summed up all these teachings in the "Golden Rule:" do to other people what you would want them to do to you. He expressed a similar truth in the instruction: "Love your neighbor as yourself". Jesus also criticized people who adopt the trappings of faith, but do so mainly because of the good impression it gives. He taught that there is no virtue in ostentatiously praying or fasting, for example, if you just do it for show. The true believer concentrates on heavenly rewards, not earthly ones.

Jesus's teaching explores many facets of normal life. He supported marriage, opposing divorce as well as condemning adultery. He also valued family life, especially children. At the same time, he remained single himself, with his community of followers as his family.

JESUS'S FOLLOWERS

The Christians who carried Jesus's teaching around the Mediterranean after his death and resurrection were especially influential. Most influential of all was the great missionary St. Paul. Paul sees human nature as flawed—we often have good intentions but our sinful human nature leads us to do the wrong thing. Jesus is able to set us free, leading us from death to new life. Paul's letters to the various early Christian churches also offer more specific advice to their members. For example, Paul praises marriage and, like the other early Christians, sees the husband as the head of the household, while also stressing such virtues as kindness and self-control. This view of human

Jesus proved his own worth to preach God's word and take his place in Heaven when he overcame temptation by the Devil in the desert.

The Lord's Prayer includes the lines "Your kingdom come/Your will be done"—the doctrine that God's kingdom comes to those who do his bidding.

relationships is, like many Biblical teachings, very much of its time. But Paul makes more general remarks that are relevant in any place or time, and that have inspired Christians ever since. Above all, he follows Jesus in stating that all behavior should stem from love. One result of this is the notion that all people should care for one another: Christians should help others, give others encouragement, and pray for their fellow humans. These caring values lie at the heart of Christian ethics to this day.

Good Friday, when Christ was crucified, is commemorated with elaborate rituals in many Catholic countries. In Ecuador, shown here, literally thousands of devotees attend colorful processions in their towns to remember Christ's crucifixion and show penitence for their sins.

PRACTICES AND FESTIVALS

The Christian churches have a rich tradition of ritual and worship. At the heart of this worship are the sacraments, including baptism and the Eucharist. Christians also use prayers, music, Bible readings, and sermons to praise God and reflect on the meaning of their faith.

From Christianity's early beginnings, prayer has played a key part in worship. Prayers are central to every Christian service and, as the main medium through which Christians talk with God, are also central to the private devotions of believers. Prayer was so important to Jesus that he made a special effort to teach his followers how to pray for the best communication with God. He told them that there was no need for them to pray loudly or ostentatiously, as was the custom among many Jewish people at the time, because God, who is omniscient, would know what they

The cross is often worn by Christians as an outward sign of their devotion to their faith.

were going to say even before they said it. The Christians adopted the Psalms for their own worship from quite early on in the history of their faith. Luke claims in his Gospel that the Psalms provide a source of guidance; and Paul urged the Christians of Ephesus to give thanks to God in "psalms and hymns and spiritual songs." Early monks and nuns aimed to say or sing all the Psalms every week to show their devotion to God and to the faith. Many of the Psalms were intended to be sung to music, and today some Protestant denominations sing little else. Over time Christians added their own devotional

"THIS IS MY BODY WHICH IS GIVEN FOR YOU"

Luke 22:19

were going to say even before they said it. Rather, they should pray quietly, undemonstratively, and often privately. Like many other Jewish teachers of the time, Jesus taught his disciples a particular prayer for their own use. Known as the Lord's Prayer, this has been used as the main prayer in Christian worship ever since.

MUSIC AND WORSHIP

The Psalms of the Old Testament were the hymns of thanksgiving, laments, and songs of praise of the Jewish people, who sang them in the temple as part of

hymns to their worship. These were valued for their direct language and simple, singable tunes.

Around the middle of the 1st century CE, the church in the West adopted the practice of congregational singing—worshippers joining together to praise God in words and song. By the Middle Ages, most worshipful singing was performed by the church choir, although the Reformation (*see p.88*) brought back the widespread practice of congregational hymns—a tradition that many Christian churches continue to follow to this day.

A Mass held at Keur Moussa Abbey in Senegal, Africa. This Roman Catholic ritual pays homage to the sacrifice of Jesus on the cross.

Some branches of Christianity, such as the Anglican high church, added still more forms of music to their worship—for example, settings of Biblical and other holy texts that are sometimes sung by a choir rather than by the congregation as a whole.

HOLY COMMUNION

The most central and widely affirmed of the Christian sacraments—the rites instituted by Christ—is the sharing of consecrated bread and wine. This is known in different churches as the Lord's Supper, Holy Communion, the Eucharist, or Mass. This ritual is a re-enactment of the Last Supper that Jesus shared with his disciples, at which he identified the bread and wine with his own body and blood. The rite commemorates the sacrifice that Jesus made for his followers.

There has been controversy in the past over the exact nature of what happens during Holy Communion. Catholics believe in the doctrine of transubstantiation—that the bread and wine actually become the body and blood of Christ when consecrated.

Choirboys sing a hymn during a church service. Devotional singing by Christian worshippers was first practiced in the century following the Crucifixion.

The resulting "real presence" of Christ has resulted in Catholics' deep devotion to the sacrament of the Eucharist. Protestants, however, do not all accept this doctrine, some believing that the body and blood are spiritually present, and others that the ritual is purely symbolic.

THE WORD OF GOD

At Christian services, there is a concentration on the word of God as it appears in the Bible. There are usually readings (known as lessons) from the Bible, and in many churches the priest or minister preaches a sermon related to one or more of the readings. Sermons offer moral instruction, guidance on how to live a better life, and direction in how to interpret the Bible. For many Christians, reading and thinking about the text of the Bible is the most important religious activity, and for them the lessons and sermon are at the heart of regular worship.

CYCLE OF LIFE

Most Christians mark the various stages of the believer's life with ceremonies (the major exception being the Quakers, who do not observe outward ritual sacraments). The first of these is baptism, which marks a person's entry into the church. Holy water is central

Jesus is baptised in the waters of the River Jordan, after which God acclaims Jesus is his son.

to the ritual, and a lighted candle symbolizes the light of Christ come into the world. In most Christian churches, baptism occurs during infanthood. The priest splashes water on the baby's head or uses the water to make the sign of the cross on the brow. This practice has been common in Christian churches since the 4th century CE.

The Baptist churches baptize only adults and the ceremony involves complete immersion in water. Many churches follow baptism with the rite of confirmation, in which, usually, older children or adults confirm their membership of the church when they are old enough to understand the commitment that they make. The other key life-cycle rituals are marriage, centering on the exchange of vows in front of the priest or minister and before God, and funeral rites, which may involve either cremation or burial of the body.

THE SACRAMENTS

In the Catholic Church, baptism, confirmation, and Marriage are, like Mass, all regarded as sacraments, outward and visible signs of internal and spiritual grace. The other Catholic sacraments are the ordination of priests, unction (the anointing of people, usually the sick or the dying, with holy oil), and the process of penance, in which the believer confesses their sins to a priest, and the priest announces forgiveness in the name of the Father, Son, and Holy Spirit, then prescribes the

During Anglican Communion the minister offers worshippers consecrated bread, which represents the body of Christ.

penance to be done. The Protestant churches recognize only baptism and the Eucharist as sacraments.

Confirmation in the Catholic Church is carried out by a bishop and is believed to confer divine grace and make perfect the recipient's bond with the Church.

THE CHRISTIAN YEAR

For Christians, the year is marked by a number of festivals and holy days that commemorate the key events in Jesus's religious study, and, traditionally, fasting. This period commemorates Jesus's fast in the desert immediately before his crucifixion. Easter itself is the heart of the Christian year, when

"TODAY YOU WILL BE WITH ME IN PARADISE."

Luke 23:43

life, his crucifixion and resurrection, and the foundation of the church by his disciples. The Christian year begins with Advent, several weeks at the end of the calendar year during which believers prepare for Christmas. Traditionally, the preparation was marked by fasting, although this practice is no longer widespread. At Christmas, on December 25, Christians celebrate Jesus's birth with feasting, gift-giving, and special church services. The 40 days from Ash Wednesday to Easter make up Lent, a period of reflection,

Christians commemorate the Crucifixion on Good Friday and then celebrate Jesus's Resurrection on Easter Day.

Other key festivals are Ascension Day, 40 days after Easter, which marks Jesus's return to Heaven, and Pentecost (or Whitsun), 10 days after Ascension, which marks the birth of the church, when the Holy Spirit descended upon the apostles as tongues of flame. Some Christians, especially Catholics and Orthodox Christians, also celebrate days associated with certain saints—especially with the Virgin Mary.

BRANCHES OF CHRISTIANITY

From the ancient Orthodox churches to new churches in the developing world, Christianity has produced a multitude of branches. Many of these first appeared during the 16th century with the explosive changes of the Reformation.

ROMAN CATHOLICISM

Rome, Italy   1st century CE   1.1 billion

The Roman Catholic Church is the largest and oldest of the Christian churches. It has a hierarchical structure (*see below*) and its leaders, the popes, have claimed to be the descendants of St. Peter, who founded the first Christian church in Rome in the 1st century CE. This line from St. Peter, known as the Apostolic Succession, connects the pope directly with the first followers of Christ, and thus is said to give the leader of the Church a unique authority: the pope is considered to be infallible (incapable of error) when ruling on key articles of faith.

THE SACRAMENTS

Catholics celebrate seven sacraments: baptism, to admit a person to the faith; confirmation, usually at around 8 years old; ordination, the admission of a person to the priesthood; Mass, which in the Eucharist re-enacts the sacrifice of Jesus Christ; marriage; penance, to obtain pardon for one's sins; and unction, anointing the sick with holy oil. The central sacrament is Mass, which practicing Catholics usually attend at least once a week, and which involves the taking of consecrated bread and wine. Catholics believe that the bread

THE CATHOLIC HIERARCHY

The pope stands at the head of the Catholic Church. Below him are, in descending order, the cardinals, bishops, and priests. The cardinals assist the pope in governing the Church, and elect a new pope from their number when their leader dies. The bishops each lead a specific geographical area called a diocese. Bishops confer holy orders on the priests of their diocese and preside over the Confirmation of lay members of each church community within the diocese.

Catholic bishops assist the pope on matters such as ecclesiastical law. Catholics believe their bishops to be descended from Christ's apostles.

and wine are turned by the act of consecration into the body and blood of Christ, a doctrine known as transubstantiation.

CHURCH AND WORSHIP

In a Catholic church, the focus is on the altar, to which members of the congregation bow or genuflect as they enter. The church usually contains a Lady Chapel (dedicated to the Virgin Mary) for private prayer and contemplation, and statues of saints and the Stations of the Cross (the actions of Jesus on his walk to the Crucifixion) around the walls. There are also boxes where priests can hear the confessions of church members. The worship that takes place in Catholic churches is generally more formal than in many other Christian denominations. It usually makes use of incense, chants,

A processional cross, usually mounted on a long staff, is carried at the front of a procession to guide worshippers along the route.

and processions, and congregations follow set forms of words laid down in a service book called a missal.

TEACHINGS TODAY

In recent decades, Catholic teaching on some issues has brought the church into controversy. The Church holds contraception to be wrong, because it puts an obstacle in the path of God's creation. It also bans abortion, which it equates with murder because human life is said to begin at the moment the woman's egg is fertilized by a sperm. Many individual Catholics do practice contraception, however, and there is increasing pressure on the Church to modify its strict views in the light of the worldwide AIDS epidemic.

Catholic cathedrals, such as Notre Dame in Paris, France, are often amazing feats of architecture with a huge altar as the centerpiece.

EASTERN ORTHODOX

Constantinople (Istanbul)   1054   150–350 million

The Eastern Orthodox churches of eastern Europe and western Asia arose from a split between the western Catholic church and the churches of the Byzantine Empire in 1054. This split was caused by differences in the churches' views of the Holy Trinity (*see pp.90–91*). Westerners believed that the Holy Spirit proceeds from both God the Father and God the Son, whereas the eastern churches saw the Holy Spirit as proceeding only from the Father.

Each Orthodox church is led by a patriarch, who heads up a hierarchy of bishops and priests.

In addition, the western church tends to stress humankind's sinful nature, while the eastern church recognizes our essential goodness; the western church focuses on dogma, while the eastern is more centered on worship.

All of the Orthodox churches celebrate seven sacraments, like those of the Catholic church (*see p.104*), but they are referred to as mysteries.

RITUALS AND ICONS

The mystery at the heart of the faith is emphasized by the fact that large parts of the Eastern Orthodox service take place out of sight of the congregation, behind a screen called the iconostasis. When the door in the iconostasis is opened, this action symbolizes the revelation of Christ to the people.

Orthodox churches are famous for their icons—small, stylized images of Jesus, Mary, or the saints. These paintings show how God has worked in the world through such figures.

Greek Orthodox churches, such as this in Santorini, Greece, are often roofed with striking blue domes.

ORIENTAL ORTHODOX

📖 Various   🕴 Various   ⛪ 36 million

The Oriental Orthodox churches, which include the Armenian Church (*see below*) as well as the Coptic Church and those of Syria and Ethiopia, share the view that Christ has one nature (that his human and divine aspects are inseparable). All the Oriental Orthodox churches trace their origins back to the early centuries of Christianity.

The Coptic Church is Egypt's national Christian church, with roots in the 3rd century CE, although Coptic Christians also claim St. Mark as their founder. St. Pachomius (who died in 346CE) created the first Christian monasteries in Egypt and monasticism is still a strong element of the church. The Ethiopian Orthodox Church was founded around 340CE as a branch of the Coptic Church. Despite this, it follows several Jewish-influenced practices, such as observing a day of rest on the Sabbath, circumcision, and certain dietary rules.

The Syrian Orthodox Church has members in southern Turkey, Iran, Iraq, and India, as well as in Syria itself; the leader of the church, the Patriarch of Antioch, is based in Syria's capital city, Damascus. The Syriac language is used in worship, and the liturgy is one of the richest of all the Christian churches.

ARMENIAN CHURCH

📖 Etchmiadzin, near Yerevan   🕴 *ca.*294CE   ⛪ 4 million

Armenia was the first country to make Christianity its state religion—St. Gregory converted its ruler King Tiridates III in the late 3rd century CE. The Armenian Church had been close to the Orthodox churches, but around 506CE, they split over the nature of Christ. The Armenian Church sees Christ as having one nature—his human and divine aspects cannot be untangled. Today, it still holds this position—a unique record achieved in spite of terrible persecution by the Ottoman Empire in the 19th and 20th centuries. Today, Armenian Christians worship in their own language using a 5th-century translation of the Bible. Their churches are plain and they have two kinds of priests: parish priests, who must marry before ordination (unless they are monks), and doctors, who are celibate, and may become bishops.

Armenians hold a Service of the Light in Jerusalem at Eastertime, to celebrate Christ's resurrection.

LUTHERAN

⚑ Germany   **⌛** 1520s   **♜** 84 million

Like other Christians who followed the ideas of the great 16th-century reformers, Lutheran Protestants see the Bible as the only guide to doctrine. They believe that salvation is the gift of God, and that people come to God through faith in Jesus Christ, not through good works—Lutheran theologians insist on the fallen state of humanity, and believe that it is impossible to please God by doing good in the world. Lutheranism is a word-based faith, and preaching is central to Lutheran worship.

> ### CALVINISM
> Another movement that, like Lutheranism, is founded on the ideas of an early reformer and firmly Bible-based, is Calvinism. French reformer John Calvin (1509–1564) saw humankind as inherently sinful and the Bible as the word of God and the ultimate moral standard. Later Calvinists placed a special emphasis on predestination, asserting that God decides who is saved. Calvinism spread to North America in the 17th century.
>
> **JOHN CALVIN**

THE SPREAD OF LUTHERANISM
Adherents trace Martin Luther's ideas in his many writings, especially the Book of Concord, a summary of his teachings that was assembled by his followers after his death. In the 16th and 17th centuries, Lutheranism spread quickly with Reformation ideas across northern Europe.

The Lutheran Church of the Holy Ghost in Jawor, Poland, was completed in 1655 and represents the changing face of Christian institutions in that era.

Today, the Lutheran churches are still strong in northern Europe—notably in Germany, the Baltic countries, and Scandinavia—and in the US, especially in those states where there is a high proportion of people with German or Scandinavian roots. But although there are many Lutheran churches, they are all brought together under the umbrella of the Lutheran World Federation, an association of around 70 separate Lutheran churches.

PRESBYTERIAN

Scotland   16th century   60 million

Presbyterian churches are so-called because, although they involve all church members in the governance of the church, they are governed principally by presbyters—ministers or elders who occupy a role similar to priests in other churches—and have no bishops. This form of Protestantism is based on an interpretation of how the New Testament describes the structure of the first Christian churches.

A VARIETY OF CHURCHES

Some early heretical Christian groups were governed by elders, but the idea became popularized by leaders such as John Calvin (*see box, opposite*) during the Reformation. This form of governance particularly attracted religious leaders in Scotland, who were looking for a way to run their churches that involved the whole community and left the way open for subsequent reforms. In other places, Congregationalism (which emphasized the power of the congregation) developed as a response to similar needs. The early Presbyterians and Congregationalists did not intend to found new churches, but their ideas led over the years to the development of many separate churches.

During the late 20th century, the two movements joined together in the World Alliance of Reformed Churches. The alliance is composed of around 150 churches with some 60 million members. The patterns of worship in the Reformed Churches still vary quite widely from one church to another, but all members see salvation as the gift of God, given through the sacrifice of Jesus Christ. The Holy Spirit delivers salvation to those who the Father wants to receive it, in the process preparing the individual to receive this divine gift.

The plain exterior of a Presbyterian church in the US is typical of the denomination's modest and upright ethic.

THE ANGLICAN CHURCH

London, England   1534   78 million

In the 1530s, King Henry VIII announced that the English church would break from Rome, reject the pope's authority, and make the English sovereign the head of a Church of England.

HIERARCHY AND RITUAL

Initially, the Anglican Church kept many of the features of Catholicism, including the structure of bishops and priests and much of the ritual, but later it came under the influence of Protestant reformers. Today, Anglicans describe their church as "both Catholic and reformed," with members who favor elaborate ritual and refer to their faith as "Anglo-Catholic," as well as those

King Henry VIII broke from Rome because he wanted to divorce his first wife, Catherine of Aragon.

who are "Evangelical" and hold simpler services. In all, the Anglican Church embraces the beliefs of more than 30 autonomous churches around the world— known collectively as the Anglican Communion. These bear different names in their different countries—for example, the Episcopal Church of the US, the Church in Wales, and the Church of Ireland. All Anglicans believe in the importance of Holy Scripture, accept their unbroken line of bishops (tracing it back to the apostles), and heed two sacraments—baptism and the Eucharist.

The different churches of the Anglican faith share a similar structure, with an archbishop at the head, bishops leading local areas called dioceses, and vicars or rectors, who are responsible for individual parishes.

Westminster Abbey in London is one of the most famous landmarks of the Anglican faith, partly due to its association with royal coronations.

THE METHODIST CHURCH

📕 England   ⏳ 1720s and 1730s   🏛 50 million

In the mid-1730s the English Anglican priest John Wesley hoped simply to inspire a renewal of Christianity within the Church of England. However, his religious movement of Christians living according to the rules or "method" laid down in the Bible eventually became a denomination in its own right.

THEMES AND DEVELOPMENT

John Wesley preached that salvation was obtained by the grace of God, through faith in Jesus Christ. Salvation was open to all whose faith brought them to God, and was not possible through good works alone—although it was nevertheless right to live a good and holy life. Through the inspirational preaching of John Wesley and his brother Charles, the faith spread quickly and by the end of the 18th century, Methodism had become a church in its own right. Since then, internal divisions have given rise to a number of separate Methodist churches (such as Primitive Methodists and Wesleyan Methodists), but more recently the trend has been toward reconciliation and the church has evolved a highly organized structure.

SCRIPTURE AND PREACHING

Methodists place a major emphasis on scripture. Their churches are usually plain, and their services, which involve prayers, hymns, and sermons, are unritualistic. Ministers lead services, celebrate Communion, and provide pastoral care, but services may also be led by trained local lay preachers.

METHODIST VALUES

The church stresses the importance of preaching, both locally and in a wider world mission to bring others to the faith, to promote understanding between different churches, and to bring about a better society.

John Wesley, the founder of Methodism, was an energetic Christian Evangelist, who preached his faith vigorously.

AMISH

 Switzerland   Late 17th century   128,000

The Amish are members of a strict Protestant group originating in Switzerland, but now mostly living in the US, centered in Ohio, Pennsylvania, and Indiana. The most distinctive of the Amish groups are the Old Order Amish, who set themselves apart from the rest of society by adopting traditional clothes, shunning modern developments such as motorized transportation, and running their own schools, preferring mutual aid rather than relying on state benefits.

An Amish man displays some of the products of the Amish agricultural way of life.

EUROPEAN ORIGINS
The Amish began under the leadership of Jacob Amman, a Swiss Mennonite minister (*see p.115*) who wanted to follow a more rigorous religious path than that of the other elders of his church. He and his followers took the Lord's Supper (sacramental bread and wine) more frequently than the Mennonites,

wore plain clothes, and shunned people who had been excommunicated. Amman soon attracted followers in Switzerland and Alsace, and in the 18th and 19th centuries, most of their descendants emigrated to the US.

OLD ORDER AMISH
Of several groups of Amish that exist today, the largest is the Old Order Amish Mennonite Church, who wear 18th-century-style clothes, including bonnets and aprons for the women and broad-brimmed hats for the men. Worship takes place in their own homes, different homeowners taking it in turn to host the Sunday service, winning them the nickname "House Amish." They are also notable for using their own language, which is a dialect of German.

Amish children ride in horsedrawn buggies that seem borrowed from an earlier century. A rejection of "progress" is central to Amish culture.

QUAKERS

🏴 Great Britain   ⚏ *ca.*1650   🏰 300,000

The Quakers is an alternative name for the Society of Friends, which began in the 17th century under the leadership of George Fox (1624–1691). The name Quakers originated in 1650, when Fox told a magistrate to quake at the name of the Lord. Fox believed that the organized churches put obstacles between the believer and God and he wanted to get back to a more basic, apostolic faith. He and his followers had no clergy, no sacraments, and no formal liturgy, believing that the Friends would communicate directly with God, and that when Friends gathered together, Christ would be with them.

They also opposed warfare and refused to take oaths. All this put the Quakers at odds with 17th-century religious laws, and they were widely persecuted. But they stayed true to their beliefs and are now admired for their campaigns for peace, for prison reform, and against slavery. Modern Quakers still emphasize direct contact with God, gathering together in silence until the Spirit moves a member to speak.

This Quaker meeting house in Burlington, New Jersey, was built in 1683. A plain, unadorned building, it provided a well-lit space in which Friends could meet.

SHAKERS

🏴 Great Britain   ⚏ *ca.*1758   🏰 Very few

The British religious leader Ann Lee (1736–1784) was a member of the "Shaking Quakers," a name that derived from the trembling experienced by members in religious ecstasy. Soon after her conversion, Ann had revelations telling her that she was the female counterpart of Christ, and she began to attract her own followers. This group became known as the United Society of Believers in Christ's Second Coming (more informally, the Shakers) and their leader was referred to as Mother Ann. Persecuted in England, Ann and her followers emigrated to the

US, where they held their possessions in common and were strictly celibate. By the time of the Civil War in 1861, there were Shaker communities as far apart as New York, Kentucky, and Indiana, with a total of around 6,000 members. In the 20th century, however, membership declined, and today members amount to only a handful. Despite their dwindling numbers, the Shakers are remembered and respected for their austere lifestyle and for their distinctive crafts, in which they created furniture and other household items with both simplicity and beauty.

PLYMOUTH BRETHREN

Plymouth, England   1831   2 million

The Plymouth Brethren began as a group of Christians who rejected the sectarian nature of the existing Protestant churches and wanted a less formal kind of religion. They shunned the idea of a fixed order of worship and believed that all should have equal access to their Christ-centered faith, so they ordained no priests. They were enthusiastic preachers, emphasizing the importance of regular worship, Bible study, and missionary work. In time they divided into two broad groups, the Open and the Exclusive Brethren. The Open Brethren are organized like the Presbyterian churches (see p.109) and are generally more willing to show unity with other Protestant congregations. The Exclusive Brethren have a more centralized form of church organization and tend to separate themselves from other Christian groups. The name Brethren is also used by other Christian sects, including the Brethren in Christ, which was founded by two Swiss Mennonites (see opposite, below).

MORAVIANS

Saxony, Germany   1722   750,000

After the end of the Thirty Years' War in 1648, a number of Protestant refugees from Moravia (now in the Czech Republic) settled in Saxony in Germany. In 1722, a count named von Zinzendorf invited a group of these refugees to form a community on his estate. This became the Unitas Fratrum (Unity of Brethren), or the Moravian Brethren, a Protestant church that looks to the scriptures for guidance on both faith and conduct. The Moravians do not overemphasize doctrine, and prefer a religion that comes from the heart and is to be shared freely with others. To this end, the Moravians are highly evangelical, sending missionaries all over the world to convert people to their faith. A key element of Moravian worship is the sharing of a communal meal (known as the Love Feast), while the minister speaks informally.

The Moravians set up mission stations all over the world. This one is in South Africa.

SEVENTH-DAY ADVENTISTS

ᴘᴜ Battle Creek, Michigan   ☗ 1863   ♖ 10.5 million

Adventists are Protestant Christians who believe in the imminent Second Coming of Jesus Christ. They believe that a time, which they refer to as Advent, will soon come when the

Seventh-Day Adventists are devoted to preaching as they believe that Christ will come again when the Gospel has been taught throughout the world.

righteous will be taken to Heaven to live there for a millennium, while Satan rules on Earth for the same period. Then Christ will return to Earth, destroy Satan, and create a new world.

American Adventist William Miller preached that this process would begin in 1843–1834. When it did not, he blamed people's refusal to keep the Sabbath—hence the term Seventh-Day Adventists and, eventually, the formal foundation of the church, which took place in 1863. Adventists follow the dietary rules of the Old Testament, eschew worldly pursuits, such as gambling, dancing, and the theater, and, of course, observe the Sabbath.

MENNONITES

ᴘᴜ The Netherlands   ☗ 1530s   ♖ 1.25 million

The Dutch preacher Menno Simons, originally a Catholic who joined the Anabaptists in 1536, attracted many followers with his views in favor of church reform, pacifism, and the baptism of only adult believers (not infants). Simons's followers, who became known as Mennonites, grew in numbers in various parts of Europe, and when the Russian Mennonites suffered persecution, many moved to North America and started Mennonite churches there. Today, most Mennonites live in North and South America. Mennonites do not emphasize doctrine, instead pursuing a Bible-based faith, expecting the second coming of Christ, and aiming to live a life of holiness and prayer. Missionary and relief work is important to the group.

Bolivian Mennonite farmers riding in a carriage. Their simple agrarian lifestyle reflects the plain humility of their faith.

BAPTISTS

📖 The Netherlands and England   ⌛ Early 17th century   👥 100 million

The first Baptists were early English Protestants, some of whom were in exile in the Netherlands. Their Bible-based faith has, over time, brought them many followers throughout the world.

Simple, unadorned buildings, such as this one in New Zealand, characterize Baptist chapels.

BAPTIST BELIEFS

The Baptists are so-called because they believe that a person should not be baptized until they are able to make their own personal profession of faith. In most cases, individuals are not considered to be full members of the Baptist church until this ritual has taken place.

The practice of adult believers' baptism, along with other Protestant beliefs such as the primacy of the Bible and the authority of local churches, were the doctrines put forward by early Baptists such as the Englishman John Smyth, who preached while in exile in the Netherlands at the beginning of

the 17th century. In 1612, his colleague Thomas Helwys returned to England and founded the first Baptist church.

The independence of the Baptist churches gave rise to a number of separate groups, including the Particular Baptists, who held that Christ died only for the Elect (those chosen by God for salvation), and the General Baptists, who believed that he died for all humankind. In time many Baptists, concerned about religious persecution, moved to North America, and by the 18th and 19th centuries, Baptist churches had spread widely across the US. The ideas of the Baptists did not appeal only to settlers from Europe. Many black people also became Baptists and Baptist churches are still popular among the African-American community in the US. The denomination has expanded widely elsewhere, too, and today the Baptist churches make up one of the world's largest Christian groups.

Baptism by full immersion is a defining feature of the Baptist faith. It may take place in a tank (a baptistery) in a church, in a river, or in the sea.

SALVATION ARMY

London, England ☒ 1865 ♔ 1.5 million

In the mid-1800s, William Booth, a Methodist minister, left his church to do social and evangelical work in London, eventually founding the Salvation Army. Booth's beliefs, including redemption for all, were strongly influenced by his Methodist background, but the organization of Booth's sect was different from that of other Protestant churches, taking its inspiration from the military. The leader of the church is called its General and the ministers are officers and wear uniforms. The structure of the church is divided into territories and the places of worship are known as citadels. This military model emphasizes Booth's concern to do both missionary and social work on a large, organized scale. The Salvation Army soon acquired a reputation for helping the poor, and for bringing the Gospel to the people.

Brass bands often provide the music for hymns (called songs by Salvationists), which play an important part in the Salvation Army's worship.

HOLINESS CHURCHES

New York City ☒ 19th century ♔ 1.5 million

The Holiness churches embrace the doctrine of perfection or perfect love, a notion championed by John Wesley, founder of Methodism (*see p.111*), and by various Evangelical leaders in the US in the 19th century. According to this doctrine, a convert to the faith undergoes a process of sanctification and regeneration by grace and through faith, in which sin is removed. From then on, it is possible to live a life free from sin, although the convert may experience episodes of non-deliberate failing, or "weakness." The Holiness churches believe that faith is shown by leading an ethical, spiritual life.

A number of separate Holiness churches, such as the Pilgrim Holiness Church and the Church of the Nazarene, have been founded—at one stage there were thought to be 150 different Holiness churches, although many of these have now amalgamated.

Nevertheless, all Holiness churches place a strong emphasis on Christian education and on living a holy life. A prominent church that has drawn on the ideas of the Holiness movement is the Christian and Missionary Alliance, whose evangelical work has seen it spread across six continents since it was founded in North America in 1887.

PENTECOSTALS

📍 Topkepa, Kansas; Los Angeles, California   ⌛ 1900–1906   👥 105 million

The Pentecostal churches take their name from the first Pentecost, when, according to the Book of Acts, the Holy Spirit descended on the apostles as tongues of flame. These churches emphasize spiritual experiences, such as healing, exorcism, and prophecy. Today's Pentecostal churches have their roots in the work of Charles Parham. Central to Parham's beliefs was the concept of the Holy Spirit entering the believer, often accompanied by events such as speaking in tongues. One of Parham's students, William J. Seymour, founded the Apostolic Faith Gospel Mission in Los Angeles, which inspired

Pentecostal worshippers often make energetic demonstrations of their involvement in praise, such as raising their hands, clapping, and dancing.

the worldwide founding of Pentecostal churches. They are especially numerous in the developing world, and in poorer communities in the developed world.

CHARISMATIC MOVEMENT

📍 Various   ⌛ 1950s and 1960s   👥 300 million

The Charismatic movement is a worldwide movement of Christian revival. At its heart is the belief in the *charismata*, or gifts of the Holy Spirit—gifts or inspiration that are granted by God to the faithful and that empower the recipients in such fields as wisdom, healing, faith, prophecy, and glossolalia (speaking in tongues). The beginnings of the movement, which is sometimes also known as neo-Pentecostalism, have been traced to the 1950s and 1960s in

both Roman Catholic and Protestant churches. In churches that are influenced by the Charismatic movement, worship tends to be informal and the Second Coming of Christ is often seen as imminent. The movement also stresses the empowering presence of the Holy Spirit, which is said to enter believers during baptism.

Adherents of El Shaddai, a Catholic Charismatic movement based in the Philippines, pray during a celebration in Manila.

CHRISTADELPHIANS

⚑ Richmond, Virginia ⚊ 1848 ⚏ 55,000

The name Christadelphians derives from the Greek, meaning "Christ's brothers", and was chosen to reflect the desire of the church's founder, John Thomas, to return to the faith of Jesus's first disciples. Thomas, an Englishman who had emigrated to the US, refused to use the term "Christianity" for his faith because he believed that the Christian churches had distorted Jesus's true message.

Christadelphians follow Jesus's teachings, although they reject the doctrine of the Holy Trinity (God the Father, God the Son, and God the Holy Spirit; *see p.90*). They look forward to the Second Coming, when Christ will return to rule, building a worldwide kingdom from the city of Jerusalem.

The church does not ordain priests and is organized in local congregations called ecclesias, which elect their own officers. Its members do not vote or take part in politics and they reject military service. Christadelphian worship typically takes place on Sundays in dedicated buildings, known as Christadelphian halls. However, because the space for worship does not have to be consecrated, many believers also hold simple gatherings in their own homes.

UNITARIANS

⚑ England ⚊ 1774 ⚏ 500,000

Unitarians believe in one God, but not in the Holy Trinity (*see p.90*). Their religion is typified by a search for truth based more in human experience than in religious doctrine. Congregations are independent of one another and there is no church hierarchy.

Unitarian ideas began to emerge during the Reformation (16th century), in Poland, Hungary, and England. Early Unitarians were inspired by the Spanish theologian Michael Servetus, whose book *De Trinitatis Erroribus* (*On the Erroneous Understanding of the Trinity*) appeared in 1531. There were Unitarians in England in the 17th century, but the first Unitarian church was not founded in England until 1774, and in the US until 1781. The American preacher and writer William Ellery Channing gave a boost to the movement with his sermon on Unitarianism in 1819. Numbers declined in the 20th century, but there are still thriving congregations in the US and Europe.

Unitarian ceremonies, such as this naming, are free from rules; celebrations are tailored to meet needs.

CHURCH OF CHRIST (SCIENTIST)

Boston, Massachusetts   1879   400,000

Mary Baker Eddy dedicated her life to reviving the early healing ministry of Jesus after she was cured from an injury without medical treatment. Her book, *Science and Health with Key to the Scriptures,* appeared in 1875, and in 1879 she founded the Church of Christ (Scientist). The Bible and Eddy's own writings form the basis of the ideas of Christian Science. Services feature readings from both, but there are no sermons. Healing is central to Christian Science, and it is believed that we can nurture physical and spiritual health by seeking the truth and by following God.

Mary Baker Eddy claimed to be a spiritual healer able to cure the sick through God's grace.

Christian Scientists believe God is Spirit and that Spirit is Truth, Life, and Love. Jesus embodied caring, spiritual Love in his healing ministry, and Eddy believed that those who could understand the link between God and love, and who followed her example, would be able to become spiritual healers too. By ridding herself of any thought of ill health or weakness and opening herself up to the spiritual power of God, she claimed to be able to heal the sick through God's grace. This healing ministry became popular, and Christian Science grew steadily in 80 countries.

Convinced that ignorance was a barrier to well-being, Eddy emphasized the importance of Bible study, and the church set up many reading rooms where the Bible and her own book could be read. A successful newspaper, called the *Christian Science Monitor*, also helped to give the religion a high profile.

The Christian Science Center, in Boston, is the international administrative headquarters of the faith and occupies 14 acres of Massachusetts land.

JEHOVAH'S WITNESSES

Pittsburgh, Pennsylvania   1872   6 million

The Jehovah's Witnesses have their roots in the International Bible Students' Association (founded by independent preacher Charles Taze Russell in 1872) and the Watch Tower Bible and Tract Society (of 1882). They adopted their current name in 1931. They believe that Jesus Christ was not himself God, but was God's first creation. They anticipate the coming of the kingdom of God, which will be heralded by the Battle of Armageddon. Jehovah's Witnesses believe that 144,000 believers will rule in Heaven, which will be populated with the other people of goodwill. They hold to rigid rules of conduct: blood transfusions are prohibited; they reject nationalism (members do not do military service and will not salute national flags); they dispute doctrines such as the Trinity, and the immortality of the soul. The church preaches vigorously, producing a magazine, *The Watchtower*, and engaging in door-to-door proselytizing, hoping to convert others to their faith.

MORMONS

New York   1830   13 million

The Church of Jesus Christ of Latter-Day Saints, popularly known as the Mormons, was founded by Joseph Smith. According to Smith, a revelation from an angel told him the location of gold tablets bearing the words of God. These Smith translated as *The Book of Mormon* (1830), which tells of lost tribes of Israel who traveled to the US, the last survivors of whom were a man named Mormon and his son Moroni. It goes on to predict that Jesus Christ will reappear and rule in the US. *The Book of Mormon* along with the Bible and other Mormon texts form the sacred writings of Smith's church. Smith also claimed the right to guide the church through further revelations, one of which included permission for polygamous marriages and the possibility for all men to become gods.

The early Mormons were persecuted for their views, and Joseph Smith was murdered in 1844. After this, Mormon leader Brigham Young took most of the church's members to Utah, where the church remains strong.

Brigham Young's Mormons had a strong missionary focus, and now there are followers all over the world.

NEW CHRISTIAN CHURCHES

In many parts of the world, especially in western Europe, Christianity is in decline. However, there has been a huge expansion in the faith in the developing world, particularly in South America and Africa. This expansion has often taken the form of new independent churches that demonstrate the ability of Christianity to attract people from a wide range of cultures and backgrounds.

NEW AFRICAN CHURCHES

The last 100 years have seen an explosion of Christianity in Africa south of the Sahara. In the late 19th century, Africans began to react against the Christianity brought to them by western missionaries, creating new African independent churches. Some of these are small and locally based, while others have expanded widely. The largest include the Kimbanguists, named for its founder Simon Kimbangu, from the Democratic Republic of the Congo, which has some ten million members; and the similarly sized Celestial Church of Christ, which originated in Benin. Many of these churches share key features, such as having their origins in times of persecution, a strong sense of sacred places where worshippers may encounter God, and the use of hymns and songs.

NEW PENTECOSTAL BRANCHES

In the developed world, several new Christian churches have aligned themselves with Pentecostalism (*see p.118*). While many of these churches embrace a traditional Christianity, some have diverged. One divergent group is made up of

Brazilian Pentecostal believers read from the Bible in a subway station in a public demonstration of their faith.

Movement in the US, developed out of the counterculture movements of the 1960s. Several of these alternatives offered a way for people to live together communally in Christian fellowship. One or two moved far from the norms of Christian orthodoxy—Jim Jones's notorious People's Temple, based at Jonestown, Guyana, ended with the mass suicide of more than 900 members in 1978. But other new Christian spiritualities have sought ground in the basics or the history of the faith. For example, many have sought Christian renewal by studying the church's early Celtic history and finding inspiration in its saints and monks.

the "Oneness" Pentecostal churches, which baptize in the name of Jesus Christ only, not the Holy Trinity. Another preaches the controversial message of "prosperity spirituality," offering wealth to God's followers.

ALTERNATIVE SPIRITUALITIES

Some of the new churches, such as the British-founded Jesus Fellowship (formerly the Jesus Army) and the Jesus

Pilgrims of the Zion Christian Church, which has around six million members, in Moria, South Africa.

ISLAM

The most recently revealed of the three great monotheistic religions, Islam spread quickly from its roots in the Middle East and has been hugely influential in both scholarship and politics all over the world. Although this influence has been complex, the essence of the faith is simple: a belief in one God and that Muhammad is his principal prophet.

Muslims (followers of Islam) believe that the Islamic sacred text, the Qur'an, contains the words of God himself. These words were revealed to the prophet Muhammad over a period of years, beginning in 610CE. Although this was when the message of Islam was first made manifest on Earth, Muslims believe that their faith, based on the words of the eternal God, has always existed, and that earlier prophets of the monotheistic religions, such as Moses in Judaism and the Christian Jesus, are precursors of Muhammad himself. Muhammad has a special significance, as he was chosen to receive the Qur'an.

The importance of reading God's actual words in Arabic—the language in which they were revealed—has meant that literacy and education have always been paramount in Islam.

Muslim scholars not only learned how to read the Qur'an, but also became leading scientists and writers. They used their learning to preserve the work of their predecessors. For example, many of the discoveries of the Ancient Greeks, which had been lost to the West, were preserved by Islamic scholars. Islamic scientists made many discoveries of their own, too, in fields ranging from chemistry to astronomy.

In the centuries after Muhammad received the faith, news of Islam spread. Arab merchants carried their religion along trade routes across Asia, to areas such as India and Indonesia. They also traveled through Africa, taking Islam across North Africa and southward to the west of the continent. There were also Arab conquests, which brought the faith to Central Asia and Spain. Today, most people in North and West Africa, the Middle East, and Indonesia are Muslim. With many converts in the West, too, the voice of Islam has never been more widely heard.

The Friday Mosque in Herat, Afghanistan, shows off the use of calligraphy and geometrical adornment that is typical of Islamic art.

ORIGINS AND HISTORY

The early prophets, including Musa (Moses), tried to show people the truth about the one everlasting God. However, it was not until the 7th century CE that the Muslim faith was revealed, when an Arab merchant named Muhammad received God's teaching.

THE REVELATION OF ISLAM

Muhammad (570–632CE) is so revered among Muslims that many make the blessing "may peace be upon him" when they mention his name. He was a member of the Quraysh, the most powerful Arab tribe of the period, and lived in the city of Mecca, but his work took him on travels around the Arabian Peninsula. As a young man, he became known

Jibra'il, the archangel Gabriel, appeared to Muhammad to reveal the sacred words of the Qur'an.

as a person of integrity and high moral standards. It was his habit during the month of Ramadan (see p.139) to go to Mount Hira near Mecca to meditate, and, according to tradition, it was here in 610CE that Muhammad felt the presence of the divine. God's messenger Jibra'il (the archangel Gabriel) commanded him, "Recite," and presently the Prophet found himself

speaking the words of God. Muhammad was illiterate, but these words were later collected in the Qur'an, the sacred book of Islam. Muhammad understood that there was one God, who should be known as Allah, meaning "the one who is God."

FROM MECCA TO MEDINA

Muhammad shared his vision with people in Mecca, attracting a small group of followers. However, threatened by Muhammad's attack on immorality and believing that their power was being undermined, the Quraysh leaders began to persecute Muhammad's people. In 620 CE, Muhammad advised his followers to flee to the city of Medina, about 200 miles (320km) north of Mecca. Muhammad himself remained in Mecca for another two years. His

AYAT AL-KURSI

Ayat al-Kursi, the Throne Verse, is part of the second sura (chapter) of the Qur'an. It expresses the almighty power of God, whose "throne extends over the heavens and the Earth," saying that: "All that is in the heavens and the Earth belongs to him." Because the Throne Verse deals with the greatness of God, Muslims hold it in especially high esteem. They memorize it and often quote and reproduce it in posters and prints, and inscribe it on amulets to ward off evil.

An ancient text of the Ayat Al-Kursi. Some say that the meaning of the word *kursi* is known only to God, others that it refers to the knowledge of God.

eventual flight to Medina in 622CE, called the Hijrah, is a major event in Islamic history and marks the start of the Islamic calendar.

When Muhammad arrived in Medina, he found the local tribes at war and faced opposition from the region's Jews, who would not accept him as a prophet. Nevertheless, Muhammad's leadership established unity for many people, and in 624CE the Prophet was able to fight off a challenge for power by a large army from Mecca, whose forces he defeated decisively in 630CE. He banished polytheism and idol worship from Mecca before dying after a short illness in 632CE.

According to tradition, the Prophet left the mortal world after a magical trip to Jerusalem known as the Mir'aj or Night Journey. Jibra'il (Gabriel) woke Muhammad from his sleep one night and led him to a magical horselike creature, called the Buraq. Muhammad climbed on to the back of the Buraq, which bore him to Jerusalem, where he ascended to heaven.

THE CALIPHATE

When Muhammad died, leadership of the Islamic community passed through his close companions. These leaders were known as Caliphs (Khalifa). Muslims deeply revere the first four Caliphs—

The Grand Mosque in Damascus, Syria, is one of the oldest mosques in existence. It was built in the 7th century CE.

THE SULTAN

For more than 400 years, since the Ottoman Turks conquered the city of Constantinople, naming it Istanbul in 1453, the Ottoman Empire was the linchpin of the Islamic world, led by the Sultan. One highly successful sultan was Suleiman I (ruled 1520–1566). Known in the West as "the Magnificent" and in the Ottoman Empire as "the Lawgiver," he extended the Empire, patronized artists and architects, and built the Suleimaniye mosque in the center of Istanbul.

Portrait of Suleiman II, who was Sultan of Turkey between 1687 and 1691. He built Ottoman power through political reform and military conquest.

Abu Bakr, 'Umar, 'Uthman, and 'Ali. They are known as the Rightly Guided Caliphs, because they followed Muhammad's example closely.

However, there was a dispute among Muslims about the Caliphate. Some people felt that 'Ali, Muhammad's son-in-law and cousin, should have been made Caliph earlier. 'Ali's supporters became the Shi'i Muslims, while those of Abu Bakr became the Sunni (*see p.144*). After the death of 'Ali, the Caliphate passed to the leaders of two important dynasties of the

Khajou Bridge in Isfahan, Iran. Built during the 15th century, it is tangible evidence of Islamic culture's engineering prowess during that period.

Quraysh, the Umayyads (661–750CE) and the Abassids (750–1517), before passing to the Ottoman dynasty of Turkey, until the abolition of the Caliphate in 1924.

This history of overall leadership reinforced the idea of an *umma*, or overarching Islamic community, and stressed the unity of Muslims all over the world. During the period of the Caliphate, Islam began to expand its influence. For example, Muslim armies made conquests in central Asia and Spain, while Arab merchants carried news of their faith along trade routes in the Middle East and North Africa. Islam spread to lands whose rulers

made treaties with the Caliphs, too. From small beginnings in the Arabian Peninsula, the world of Islam had grown into a global presence.

ISLAM TODAY

Roughly one-quarter of the population of the modern world is Muslim. In most Middle Eastern countries, nearly everyone is a Muslim, and this is also true in North Africa, Indonesia, and some central Asian countries. Many western countries, including France, Germany, Great Britain, and the US, have large Muslim minorities.

Although united by their faith, the world's Islamic communities vary widely in their outlook, and Muslim countries show varied approaches—from highly traditional nations, such as Saudi Arabia, to determinedly secular states, such as Turkey. Such differences have led Islamic communities to bitter divisions, as with disputes between Sunni and Shi'i Muslims. And differences, sometimes extreme, with

The siege of Vienna in 1529, led by Sultan Suleiman I, marked the end of Ottoman advancement in Europe and the most northerly outreach of Islam.

the West have blighted relations between some sections of Muslim society and the non-Muslim world during the recent decades. But Islam also has great capacity for respect for others, especially for the other "peoples of the book"—the Christians and Jews who, like Muslims, believe in one God.

"PRAISE THE NAME OF THE LORD MOST HIGH."

Qur'an, Sura 87

CORE BELIEFS

At the heart of Islam is a single core belief: that there is One God, who is eternal, uncreated, and controls the entire cosmos. This belief directs and illuminates every aspect of Muslim life, from the mosque to the workplace and from birth to death.

THE ONE GOD

In the Qur'an, the sacred text of Islam (*see pp.132–133*), God is referred to as Allah. He is the only God in Islam and, for Muslims, the sole creator of the cosmos. His divinity is beyond human understanding. Muslims believe that all living things owe their breath to the life-giving power of Allah, and if at any time he withdraws this power, all living things will die.

Calligraphy is highly valued in Islam and is often used to adorn mosques. This text spells "Allah."

Along with this omnipotence, Allah exhibits the qualities of goodness and compassion. Muslims commonly use the Arabic phrase, "*bis millah hirahman nir rahim*" (which means "in the name of God the merciful, the compassionate") as a blessing before undertaking an important action; these words also precede every sura (chapter) except one of the Qur'an.

The other key characteristics of Allah—his Oneness, his uniqueness, and the fact that he has always existed—are expressed in Sura 112, known as the Sura of Unity. An English translation of this sura reads: "Say: 'He is God, One, the ever self-sufficing, God, the Eternal. He does not beget and he was not begotten, and there is not any one like him.' " The Arabic term for this assertion of God's Oneness is *Tawhid*. In Islam it is important not only to believe in *Tawhid*, but to affirm it—and in making that affirmation to reject any notion of idolatry or polytheism (the worship of many gods). When Muslims repeat the Sura of Unity with conviction, it is said that their sin falls away

THE PROSCRIPTION OF IMAGES

The Qur'an forbids the worship of idols and in the Hadith (the account of the life and teachings of Muhammad) there is a specific ban on figurative representation of humans and animals. There is also a strict ban on portrayals of God and, in most cultures, of the Prophet. This meant that Islam developed a style of art that draws heavily on abstract patterns and repeated plant motifs. In some Muslim countries, figurative art has been permitted outside the mosque, while artistic traditions that portray the Prophet show him without any facial features.

from them in the same way that the leaves fall away from a tree in autumn; whereas to deny *Tawhid* is to commit the sin *shirk* (*see p.137*).

SUBMISSION TO GOD

The name "Islam" is commonly interpreted as "submission to the will of God," but actually comes from the Arabic word *slm*, which means "to be in peace." So, a more precise translation of the name Islam is "peace through submission to God."

The first man and woman, Adam and Eve, originally submitted to God's will and lived in peace in the Garden of Eden. But when they disobeyed God and abandoned their submission, they were no longer at peace. The Muslim submission to God directs a devotee's entire life. Muslims aim to dedicate all their actions to God —not just their prayers and their reading of the Qur'an but

The Nabawi Mosque in Medina is the Prophet Muhammad's final resting place. He built the mosque that first stood on this site.

everything they do, from their financial affairs to their work, from caring for other members of their community to their political beliefs. For this reason, Muslims often introduce God when they are talking about anything of importance. For example, before making a promise, it is common to say "*inshallah,*" which means "God willing." So in Islam it is impossible to separate the church from the state or religious from secular life— Islam covers both.

Because of their submission to God's will, Muslims sometimes refer to themselves as *abd-Allah*, "slave of God." But they balance this by also seeing themselves in another way. They are *khalifa*, vice-regents, people whose status is high compared to the rest of the living world. This position brings with it responsibilities. Muslims should do their best to make the world a better place, to ensure that, in as many ways as possible, it too conforms to the will of God.

THE QUR'AN

The Muslim sacred book, the Qur'an, stands in a tradition of revelations to prophets stretching back to figures such as Moses. But the Qur'an is on a higher level than these other revelations, because its words are believed to be the words of God himself. This is why Muslims read the text of the Qur'an in the original Arabic, the language in which it was revealed to the Prophet Muhammad.

THE WORDS OF GOD

The name Qur'an means recitation, but the text is also known as al-Furqan, which means discrimination (between truth and falsehood), and Umm al-kitab, meaning the mother of all books. The revelation of the Qur'an began one night in 610CE, an occasion now known as the Lailat ul Qadr ("Night of Power"). The angel Jibra'il (Gabriel) appeared to Muhammad and told him that he was going to be a prophet and that he should bring himself closer to God. When Jibra'il commanded Muhammad to "Recite" and began to reveal God's words to him, the Prophet started to speak and memorize them.

Jibra'il's revelations continued over a period of 22 years and Muhammad, who could not read or write, committed them all to memory. His followers memorized them, and they also wrote them down. At first their accounts were fragmented, written on pieces of skin, bark, and other materials, but eventually, during the reign of the third Caliph, 'Uthman, in the 7th century CE,

This decorative tile in an Algerian mosque bears a calligraphic verse drawn from the Qur'an.

the complete Qur'an was written down in the form that Muslims use to this day.

Because it is made up of God's words, Muslims always reproduce the text of the Qur'an with the greatest accuracy, and in the original Arabic. The Qur'an is often written in calligraphic form: Muslims admire the art of calligraphy both for its ingenuity—because calligraphers form patterns and shapes with their letters—and for the combination of beauty and clarity with which the words of God can be written on a page.

A BOOK TO LIVE BY

The central message of the Qur'an is that Muslims must believe in One God and put him first, giving him precedence over even one's family. The Qur'an's text is divided into 114 suras, or chapters (themselves divided into many *ayat*, or verses), making up a total of around 78,000 words. These include appeals to people to believe in God and to live just lives; stories of the punishments meted out to earlier peoples who disobeyed God; signs of God in nature; sermons; stories; and juridical instructions. The text provides a source book for Islamic law on such matters as divorce, inheritance, and warfare, as well as on more obviously religious matters, such as fasting and worship. Because it provides the framework for every aspect of life, Muslims greatly revere the Qur'an. Many of its suras are admired for their clarity of language, while Muslim scholars have explained the more difficult passages in the writings known as the Hadith (*see p.134*). There is, however, a resistance to interpreting the words

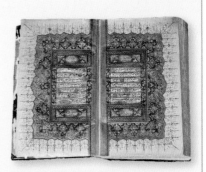

The words of God are supremely important in Islam and often written with the utmost care and beauty, as in this medieval manuscript.

of God where this is not necessary, and many Muslims feel uncomfortable with translations of the text, which are also held to be acts of interpretation.

Many Muslims learn the words of the Qur'an by heart—a person who has done this is known as a *hafiz*, and is accorded great respect.

ETHICS, MORALITY, AND LAW

Islam is a practical religion. It offers its followers a body of instruction about how to live their lives, and has established a system, called *shari'ah*, of coming to moral and legal decisions. Rooted in the Qur'an, this moral instruction also embraces the opinion of religious leaders.

THE NATURE OF SHARI'AH

Islam affects every aspect of the Muslim's life. The faithful are expected to follow the instructions of the Qur'an and the system of law and morality called *shari'ah*. Although often referred to in the West as "*shari'ah* law," and although it contains many precise instructions as to how a person should live, this system is not a legal code in the Western sense of the term. Its true nature is revealed by its name, which means "path to water:" *shari'ah* is the path that the Muslim must follow in order to live a good life. Although it can be strict and exacting, *shari'ah* is also highly practical. For example, it prohibits a woman revealing certain parts of her body to a man other than her husband, but these prohibitions may be lifted if the woman is ill and the only doctor who can treat her is a man.

QUR'AN AND HADITH

Shari'ah is made up of four elements. The first and foremost element is the Qur'an itself. As the word of God, this

THE CRESCENT

In the Qur'an the waxing and waning of the moon is seen as an indication that God's purpose is eternal and unchanging. The Prophet recognized this by declaring his faith in God whenever he saw the new moon. But the use of the crescent as a symbol of Islam did not begin in the Prophet's time. The symbol was at first adopted by the Ottoman Turks in the 15th century, before being adopted by the whole Islamic world. Crescents are often placed on the domes of mosques, where they point toward Mecca.

text is paramount and the legal instructions it contains are the first place to which Muslims look for guidance. The second element is the *sunnah*, which concerns the way in which the Prophet Muhammad and his followers lived, and what they said and did. The *sunnah* forms a kind of living commentary on the Qur'an, showing Muslims the "example of the Prophet," and it is collected in the scholarly writings of the Hadith. So, if a Muslim faces an ethical question that is not covered in the words of the Qur'an, they look to the Hadith for an answer. For example, whereas the Qur'an tells Muslims simply to give alms, in the Hadith, Muslims learn that Muhammad laid down the details of what

Zakat, **or the giving of alms,** is one of Five Pillars or tenets of the Islamic faith. Here a Muslim worshipper places a coin in a community alms collection box.

a Muslim should pay and how payment should be collected. The Hadith is, therefore, an aid to virtuous conduct.

IJMA' AND IJTIHAD

Even the Hadith does not cover every issue, however. To resolve questions outside the scope of the Qur'an and Hadith, Muslims turn to the two other elements of *shari'ah*, *ijma'* (consensus) and *ijtihad* (reason). To come to a consensus or to apply reason, Muslims (in the early days, the whole Islamic community; nowadays, the community of scholars) come together to discuss the issue, always with reference to the instructions in the Qur'an and Hadith, eventually arriving at agreement. As an extension of this system of reason and consensus, local imams offer ethical advice and instruction to members of the congregation of their mosque.

The stress laid on the views of scholars and religious leaders is different in Sunni and Shi'i Islam (*see pp.144–5*), with Shi'i Islam placing more emphasis on the opinions of the scholars. In both branches of Islam, however, the most important thing is for individual Muslims to think for themselves and to take responsibility

Islamic moral codes extend to practical as well as spiritual matters. For example, some of the earliest *shari'ah* laws promoted fair trading in markets.

for their own actions. Muslims believe that their capacity for reason is God-given, and that it is their duty to use this gift that comes from God.

LEGAL DISPUTES

Sunni Islam has four main schools of law: the Malaki (dominant in western Asia and West Africa), the Hanafi (in the countries that were part of the Ottoman Empire and in India), the Hanbali (in Saudi Arabia and Qatar), and the Shafi'i (in Indonesia, Malaya, and the Philippines). From the 8th century, these four schools have interpreted the laws of Islam in various ways. Shi'i Islam interprets Islamic law differently again, and itself has several schools. The schools of both Sunni and Shi'i Islam vary in the extent to which they draw on consensus and reason in making judgments, with the Hanbali school of Sunni Islam being the one that restricts itself most scrupulously to the Qur'an and Hadith.

The differences between Sunni and Shi'i interpretations of the law have led to disputes between these two branches of Islam. For example, in Sunni law, people are not expected to try to overthrow a bad ruler, provided that he upholds Islamic law and defends Islam if it is attacked. The theory goes that everyone aside from the Prophet is sinful, so we should expect even rulers to have their flaws. Shi'i law, however, says that Muslims are obliged to depose particular reasons, are prohibited. So Muslims distinguish between what is permitted, or *halal*, and what is prohibited, or *haram*. The best-known example of this is in the dietary rules that limit the things a Muslim may eat. Meat may be eaten, with the exception of pork, but in order for the meat to be *halal*, the creature must be killed in the

"ALLAH IS KNOWER OF ALL THINGS."

Qur'an 2:282

unjust rulers. This division has led to disagreements and even wars between Islam's two branches.

HALAL AND HARAM

According to the Qur'an, everything that God has created is for human use. But there are some things that, for

Berber boys sit around a fire by a tent in Morocco. The Berbers are an ancient, indigenous people of the Nile Valley and helped to spread Islam.

correct way—by severing blood vessels with a sharp knife while the slaughterer pronounces the name of Allah over the animal. The rules, which are carefully observed, lay down that the animal must not see the knife, and that no other animal should be able to see the act of killing. Aside from pork and improperly slaughtered meat, Muslims may not eat meat if its method of slaughter is unknown.

Coffee served in Oman: the fabric of Islamic culture is underpinned by social rituals.

Muslims believe that God has set down dietary prohibitions for their protection, so there is an important exception. If people find themselves faced with a choice between starving and eating banned foods, the Muslim should eat. The other main dietary prohibition covers intoxicants, such as alcohol. Muslims learn that God has provided all kinds of foods for human enjoyment, but that it is wrong to misuse these gifts. For example, the fruit of the vine is good to eat, but fermented fruit produces wine, an intoxicating drink that brings with it corruption and evil—and is therefore prohibited.

SERIOUS SINS

Islam defines a number of serious sins, which the faith condemns and which may be punished severely. Several of these, such as murder, theft, and adultery, are recognized as sins in most cultures, but others are specific to Islam. The most serious and fundamental sin of all is *shirk*, the sin of associating anything with God other than God himself or putting something else in place of God. Having false gods, exalting human hero-figures, such as pop stars or sports personalities, or being an atheist (replacing God with nothingness) are all examples of the sin of *shirk*. Other serious sins in Islam are *riba*, or money-lending for profit, which is wrong because those who can do so should freely help others in need; *juba*, or cowardice; *qadhf*, or slander, which includes gossip and bad language; and

A Muslim woman in traditional modest dress, with only the hands and face exposed.

the use of intoxicating drugs (including alcohol; *see left*), which make people lose control of their actions, something condemned in the Qur'an.

PUNISHMENTS

Some Islamic societies may punish these sins very harshly. For example, theft may be punished by the amputation of the criminal's hands, and the traditional punishments for adultery and apostasy (renouncing belief) are, respectively, flogging and death. Some Muslim countries also give harsh corporal punishments for the production, sale, or consumption of alcohol. On the other hand, some Muslims argue that such punishments are unfitting in the majority of cases, so there are a number of exemptions. For example, a thief will not undergo amputation if he or she has stolen because of genuine economic need. Nevertheless, a strong belief among many Muslims is that these punishments, sanctioned in the Qur'an, have been laid down by God and should be used; that they keep the crime rate low in countries where they are enforced; and that there are cases in which flogging is preferable to depriving a person of his liberty with a long prison sentence.

PRACTICES AND FESTIVALS

The most important practices of Islam are known as the Five Pillars. In many ways these define and, as their name suggests, support the entire religion, covering the expression of faith, regular prayer, and three key activities—supporting the poor, fasting, and pilgrimage.

SHAHADAH: THE DECLARATION

The first Pillar of Islam is the *shahadah*, or declaration of faith: "I bear witness that there is no god but God and Muhammad is his Messenger." This declaration is the central belief of Islam, and a person who makes the declaration sincerely, using the original Arabic words, is a Muslim. The first part expresses belief in the one creator, and submission to him. The second part, which recognizes Muhammad's role as Prophet, signifies that the Muslim accepts God's teaching, as revealed to the Prophet in the words of the Qur'an (*see pp.132–133*).

Money obtained through the third Pillar of Islam (*zakat*) may be used to build drinking fountains.

SALAH: PRAYER

The Qur'an instructs Muslims to pray regularly, to praise God, and to keep God in their minds throughout the day.

This regular prayer (*salah*), five times a day at set times, is the second Pillar of Islam. The times for prayer are at dawn (*fajr*), just after noon (*zuhr*), at mid-afternoon ('*asr*), at sunset (*maghrib*), and in the evening ('*isha*). On most days of the week, prayer may take place at home or at work, but every Friday Muslims usually go to the mosque at midday for communal Friday prayers. Before prayer, Muslims wash themselves ritually, using running water from a fountain at the mosque or a tap at home. While doing this they turn their thoughts toward God, so that they are prepared mentally as well as physically for prayer. When this preparation is complete, the devotee removes his or her shoes and, standing on clean ground or on a prayer mat, faces the direction of Mecca and begins to pray. The prayers themselves take place in a prescribed way, beginning with the words "*Allahu Akhbar*," meaning "God is greater (than all else)." The words of prayer are accompanied by a number of movements that involve standing, bowing down, prostrating, and sitting. Collectively, these movements are known as a *rak'ah*.

ZAKAT: ALMSGIVING

The third Pillar of Islam is *zakat*, the payment of a tax, the money from which is then used to help the poor and needy. How much a person pays is based on their income—the amount

CLERICS AND SCHOLARS

Muslim congregations are led by imams, who are not ordained in the way that Christian priests are, but are men known to be of good standing in the community and often learned in theology. This reflects Islam's enormous respect for learning and scholarship. Imams act as Islamic teachers and community leaders, and give advice and guidance on all aspects of life to the members of their congregation. They also give the sermon at Friday prayers and often lead prayers in the mosque. In Shi'i Islam, they have higher authority and are seen as successors to the Caliphs (*see p.129*).

is calcuated as 2.5 percent of a person's wealth, but the value of that person's home and other essential possessions is not counted in the assessment. Through paying *zakat*, Muslims express their love of God by taking care of other people. They may also make additional donations to charities that will help the Muslim community, funding facilities such as hospitals and aiding the victims of natural disasters.

SAWM: FASTING

The fourth Pillar, *sawm*, is the practice of fasting and abstention during Ramadan, the ninth month of the Islamic calendar. Ramadan is important because the first revelation of the Qur'an to Muhammad occurred during this month. Throughout Ramadan,

Pilgrims praying at Mina, just outside Mecca, overlooking the tents of two million pilgrims on the annual Hajj, or great pilgrimage to Mecca.

Muslims abstain from food, drink, and sexual relations in the hours from dawn to dusk. Several groups of people— the old, the sick, young children, and pregnant women—are excused from the fast. However, if possible, those who cannot fast during Ramadan are encouraged to practice the abstention the following year. During the last ten days of the month of Ramadan, Muslims are encouraged to dedicate as much time as possible to coming closer to God. People go to the mosque more frequently and devote more time to reading the Qur'an. At the end of Ramadan, the festival of 'Id al-Fitr (*see p.141*) marks the breaking of the fast.

HAJJ: PILGRIMAGE

Every Muslim who is physically able and who can afford the journey is required to go once on pilgrimage or *hajj* to

Mecca, in Saudi Arabia: this is the fifth Pillar of Islam. The Hajj takes place every year in the 12th month of the Islamic calendar. It involves a series of rituals and prayers that bring together the vast Muslim community: Muslims from all over the world and from all walks of life gather in Mecca, the birthplace of the Prophet Muhammad, to foster a spirit of equality and unity and a perception of the greatness of

Muslim graves, such as these in Bosnia, are raised above ground to prevent mourners from walking on them. Cremation is forbidden in Islam.

who have undertaken the pilgrimage are accorded great respect among the entire Muslim community.

THE MOSQUE

The spiritual heart of the Islamic community is the mosque, which is primarily a place for prayer. The largest

"HASTE UNTO REMEMBRANCE OF ALLAH."

Qur'an 62:9

God. The rituals of the Hajj include wearing special white garments symbolizing the state of consecration or holiness, known as *ihram*, as well as walking around the Ka'aba—a cubic monument in the center of the mosque at Mecca—seven times, reciting certain prayers during the procession. To go on the Hajj is one of the greatest moments of a Muslim's life and those

space in a mosque is the prayer hall. This is a room with a niche called a *mihrab* at one end, which indicates the direction of Mecca, toward which Muslims must face while praying. Mosques traditionally have at least one tower, called a minaret. From here, five times a day, an official called a muezzin gives the call to prayer. There is also often a courtyard, which offers a quiet area for reading or meditation, and at the entrance there are fountains where Muslims perform their ritual of washing before prayers. In addition, mosques may have rooms where teaching or religious discussions take place, or there may be other rooms, allowing the building to take on the functions of a community center.

THE CYCLE OF LIFE

When a baby is born in a Muslim family, it is customary to whisper the profession of faith or the call to prayer into the child's ear. Seven days after the birth, there is traditionally a naming ceremony, a common part of which involves shaving the child's hair and offering the weight of the shorn hair in silver to the poor.

When Muslims reach adulthood, they are encouraged to marry, for marriage is believed to be a state that was designated by God. In addition, the family is seen as a positive force for stability, and marriage marks the unification of two families, helping to bind the Muslim community together. The marriage ceremony itself may be held at the house of the man or woman, or at the mosque, and it is usual to ask the local imam (Muslim leader) to preside. The details of the ceremony and celebration vary from one place to another, but generally the

The Muslim community is so widespread that wedding practices are extremely varied. This ceremony is taking place in London, England.

man gives a dowry or bride-gift to his new wife, the exact size and nature of which depends on his means, but which becomes his wife's sole property, for her to do with as she wishes.

Burial customs also vary in Islam, but generally Muslims prefer to bury their deceased as soon as possible after death. Funerary prayers consist of a *salah* with the addition of extra prayers.

MUSLIM FESTIVALS

A number of Islamic festivals celebrate key dates in the life of Muhammad, notably Mawlid an-Nabi (the Birth of the Prophet). But the most important Muslim festivals are linked to the Five Pillars. The first, 'Id al-Adha, the feast of sacrifice, marks the culmination of the Hajj, the pilgrimage to Mecca, and is celebrated with a communal prayer and the sacrifice of an animal. The other major festival is 'Id al-Fitr, the festival that occurs at the end of the month of fasting, and marks the close of Ramadan. At 'Id there is a special prayer, performed by the whole community together; alms are given, and celebrations go on for three days.

Muslim families often read religious texts together. Islam touches on all aspects of daily life, including hearth and home.

Muslims flock to Mecca in the thousands to commemorate the day when the Prophet Muhammad began to receive the Qu'ran. The celebration—one of the most important in the Islamic calender—is called Laylat al-Qadr and occurs on the 27th night of Ramadan.

BRANCHES OF ISLAM

Islam has two main branches, Sunni and Shi'i. The division occurred soon after Muhammad's death, when there was a dispute over his successor. In addition, several smaller Islamic sects, such as the Sufis, have had an influence beyond their size.

SUNNI

⚑ Arabian Peninsula   ⌛ 7th century CE   ⛪ 1 billion

Shortly after Muhammad died, the Prophet's close follower Abu Bakr was elected as Caliph, the leader of the Muslim community. However, some Muslims thought that the Prophet's son-in-law, 'Ali, should have become the first Caliph. Eventually, 'Ali succeeded as the fourth Caliph, but there were still those who objected to him, and he was assassinated in 661CE. Those who agreed with the view that Abu Bakr was the Prophet's own choice of successor became known as Sunni Muslims—that is, followers of the *sunnah*, or custom, of Muhammad (*see p.134*). Those who supported 'Ali became known as the *shi'at 'Ali* ("the party of 'Ali"), or the Shi'i Muslims (*see opposite*).

Sunni Muslims view the Four Caliphs (from Abu Bakr to 'Ali) as the spiritual leaders of Islam.

FOLLOWING THE SUNNAH

Sunni Muslims recognize the first four Caliphs (up to and including 'Ali), but do not see the descendants of 'Ali as fulfilling any special religious or political role. Because they follow the custom of the Prophet as laid out in the *sunnah* and show less regard for the advice of imams than do Shi'i Muslims, Sunni Muslims are often known as Orthodox Muslims. Every Sunni Muslim follows one of the four schools of law—Malaki, Hanafi, Hanbali, and Shafi'i—which vary in the way that they use consensus and reason to supplement the Qur'an (*see p.135*). Individuals are free to choose which of the schools of law they adhere to, although most Sunni Muslims tend to adopt the same school as their father.

A SUNNI MAJORITY

More than 85 percent of the Muslim population is Sunni. This means that in most Islamic countries, the majority of Muslims are Sunni, with the notable exceptions of the people of Iran, and the substantial Shi'i populations in Iraq, Azerbaijan, and Yemen, as well as some of the Gulf States.

SHI'I

Arabian Peninsula   7th century CE   180 million

The Shi'i Muslims began as the supporters of 'Ali (Muhammad's cousin, and the husband of the Prophet's daughter Fatima), and opposed the Sunni choice of Abu Bakr (*see opposite*) for the Caliphate. 'Ali finally became Caliph in 656CE, but then the Sunni and Shi'i Muslims disagreed over how they should select future Caliphs. Shi'i Muslims held that Caliphs should be descendants of 'Ali and Fatima, while Sunnis wanted them elected.

THE DEATH OF HUSSAYN

The division between the two branches of Islam deepened in 680CE, when Hussayn, son of 'Ali and Fatima, led a revolt against a Sunni Caliph of the Umayyad dynasty (*see p.128*), Yazi ibn Mu'awiyah. Hussayn's supporters failed to back him and Hussayn was killed at the Battle of Kerbala (in modern Iraq). Shi'i Muslims mark the anniversary of Hussayn's death with a period of mourning, some even scourging themselves to atone for the supporters who abandoned Hussayn.

THE SUCCESSORS OF 'ALI

Most Shi'i Muslims identify 'Ali and eleven of his successors as the spiritual leaders of the faith. These Muslims are known as the "Twelve-Imam Shi'is." Another group of Shi'i Muslims, the Seven-Imam Shi'is, do not recognize the last five Imams in this lineage. Precise Islamic dogma and practice varies between these groups and Sunni Islam. Practices of the Twelve-Imam group that distinguish them from other Muslims include adding extra lines to the call of prayer and variations in the funeral prayer. Both groups of Shi'i Islam have doctrinal differences with Sunni. For example, Shi'i Muslims recognize temporary marriage, believe that God changes his decisions, and, most crucially, believe in a succession of imams beginning with 'Ali.

Evening prayers at the shrine of Imam Reza in Sanabad, Iran. Imam Reza, who died in Sanabad in 818CE, is the eighth Shi'i Imam in the line from 'Ali.

SUFISM

⚑ Turkey   ⏳ 13th century   ☗ 9 million

Devotees of Sufi Islam seek a direct and personal experience of God and follow a spiritual teacher. It is not certain when Sufism began, but it seems to have been in the early period of Islam.

In order to maintain some of the simplicity of the way of life of the first followers of Islam, an early Sufi named Hatim al-Asamm established four key principles of Sufi life: to remember that no other person eats your bread for you; that no one but you performs your actions; that death is coming, so you should address your life in readiness for it; and that you are under the eye of God.

RUMI

The poet Jelaluddin Balkhi (1207–1273) was born in Afghanistan, but grew up in Anatolian Turkey. He became known as "Rumi," meaning "from Roman Anatolia," and befriended a dervish (an ascetic) called Shams. When Shams disappeared, Rumi began to write poetry as if his friend were speaking through him, offering profound religious insight. Rumi also created the dramatic "whirling" dance that was adopted by his followers, the Mevlevi order of dervishes.

DEVOTION TO GOD

Sufi devotion to God is often characterized by intense, ecstatic experiences, such as trancelike states. Such states can come about through the achievement of *dhikr*, or remembrance, a way to experience the intense presence of God. Different Sufi orders achieve *dhikr* in different ways—some through chanting, others through dancing. Sufi devotion has also produced beautiful poetry (*see box, above*) and music. Because Sufism involves practices that sometimes lead to the union of the individual with God, Sufis have been accused of turning their backs on Islam. But Sufis insist that their experience of the love of God is the anchor of their Islamic faith and that adherence to *shari'ah* (*see p.134*) is as vital to them as it is to other Muslims.

The Dervishes are an ascetic Sufi Muslim sect of Turkey. This famous whirling dance is performed to induce a state of religious ecstasy.

NATION OF ISLAM

US 1930 *ca*.300,000

In the 20th century, many African-Americans in the US were attracted to Islam, especially because of its egalitarian philosophy. In Islam, it is considered a virtuous and pious deed to give slaves their freedom, whereas in the eyes of many African-Americans, Christianity had become associated with white oppression in the first half of the 20th century were still suffering from discrimination, in spite of the fact that slavery had been abolished.

One product of the movement toward Islam was the Nation of Islam, a religious movement founded by Wallace Dodd Ford, who took the name Fard ("Righteousness") Muhammad. Although Fard Muhammad adopted many Islamic ideas, his belief system diverged in many ways from orthodox Islam. For example, he presented himself as a Messiah figure. Fard Muhammad's successor, Elijah Poole, known as Elijah Muhammad, introduced further new and unorthodox doctrines, including the notion that black people were the first humans, created by Allah, whereas white people were later creations who would be destroyed at the imminent "end of times."

Black Muslim minister and civil rights activist Malcolm X was a spokesman for the Nation of Islam in the 1950s.

MALCOLM X

Elijah attracted numerous followers, including Malcolm Little, a civil rights campaigner, who took the name Malcolm X. By replacing his surname with a letter, he was rejecting, as did many members of the movement, a name derived from that of his family's former white owners, which he saw as a sign of oppression. However, Malcolm X later broke from the Nation of Islam and became an orthodox Muslim.

NEW DIRECTIONS

This change of heart by a high-profile member of the organization led to divisions within the group and, in 1965, to the assassination of Malcolm X. In the 1970s, after this crisis, Elijah died and his son, Warith Deen Muhammad, became leader. Warith Deen Muhammad gave his part of the movement a new name, the American Muslim Mission, and directed it toward orthodox Islam. The new group looked to Sunni Muslim beliefs (*see p.144*), and was opened up to believers of all races. Most of the movement's members followed Warith Deen Muhammad and the American Muslim Mission in its more orthodox religious beliefs, though some formed the Original Nation of Islam and continued to promote the ideas of Elijah. Gradually, however, the two groups began to move together as the Original Nation of Islam became more orthodox, and in 2000 their respective leaders announced an end to rivalry between the two bodies.

The Nation of Islam and its related groups have been influential in spreading ideas about both faith and equality, especially in the US, and also in Canada and Great Britain, but the exact number of members is not known.

ZOROASTRIANISM

One of the world's oldest religions, Zoroastrianism began as the faith of ancient Persia (now Iran). In the mid-7th century CE, the arrival of Islam in Persia meant that Zoroastrianism began to lose its hold. Today it is a minority faith, practiced by a small section of Iran's population, as well as by minorities in India and elsewhere.

Zoroastrianism is named after the prophet whose Greek name is Zoroaster, although his followers usually use the Middle Persian form, Zarathustra. He preached a religion in which the creator god, Ahura Mazda, is involved in an endless struggle against the evil spirit Angra Mainyu. Followers of the faith assist Ahura Mazda in his struggle by living a good life and worshipping him.

Zoroastrians place a strong emphasis on freedom of moral choice and encourage believers to make good moral decisions in every aspect of their lives. The spiritual sphere is not considered any more important than the physical—Ahura Mazda created both body and soul, and we should aspire to live well in both. This is something to be happy about—Zoroastrians are encouraged to appreciate all the things that the Wise Lord has created, so enjoying life is seen as nothing less than a religious duty. Charity and education, which help people to live better and more enjoyable lives, are also valued highly. Zarathustra's ideas, which probably drew upon prehistoric Indo-Iranian religion and share common elements with early Hinduism, were at first transmitted orally. Eventually Zarathustra's followers wrote down his hymns. Known as the Gathas, these tell how Ahura Mazda revealed his teachings. Other early writings (including a liturgical text called the Yasna Haptanghatti, or "Worship in Seven Parts," which the prophet may also have written) were added to the Gathas to form the Avesta, the sacred book of Zoroastrianism. Adherents—both priests and lay people—still commit these texts to memory. Using the texts unites Zoroastrian adherents, who are scattered all around the world, and helps to preserve this ancient faith.

Zarathustra (known as Zoroaster in the Greek form of his name) lived around 1000BCE and was a renowned priest, scholar, and prophet.

ORIGINS AND HISTORY

The history of Zoroastrianism is bound up with the story of Persia (modern Iran) and its rulers. When Islam gained ground in Persia many Zoroastrians moved to India, and in doing so created a second major center, where followers are known as Parsis.

EARLY PERSIA

Zoroastrianism was founded by the prophet Zarathustra (Zoroaster in Greek), who probably lived around 1200BCE and came from a family of Indo-Iranians who had settled in Persia. As a priest at the age of 30, Zarathustra had a number of visions, after which he began to preach a new religious message— most significantly that there was one God, Ahura Mazda (the Wise Lord), the creator of all things and the source of all goodness.

King Cyrus helped to spread Zoroastrianism throughout his Persian Empire.

To begin with, Zarathustra attracted few followers, but his faith did take hold in northeastern Persia, when he converted a local ruler, King Vishtaspa, who adopted Zoroastrianism as his kingdom's official religion. Little is known about the early centuries in the history of Zoroastrianism, but in the 6th century BCE, a ruler named Cyrus came to power in Persia. Cyrus carved out a large empire that included Babylon and Turkey, as well as Persia itself. His dynasty, the Achaemenids, was Zoroastrian, and it spread the faith around its lands. The Achaemenids employed royal priests called Magi, who traveled with the emperors on their diplomatic missions and military campaigns, and settled in the emperors' territories. Both learned and powerful, the Magi were good ambassadors for their religion, and helped to spread news of Zoroastrianism around western Asia.

FROM PERSIA TO INDIA

In the 2nd century BCE, the Parthian dynasty took over the rule of Persia. The Parthians collected together the surviving teachings of Zarathustra, as well as the other teachings of the faith, to put together the Zoroastrian sacred book, the Avesta. In 224BCE, the Parthians were succeeded by the Sassanians. This new family was also Zoroastrian, and its members promoted the faith. The Sassanians and their high priests regarded the church and state as unified, giving both political and religious leadership. This both promoted the Zoroastrian faith and gave the high priests a great deal of power. However, in the 7th century CE, the religion of Islam (see pp.124–147) spread across Persia, and Zoroastrians quickly found themselves in a minority

The desert villages of Persia (modern-day Iran) were the cradle of the Zoroastrian religion. The faith is still alive in Iran, but it is now a minority belief.

that often suffered persecution. Wanting to be able to practice their faith freely, from the 8th century CE onward, a number of Zoroastrians decided to leave their homeland to find a new place to live and worship. They settled in Gujarat, in northwestern India, where they became known as the Parsis, meaning the people from Persia.

The story of the emigration of the Parsis to India is told in the *Tale of Sanjan*, a book written by a Parsi priest in 1600. Because it was composed so

A Parsi priest offers prayers at a Zoroastrian temple. He wears a mouth-veil so that his breath does not pollute the sacred fire that burns in the temple.

in trade and later in shipbuilding. They also developed their faith, making it more accessible, partly in light of advice that they read in 19th-century Western studies of Zoroastrianism.

THE FAITH TODAY

Over the last few decades, Iran has been a strictly Muslim country and there are relatively few Zoroastrians

"ABSOLUTE IN POWER MAY THE HOLY BE."

Avesta, Yasna 8:6

long after the migration, it is not known how accurate it is historically, but it tells how the local Indian ruler gave the travelers permission to settle, provided that they learned the local language, observed local customs about purity and marriage, and carried no arms.

Although not much is known of their history, the Parsis appear to have lived for centuries in peace with their neighbors in Gujarat, prospering

left there today—the Iranian government puts the number at around 90,000; other estimates are much lower. There may be around 60,000 Parsis in India, where they tend to marry late or remain unmarried, resulting in a low birth-rate and declining numbers. There are also a few thousand Parsis in various locations around the world. However, these presently small populations are showing signs of increasing.

CORE BELIEFS

Zoroastrianism centers on the struggle between the supreme deity Ahura Mazda and his opponent Angra Mainyu. This struggle takes place on a cosmic level, but it is also supported on Earth by the faith's devotees, who live virtuously to ensure that good triumphs over evil.

THE WISE LORD

Modern scholars have found the roots of many of Zarathustra's ideas in early Hindu texts such as the Rig Veda (*see pp.170–171*), but the prophet himself believed that his experience of a series of visions came directly from God. He told his followers to worship only the supreme deity, the Wise Lord Ahura Mazda (also known by his Middle Persian name Ohrmazd). The prophet denied that other supernatural beings, such as ancient Persian deities called the *daevas*, were worthy of worship, because he saw them as spirits of destruction. However, in Zoroastrian belief, the universe's main destructive force is Angra Mainyu (Ahriman in Middle Persian), who is seen as the principal source of evil, suffering, disease, and death in the world. For Zarathustra and his followers, Angra Mainyu is the opponent of Ahura Mazda, but he is not his equal, as there

A stone head, thought to represent Ahura Mazda, found in modern Turkey. Persian conquests spread Zoroastrianism across the Near East.

is only one just and supreme God and that is Ahura Mazda. Because of its belief in a single supreme creator, Zoroastrianism is a monotheistic faith.

THE GREAT COSMIC STRUGGLE

According to Zoroastrian belief, after Ahura Mazda created the world, Angra Mainyu defiled it by bringing earthquakes. This destructive act created deep valleys in the once-beautiful, unscarred surface of the Earth, forced the sun away from its perfect position, which it now reaches only at midday, and brought sickness and death to the first human being. For 3,000 years after the Creation, Ahura Mazda and Angra Mainyu were almost evenly matched in battle, with Ahura Mazda's creative energy being constantly bombarded by Angra Mainyu's destructive forces. However, then the prophet Zarathustra was born and the balance of the battle began at last to turn in favor of goodness. Zoroastrians believe that, in their scheme of things, Ahura Mazda will be followed by a series of three saviors. The third of these figures will overcome evil in a cataclysmic battle. The Last Judgment will ensue, when Angra Mainyu will be banished and Ahura Mazda will reign supreme.

Zoroastrians look forward to this time of judgment, which they see as not the end of the world, but instead

THE AVESTA

Written in an alphabet devised specially for the purpose, the Zoroastrian sacred book, the Avesta, is actually only a fragment of the original text, much of which was lost during the period of persecution in Iran (*see p.150*). The surviving text is attributed wholly to Zarathustra, although it includes some hymns that probably predate him. An important section is the Yasna, a liturgical text that includes the Gathas, 17 hymns that were actually written by Zarathustra. Today Zoroastrians use a volume called the Khorda Avesta, which contains the essential texts for regular lay worship.

as a restoration or renovation of the cosmos, and a joining together of Heaven and Earth.

PERSONAL JUDGMENT

Zoroastrians believe that God created humanity, and that he intended for all people on Earth to take part with him in the great struggle between good and evil. For this reason, God gave the people free will. According to the Zoroastrian faith, individuals are judged twice: once when they die and once at the Last Judgment. The two judgments address, respectively, the individual's morality of thought and his or her morality of action. In both cases, moral failings are punished in Hell. However, these punishments are designed not to go on forever, but to cease when the dead person corrects their moral failing in the afterlife. At the end of the process of correction, the person goes to dwell with God in Heaven.

The Zoroastrian faith emphasizes the concept of free will, which has meant that,

for most of its history, this faith has placed a weighty significance on the moral responsibility of the individual—that in every action he or she makes, every human being has the opportunity to reinforce goodness in the world. The belief is that when all humans choose good over evil, Ahura Mazda will finally triumph over Angra Mainyu and Heaven and Earth will unite.

There was a deviation from this doctrine among some Zoroastrian believers during the Sassanian period (224–*ca*.636CE), when a third deity, Zurvan ("Time"), the parent of both Ahura Mazda and Angra Mainyu, was seen as an overarching force. The idea of Zurvan as controller of all things led to a doctrine of predestination (that our choices are already mapped out for us, so there is really no choice at all), but this idea did not endure. Today, Zoroastrians still place personal moral choice at the heart of their beliefs.

Winged guardians—*fravashis*—are angelic beings that watch over every individual, offering guidance throughout a person's life.

ETHICS, MORALITY, AND LAW

The prophet Zarathustra laid down many exacting moral rules for his followers, who are expected to adhere to these instructions sincerely. In this way, devotees can help Ahura Mazda in his struggle against evil and secure themselves a place in Heaven when they die.

WORKING FOR GOOD

Zoroastrian ethics are founded upon the concept of good—there is no notion of original sin as there is in Christianity (*see pp.90–91*). Ahura Mazda is the good God, and all his creation, which includes humankind, is fundamentally good. The Wise Lord uses his strength and goodness to struggle against Angra Mainyu (*see p.152*). As part of Ahura Mazda's creation, humanity is destined to join in with this struggle. In order to do this, every person needs to be able to distinguish good from evil, and to be able to make moral choices. So, according to the beliefs of Zoroastrianism, Ahura Mazda gave us the ability to make moral distinctions and to act freely upon them. This sets us apart from the rest of creation—other animals have no moral sense or free will—and allows us to take part in the great cosmic struggle.

A "Tower of Silence," on top of which Parsis leave their dead so that death cannot pollute Earth or Fire, both regarded as sacred.

In essence, our moral sense gives us the chance to choose between the qualities of Ahura Mazda—such as truthfulness and right-mindedness—and those of Angra Mainyu—deceitfulness and evil-mindedness. Making the right choice means that we support Ahura Mazda in his conflict with Angra Mainyu, playing our part in making the world a better place.

ZOROASTRIAN VIRTUES

The focus on moral choice makes Zoroastrianism a religion in which personal responsibility and morality are paramount. In practice, this means

upholding the various virtues outlined in the Zoroastrian scriptures. These begin with devotion to Ahura Mazda and his prophet, Zarathustra, offering regular prayers and worship, maintaining ritual purity, observing the proper rituals and festivals (*see pp.156–157*), and marrying a follower of the faith in order to preserve the religion for the next generation. Moral virtues include: telling the truth, being charitable and loving toward fellow humans, moderation in diet, being honest in dealings with others, and keeping promises. Zoroastrianism encourages hard work and industry, respect for elders and superiors, and the search for knowledge and wisdom. Followers of the faith are also encouraged to be tolerant and forgiving toward others—they are told to try to make their enemies into friends, to persuade sinners to reform, and to teach those who are ignorant or unlearned. Zoroastrians are expected to cultivate these virtues in their thoughts, language, and actions—their faith has been summed up in the phrase: "Good thoughts, good words, good deeds." In contrast, Zoroastrianism condemns vices such as anger, greed, idleness, arrogance, adultery, vengefulness, bad language, and violence, as well as those who turn away from their faith.

A Parsi priest explains the concept of guardian angels (*fravashis*) to a young girl during Zoroastrian New Year celebrations in India.

"I PRAISE GOOD THOUGHTS, GOOD WORDS... GOOD DEEDS"

Avesta, Yasna 0:4

PRACTICES AND FESTIVALS

Traditionally, Zoroastrians made sacrifices, which they offered at their temples, but today the most important form of their worship is both private and collective prayer. Communal meals to recognize the goodness of God's creation are also key to the practice of the faith.

WORSHIP

Regular worship, both at home and in the temple, is a requirement in Zoroastrianism. Much of this is private worship, usually in the form of prayers, the words of which are taken from the Avesta. Priests and the most observant lay people may pray five times a day, while others pray twice, once on rising and once on retiring at night. Those who wear the *sudreh* and *kushti* (the white shirt and the cord that are the traditional symbols of the faith) untie and retie the cord while praying, the knot acting as a symbol of their religious commitment. Another important act of worship is to light a fire in a ceremonial fire urn, feeding it

A sacred flame is kept alight in all Parsi temples to symbolize the eternal light and wisdom of Ahura Mazda.

with incense and reciting blessings as the smoke permeates the home. This fire symbolizes Ahura Mazda's divine light, energy, truth, and law.

Collective worship involves prayers at the temple, rituals around the temple fire, and a communal meal. Just as with worship in the home, fire forms the focus of temple worship: devotees keep the fire burning continuously in the temple so that Ahura Mazda's heavenly fire may merge with the ritual fire. In this way, the fire becomes a living symbol that takes on some of Ahura Mazda's holy qualities. However, although fire is central to temple worship, it is inaccurate (and offensive) to refer to Zoroastrians as "fire-worshippers"—fire is merely a tangible symbol of the single, purifying God.

LIFE-CYCLE RITUALS

Zoroastrianism's most important life-cycle ceremony is the Navjote ceremony, which takes place when a child is between the ages of seven and 12. At this ceremony, the young person takes on responsibility for upholding the faith and is given the *sudreh* and *kushti*. Although it is traditional to wear the shirt and cord, it is not essential. In places such as Iran, where Zoroastrians are still persecuted, devotees do not wear them, while they are much more often seen among Parsis in India.

A Zoroastrian woman pays her respects to an image of Ahura Mazda during an annual pilgrimage to a historic mountainside shrine.

Zoroastrianism also has distinctive funeral customs. Zoroastrians place a high importance on ritual cleanliness and in order to avoid polluting the earth (through burial) or fire (through cremation) with dead matter, they traditionally expose their dead on high platforms called "Towers of Silence" and leave nature to dispose of the flesh in its own way—often by being eaten by birds of prey.

ZOROASTRIAN FESTIVALS

Zoroastrianism has a reputation for being a faith of joyful celebration, and the Zoroastrian calendar contains many festivals. These are usually celebrated in the temple and the home, rather than outdoors, and feasting plays a key part. Celebratory meals represent a coming-together of the whole community, regardless of wealth.

The backbone of the year is formed by six seasonal festivals, called *gahanbars*, each in honor of one of the Amesha Spentas, a group of divine or angelic beings, each of which is responsible for a particular aspect of the universe. Along with Ahura Mazda, these beings create a divine group of seven, or "heptad." At ceremonial meals, followers symbolize this heptad by grouping the foods into sevens (for example, there might be seven kinds of fruit to eat). Each divine being's festival celebrates that being's specific aspect of creation; for example, the festival of Ardavisht celebrates the element of fire.

Five further festivals during the year honor five Yazatas. These are angelic beings whose name means "worthy of worship." Other days that Zoroastrians celebrate include New Year (*noruz*); the anniversaries of the birth and death of Zarathustra; Sadeh, a midwinter festival; and Pateti, a solemn day of penitence. Because Zoroastrians use three different versions of their calendar, the actual dates on which all these festivals occur can vary from one place or group of adherents to another.

At the Navjote ceremony, young Parsis are welcomed into the adult world of their faith and receive the *sudreh* (shirt) and *kushti* (cord)— symbols of loyalty.

INDIAN RELIGIONS

I ndia has one of the richest and most ancient of all religious traditions. Hinduism's roots stretch back into prehistory, while major religious upheavals have seen the birth of Buddhism and Jainism and, much later, Sikhism. These religions now have many adherents outside India, and Buddhism has developed in diverse ways among its converts beyond the subcontinent.

Hinduism is probably the oldest of today's major religions, and one of the most complex. It is likely to have begun among the people of the Indus Valley civilization in around 2500BCE, although the influence of Aryan invaders who arrived in northwest India around 1,000 years later contributed to its ideas and beliefs too. Out of this mix came Vedic religion, with its sacred texts, or Vedas,

The Hindu god Krisna (an incarnation of Visnu) is one of Hinduism's most popular deities.

which contain hymns of praise to many different gods. Later writings, and still more deities, were added in subsequent centuries to form the complex Hinduism with its myriad gods that is familiar today.

THE ROOTS OF A CULTURE
Many of the ideas central to Indian thought and life emerged from Hinduism —the system of social strata or castes, the notion of life as a series of rebirths dependent on the moral law of *karma*, the concept of an appropriate life-path or *dharma*—all these are central in Hinduism and have a strong influence on the other Indian religions, too. So is

the idea of *moksa*, or release from the round of rebirth, which some see as reaching a kind of union with the ultimate reality or god, Brahman, which acts as a supreme Absolute, unifying the diverse gods of Hinduism.

A GREAT RENEWAL
The 5th and 6th centuries BCE saw a major development in Indian religion, a kind of spiritual renewal that produced two major faiths. The first, and most influential on a global scale, was Buddhism, which is based on the teachings of the great spiritual leader Siddhartha Gautama, known as the Buddha ("enlightened one").

The Buddha taught his followers how to understand why life involves so much suffering, and promised those who followed his teachings a route out of both suffering and the round of birth, death, and rebirth. These ideas were hugely influential in India in the centuries after the Buddha's life, especially during the reign

"GOD IS NEARER TO YOU THAN ANYTHING ELSE."

Sri Ramakrishna, *Many Paths to the One God*

of the great Mauryan emperor Asoka, who in the 3rd century BCE promoted the faith all over the subcontinent. Buddhism's influence later waned in India, especially after the country was ruled by Muslims, but it spread widely—eastward to China and Japan, and southward to southeast Asia—and now Buddhism is truly international.

Meanwhile, another faith, Jainism, took hold at around the same time as Buddhism. The Jains developed one of the most exacting of all religions, in which the overriding value is non-violence. For Jains, the best way of life is that of the monk or nun, but even lay people aspire to a level of austerity that requires great strength and devotion. Jainism has always been the faith of a small but dedicated number of followers, but its ideal of non-violence has proved influential.

A Hindu meditates on a *ghat* (flight of steps) leading down to the sacred Ganges River.

A further renewal of Indian religion came with the foundation of Sikhism in the 15th century CE. Sikhs worship one God, and unlike the Hindus they believe that rather than manifesting himself in the form of gods or avatars, he communicates his will through teachers, known as Gurus. So Sikhs follow the teachings of their founder, Guru Nanak (*see p.210*), his nine successor Gurus, and the Sikh sacred text, the Guru Granth Sahib (*see pp.216–217*), which is held to be the final Guru.

Sikhism, which has a notable ethic of community service, remains strongest in its home territory—the Punjab—but there are also large Sikh communities in other parts of the world, including Britain, Canada, and the US.

HINDUISM

The ancient faith of Hinduism developed in India, where it has millions of followers to this day. Some say that there are literally thousands of Hindu deities, making the Hindu pantheon somewhat daunting for the uninitiated. However, this diversity is underpinned by a single unity: Hindus say that all of their gods are aspects of one supreme being.

The origins of Hinduism go back so far that there are no written records of its beginnings. However, it is likely that the faith originated in the Indus Valley, in what is now Pakistan, more than 3,000 years ago. Hindus believe that their faith has many founders, and that their earliest sacred texts, including hymns known as the Vedas, were revealed to ancient scholars directly from God. The Vedas are concerned with one group of gods and goddesses (known as the Vedic deities), but later texts introduce many more gods, and there are also local Indian deities to add into the mix. However, most Hindus have a special reverence for one particular god, the most popular being Siva, the destroyer, and Visnu, the protector. In addition, Hindus will make offerings to other popular deities, such as Ganesh, the god of good fortune, at times of special need; while women often worship one of the goddesses, such as Laksmi, goddess of wealth and purity. Although its myriad deities make Hinduism and its teachings extremely diverse, at its core lies the belief that all the various deities are aspects of the single eternal reality, a kind of universal spirituality or supreme existence known as Brahman.

Devotion to a deity occupies only part of Hindu belief. Like other faiths that originated in India, Hinduism is especially concerned with people's actions, and how these impact on what will happen to them when they die. Hindus believe that life consists of a continuous cycle of birth, death, and rebirth. This cycle is governed by the doctrine of *karma*, which asserts that a good life will be rewarded with a favorable reincarnation, whereas a life of sinfulness, selfishness, or indulgence will lead to reincarnation as a lower being in the next life.

The Hindu god Ganesh is depicted in Indian art with an elephant's head. In some stories, the head replaced his real head after Siva cut it off.

ORIGINS AND HISTORY

Hinduism has the longest history of all religions, its roots going back so far that it is difficult to pinpoint the origins. For Hindus, their faith has many founders and origins, unified, like their thousands of gods, by the belief that all are part of the all-embracing ultimate reality.

The beginnings of Hinduism can be traced right back to the Indian subcontinent's earliest city-based culture, the so-called Indus Valley civilization. This culture flourished in the 3rd millennium BCE, and archaeologists have unearthed its remains at the cities of Harappa, by the Ravi River, and Mohenjo-Daro, on the banks of the Indus. So far, scholars have been unable to decipher the script used by these people, so what we know about them comes from the physical remains of their buildings and the objects they left behind. From these it is clear that ritual cleanliness was important to them—their temples included large baths.

They seem to have worshipped both a goddess and a god with three faces, who is shown in the position of a yogi. This three-faced deity may be the origin of the triad of gods who later became central to Hinduism.

The priest kings of the Indus civilization ruled over both temporal and spiritual aspects of life.

During the 2nd millennium BCE, India was invaded by another people, known as the Aryans. They worshipped many gods, and saw these deities as forces of nature. We know about the Aryans' religion from texts in the ancient Sanskrit language that were written down in around 800BCE, but are probably based on beliefs stretching back centuries before.

FOUNDATIONS OF A FAITH

The Aryan scriptures, called the Vedas (from the Sanskrit word for knowledge), are the first texts of Hinduism. The oldest of the Vedas is the Rig Veda, which contains more than 1,000 hymns, each addressed to a specific god.

Among the many gods mentioned in these hymns, two of the most popular are the warrior deity Indra and the

THE ORIGINS OF THE GODS

The Vedic gods, who include figures such as Indra, Agni, and Varuna, were worshipped because they brought such benefits as health, prosperity, and victory. Some of the deities who became prominent later, such as Visnu, began as minor Vedic gods but in the later period became more complex, taking on responsibility for the entire cosmos. Other Hindu deities, such as the monkey god Hanuman, do not appear in the Vedas but come to light in later holy texts.

The monkey god Hanuman does not feature in the early Vedic texts, but appears later as an ally of Rama—an incarnation of the god Visnu.

fire god Agni. Sacrifices played a major part in the worship of these Vedic gods and the priests who presided over the rituals were among the most important people in Indian society.

A NEW SYNTHESIS

Around 600BCE the Indian religion underwent some major changes. This was the period in which Buddhism (*see p.182*) and Jainism (*see p.225*) emerged, and also when a number of other new teachings, seen by many as divine revelations, took Indian spirituality in new directions.

These new teachings, written down as the Upanishads (*see p.170*), were less to do with sacrifice and ritual and more concerned with searching for the ultimate reality. Along with other new texts, including the great Sanskrit epic poems, they introduced a whole host of new gods. The combination of these new gods, along with a much more philosophical concern with the meaning of life as well as parts of the Aryan tradition, help to make up the fascinating mixture that we now know as Hinduism.

The rich and relevant stories of its gods, especially those in the epics featuring the Lord Rama, penetrate every level of life and are always present for Hindus—Rama is invoked regularly, and his character is one that men strive to emulate, just as women look up to his faithful wife, Sita.

COMMENTARY AND INTERPRETATION

The Upanishads and Epics deal with some extremely complicated and difficult concepts, such as the meaning of reality, and tell long and complex stories involving a myriad of characters. Over a very long period, Hindu scholars began

The Minaksi Temple in Madurai, India, was completed around 2,000 years ago, although parts of its interior are far older.

to interpret the messages of these scriptures and present their essence in a way people could understand. One of the most influential interpretations was the Brahma Sutra, written in the 6th century CE, and it in turn inspired scholars and writers to produce their own summaries of Hindu philosophy.

The most notable commentators were Shankara (*ca.*788–820CE), Ramanuja (died 1137), and Madhva (*ca.*1197–1276). Shankara wrote commentaries on the Brahma Sutra and on another sacred text, the Bhagavad Gita. Influenced by Buddhist thinking, he described the world as *maya*, an illusion. Ramanuja, in commentaries on the same two texts, saw the cosmos as the body of God, but he also understood that God's nature is greater than this material aspect. Madhva, influenced by the Jains, looked to the essence of the soul for the source of each individual's destiny.

These philosophers of the Middle Ages delved deeply into the ideas behind their religion, drawing on concepts discussed by the leaders of the other Indian faiths, which

The Dakshineswar Kali Temple, India, where the philosopher and mystic Sri Ramakrishna was head priest.

had themselves at first been seen as branches of Hinduism. But they were unified in seeing Hinduism as a faith with many gods who were all in some way aspects of the ultimate God or reality, Brahman.

REFORM AND CHANGE

Another period of rethinking within Hinduism started during the 18th century, when Indians began to be influenced by the Europeans who at first traded with them and then conquered their country, bringing with them their Christian faith and values. Many Hindus were moved by the Christian story and impressed by the teachings of Jesus, but Hindu thinkers such as Rammohun Roy insisted that what was best in Christianity was already present in Indian religion.

Another hugely influential figure in Hinduism was the philosopher and mystic Sri Ramakrishna (1836–1886), who believed there was an ultimate truth that was common to all faiths, and that God, who made himself manifest in Hindu figures such as Rama and Krisna, was also present in figures such as Jesus. In his work, Ramakrishna both fostered monasticism and helped to promote educational and missionary activities. These two sides of his work were continued after his death by his followers in the Ramakrishna Mission, which helped to form a much broader understanding of Hinduism and went on to spread the faith beyond India.

A key follower of Ramakrishna was the teacher Vivekananda (1863–1902), who carried Hindu beliefs around the

Mahatma Gandhi is revered around the world as a pivotal figure in India's history. Traveling widely, he helped to spread awareness of Hindu culture.

movement was Ghanshyama, known as Swami Narayan (1781–1830), an outstanding preacher from Gujarat. His personality was so magnetic that it has attracted many devotees, including a large number of Indians in both Africa and Europe.

Another movement originating in Gujarat was founded by Sai Baba of Shirdi (died 1918). He was widely

"IN THE VASTNESS OF MY NATURE I PLACE THE SEED OF THINGS TO COME."

Krisna, in Bhagavad Gita 14:3

world, enthusing many non-Hindus with the ideas behind the faith for the first time. It was primarily the teachers such as Ramakrishna and Vivekananda who renewed Hinduism, showing how its beliefs could be relevant in the modern world.

NEW DIRECTIONS

Another group of leaders took the faith in fresh directions, founding new branches that have found many devotees. One notable figure in the

regarded by his followers as a saint and an incarnation of Siva. Sai Baba had a great interest in Islam and embraced elements of the faith in his religious outlook. The teachings of his sect about love and forgiveness later proved popular in the West.

So Hinduism, a faith that is identified more than any other with one country, India, is now a major global force. Its ability to adapt, its many gods, and its multilayered ideas have proved successful in the wider world.

CORE BELIEFS

Hinduism is the most diverse of the major faiths and one that can be interpreted in a variety of ways. The result is a complex religion, with thousands of gods, which displays no standard practice. There are, however, a few key concepts that are drawn on by all followers.

Hindu belief centers on three main ideas: the Absolute, *samsara*, and *moksa*.

THE ABSOLUTE

Hindus believe in an overall absolute reality known as Brahman. Because it is absolute, Brahman cannot be described, and is often talked about it in terms of what it is not—it is neither male nor female, nor manifest in any one form, and it does not

Laksmi, the Hindu goddess of wealth, fortune, love, and beauty, and consort of Visnu.

die. Creation, which is also infinite, is part of Brahman, and as humanity is part of creation we carry Brahman around with us, too. The part of the individual that is Brahman is the soul, known as the *atman*. This linking of the soul and the infinite, of *atman* and Brahman, is one example in Hinduism of the bonds between large and small, and God and human. For many, this is the essence of the religion.

THE PANTHEON

Another way of looking at Brahman is to see it manifested in scores of deities, the gods that make up the Hindu pantheon. Each deity is identified with an aspect of the ultimate reality, and Hindus revere them all. Of the many gods, the most prominent are a trio known as the Trimurti—a lofty creator figure called Brahma; Visnu, known as the preserver; and Siva, the destroyer of life who also recreates it. Each of the gods has his own female consort. These goddesses, Saraswati, Laksmi, and Kali, are powerful deities in their own right. In addition, Visnu has the special ability

---

BHAGAVAD GITA

The Bhagavad Gita (*see also p.170*) forms part of the Mahabharata. The hero, Arjuna, is unwilling to fight in a battle because he may kill some of his relatives. In the text, Krisna explains to him that it is his *dharma* as a warrior to fight. He goes on to say that there are three paths (of devotion to God, knowledge, and action with detachment) through which a person may reach a state of unity with God and truth. The way Krisna's words achieve a rich and deep reconciliation with the *dharma* make the Bhagavad Gita one of the most loved of all Hindu scriptures.

Krisna acts as Arjuna's charioteer in a famous scene from the Bhagavad Gita, a key sacred text in the Hindu religion.

to manifest himself on Earth in 10 different forms or avatars, the most widely revered being the noble lord Rama and the hero warrior god Krisna.

Most Hindus focus their worship on a particular god or goddess. Other gods are usually acknowledged in their worship, and a group of five (Devi, Ganesh, Narayan, Siva, and Surya) are often invoked at the beginning of Hindu worship. A believer may turn to another deity to offer prayers at a point in their life when they are coming into that deity's sphere of special influence.

SAMSARA TO MOKSA

Hindus believe in the concept of *samsara*, the continuous cycle of birth and reincarnation, and in *karma*, the law of cause and effect that links the way we live to the kind of rebirth we will have. Hindus hope to achieve a favorable rebirth by living well in their current life and thereby achieving good *karma*. Crucial to this process is *dharma*, the concept of what is right in both ritual and everyday behavior. Believers aspire to live as closely as possible to the *dharma*, the moral standard, that is right for them. But there

is also the hope that one can break out of the cycle of *samsara* by achieving *moksa* (*see p.172*), which the Bhagavad Gita describes as freedom from the body, from anger, from death, and even from *karma* itself.

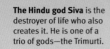

The Hindu god Siva is the destroyer of life who also creates it. He is one of a trio of gods—the Trimurti.

SRUTI AND SMRTI WRITINGS

The sacred texts of Hinduism are divided into two categories. The oldest are called the *sruti* texts. Although they are often difficult to understand, they are believed to be the holiest of the Hindu scriptures. Later and more accessible is the *smrti* literature of the great Hindu epic poems, which reveal truths through gripping stories and interesting characters.

SACRED WISDOM

Sruti literature is made up of the four collections known as the Vedas, and a much larger number of books called Upanishads. These works are known as *sruti*, or "heard," because the ancient sages went off to remote places to meditate, when they would hear or perceive sacred truths.

The word *veda* means knowledge, and the Vedas cover different areas of sacred knowledge and ritual: hymns to the gods in the Rig Veda; chants in the Sama Veda; rituals in the Yajur Veda; and rites and spells, especially those concerned with healing, in the Atharva Veda.

Indra, the Vedic god of weather and warfare, is an important deity in many Hindu tales.

The Upanishads focus on Brahman, and the relationship of the soul with this ultimate reality. Their title means "sitting down near to," just as followers of the early sages, or gurus, sat down next to their masters to learn their wisdom.

THE MAHABHARATA

The longer of the two epics that make up the *smrti* ("remembered") writings is the Mahabharata ("The Great Story of the Bharatas"). It tells of a long power struggle between two rival families, the Pandavas and Kauravas. Both of these families are descendants of a king called Bharata, whose name derives from an early name for India. The epic has a vast cast of characters and covers the whole range of human experience from love to war, interspersed with teaching on all kinds of subjects—politics, personal morality, and religion.

Saraswati, the river goddess, has been regarded in recent times as the patron goddess of knowledge, music, and the arts.

THE BHAGAVAD GITA

The sixth section of the Mahabharata is so famous that it is read as a book in its own right.

Called the Bhagavad Gita ("Song of the Adorable One"), it describes events before a great battle between two warring families. Arjuna, a member of the Pandava family, is preparing for the battle, but is overcome with horror at the prospect of war and tells his chariot driver that he cannot fight. But the chariot driver is Krisna, an avatar (manifestation) of the god Visnu. Krisna explains to Arjuna the concept of *dharma*, that each person must act according to the proper path set down for him. Finally, Arjuna understands that it is his *dharma* to be a warrior, and that, when he fights, he will be helping good triumph over evil. The Bhagavad Gita is the classic explanation of Hindu concepts, and is one of the best-loved Hindu scriptures.

THE RAMAYANA

The other Hindu epic, the Ramayana, tells the story of Rama, the seventh avatar of Visnu, and his loyal wife Sita. At its heart is a story about the abduction of Sita by a demon, Ravana, and her rescue by Rama, with the help of the monkey god Hanuman.

One of the most popular stories in Indian literature, the Ramayana appeals because it stresses the human side of Rama's character and portrays very real human emotions. It describes how its hero and heroine undergo hardship and pain, but find fulfilment through making the right moral choices and following their *dharmas*.

A pilgrim pauses on the banks of the Ganges river to read a passage from Hindu sacred scriptures.

ETHICS, MORALITY, AND LAW

The ethics of Hinduism are based on *karma*, the moral law of cause and effect, and on *dharma*, the concept of the correct moral path each person must follow. As our characters and circumstances vary, so the faith offers many ways a person can live well and follow their *dharma*.

Hindus aim to act and live well in order to produce positive *karma*. One lifetime is not enough to reach perfection and so people look forward to endless reincarnations as the cycle of *samsara* turns. Acting well is a matter of acting according to *dharma*, the path that is right. There is no single *dharma* (*dharma* means what is right in the specific circumstances), so each individual, society, and social class has its own *dharma*. Hindus also believe that *dharma* alters through a person's lifetime.

There are four traditional stages of life, each with its own *dharma*. The first stage, childhood, has a *dharma* dominated by education. The next stage, that of the household, is focused on bringing up a family. The third stage is when one becomes a grandparent, and its *dharma* involves retiring from the world of work and living a life that concentrates more closely on spiritual matters. The final stage marks the end of life, when a devout Hindu renounces the world and concentrates on the absolute.

MOKSA

The ultimate goal, which is recognized as being unattainable for most, is to move beyond the cycle of death and rebirth, and to attain a transcendent state known as *moksa*. To achieve this, the person has to realize the *atman*, the inner soul identified with Brahman, and merge with the absolute itself. There are several paths that can lead to this

Sadhus meditate and chant in a courtyard in Rishikesh, India. The Sadhus are a class of ascetic, itinerant Hindu holy men.

THE AUM

"Aum" or "Om" is a sacred syllable which is first recorded in the Upanishads. It is made up of three Sanskrit letters, and is said to be a kind of spiritual raw material that contains in its sound the beginning of all prayers and mantras. The fact that it is made up of three letters, and that writing it involves making a shape like a number 3, symbolizes the Trimurti or trio of principal Hindu gods. The silence after it is pronounced is said to stand for the absolute, Brahman.

state. One is a path of concentration on Brahman, a life of solitary meditation under the guidance of a teacher or guru and encompassing the discipline of yoga. The ascetic god Siva is an important example for those who follow this path. Another route to *moksa* is the path of action—pursuing good actions in the world, but in a way that is totally selfless. Arjuna, the hero of the Bhagavad Gita (*see p.168*), is the outstanding example of this kind of selfless action. Loving devotion to the divine is a third way a person can move toward *moksa*. The devotion of the god Krisna for his consort Rada provides a divine example of the intensity of this love, and of the fact that it is reciprocated freely by the deity.

These examples of deep holiness provide role models for Hindus who are following their *dharma*, even if they recognize that they will not necessarily attain *moksa*.

VALUES

Although *dharma* varies from one person to another, there are still Hindu values that are universal or widespread.

All life is sacred, so Hindus avoid violence, and many, though not all, are vegetarians because they object to killing animals for food. The cow is a sacred animal, and most Hindus will not eat beef or veal.

The raising of children is also very important, and traditionally, the female roles of motherhood and homemaker are valued highly. As well as keeping the home physically clean, they are also responsible for keeping it clean in a religious sense; for example, by keeping to codes of ritual cleanliness while preparing food. The women of the household are usually responsible for regular worship at the home's shrine.

CASTES AND VARNAS

Hindu society is divided into a series of social classes, called *varnas* and castes, into which people are born. Everyone's lives and actions depend on which class they are born into. A person's *dharma* is traditionally related directly to the *varna* into which they are born.

The four traditional *varnas* are the *brahman*, or priestly class; the *kshatriya*, or warriors; the *vaishya*, or merchants and farmers; and the *sudra*, or lowest division. On to this system of *varnas* fits another system of thousands of social groups or castes, which were originally defined by the work their members did and where they lived.

A child wears a red bindi mark, which once signified married status. It is now worn more widely.

The caste a Hindu is born into traditionally affects their choice of job, their choice of marriage partner, and the people with whom they may eat or from whom they may accept food. Hindu ethics fit into this class system, and obeying caste rules is important if a person is to stay ritually pure.

PRACTICES AND FESTIVALS

The long history of Hinduism has led to the development of a rich variety of rituals and other practices. Hindu observances range from quiet daily worship in front of a small shrine at home to national festivals that involve days of celebration all over India and beyond.

Hindus worship every day, either at the temple or, more commonly, at a small shrine in the home. This daily worship, known as *puja* (a word that conveys the meaning of honor and veneration), is an important and very diverse part of Hindu practice.

Puja centers on the image of a deity, which is regarded as a symbol of the god and, more than this, as part of the deity's essence. As such, images are regarded with great respect. Key elements of *puja* include ritual purity (it is common to bathe before *puja*), and the symbolic washing of the deity's image, which is treated as a guest in the house or temple.

Food, flowers, fragrant incense, and light in the form of a burning oil lamp, are offered to the deity. There may be hymns in honor of the god, especially in temple worship, and devotion can also be expressed by

Offerings of food are traditionally made during *puja*, the diverse daily worship of the Hindu gods.

dancing. A pivotal part of *puja* is *darshan*: having audience with or viewing the deity, which is done by either sitting facing the image of the deity or by walking around it.

THE CYCLE OF LIFE

There are 16 rituals, called *samskaras*, that mark the stages of a Hindu's life. The importance of children and family life in Hinduism means 11 of these are to do with babies and young children.

Many people will not celebrate all of these rituals, but the most popular are those that take place at birth (ceremonial cleansing and sacred sounds being whispered in the baby's ear) and the naming ceremony, at which songs are sung and the child's horoscope may be cast. Most important of all is the sacred thread ceremony, which is held between the ages of 6 and 14, the age variation depending partly on the family's social class. In this ritual, a boy is given a thread made of three strands of cotton yarn, symbolizing his link to God, his parents, and his teacher; he wears this sacred thread for the rest of his life.

Colorful weddings are one of the 16 *samskaras* that mark the stages of a Hindu life. Wedding customs vary, but most involve rites performed before a sacred fire.

Of the other *samskaras*, the most important are betrothal, marriage (accompanied by celebrations lasting several days), and the ceremonies that take place after a person dies.

FESTIVALS

Hinduism has many festivals, most of which are associated with specific seasons of the year. One of the most popular is Diwali, the festival of lights to the New Year in March or April. It celebrates both the spring harvest and the coming of the new year, and is marked by the relaxing of social rules, the playing of pranks, and the throwing of coloured powder, a trick once played by Krisna, whose image is carried through the streets.

Other festivals celebrate specific gods, including Ram Navami (Rama's birthday), Navami (celebrating the

"OFFER IN THY HEART ALL THY WORKS TO ME."

Bhagavad Gita 18:57

held in October or November, during which people decorate their homes, workplaces, and temples with lights. It is a time for celebration and also renewal —people decorate and clean their houses, and the goddess Laksmi is said to visit every home and to bring prosperity and happiness to those that are well decorated. Another popular festival, Holi, takes place in the lead-up goddess Durga), and Ganesh Chaturthi (in honour of the popular elephant-headed god, Ganesh). Most Hindu festivals are happy occasions, reinforcing the view that life is God-given and something to be enjoyed.

Kashmiri Pandit women light lamps during the annual Hindu festival of Jeth Ashtami, the birthday of goddess Ragni, at a shrine in Khirbhawani.

During the Hindu festival of Holi, people of all ages and castes cover themselves in brightly colored powder known as *gulal*. Holi, or the Festival of Colors, celebrates the coming of spring and remembers how the god Visnu overcame evil, demonstrating that faith prevails.

BRANCHES OF HINDUISM

There are many varieties of the Hindu faith. How people practice their religion varies in many ways, but one of the most important is the principal deity they worship. There are also several new religious movements with roots in Hinduism.

VAISNAVITES AND SAIVITES

▣ India   ⬛ c.600BCE   ⚱ 500 million (Vaisnavites); 200 million (Saivites)

One of the most popular of all the Hindu deities is Visnu, known as the preserver or sustainer of the universe. Devotees of Visnu, who are known as Vaisnavites, worship him as the supreme god, a figure unparalleled in his divine benevolence.

He is the deity who gives life to the creator, Brahma, who sits in a lotus blossom at Visnu's navel, and he also sustains and protects everything that Brahma creates. As well as inspiring devotion in his own right, he is also worshipped in the form of his avatars, especially Rama and Krisna.

The complement of Visnu is the god Siva. Known as "the destroyer," he recreates what he destroys. He also embraces other opposites too—life and death, time and eternity, and so on. This ability to bring opposites together is one of the aspects that fascinates Saivites, worshippers of Siva, about the deity. Hinduism is all about the reconciliation of diverse qualities by some higher divinity, and Siva embodies this coming together of opposites like no other deity. There is little wonder that for his worshippers he is seen as the supreme god. An especially popular depiction of Siva shows him as

Nataraja, or "Lord of the Dance". Having destroyed the universe, he then dances its recreation. As he remakes the universe with his dance, he carries fire, symbolizing destruction, in one of his hands, and a drum in another hand, representing the first sound that is made at the beginning of creation.

The Hindu god Visnu rides on the winged creature Garuda, accompanied by two consorts. One of the most popular Hindu deities, he is worshipped widely.

DEVOTION TO THE GODDESS

⚑ India   **✎** *ca.*600BCE   **♟** Not known

Each of the three gods of the Trimurti—Brahma, Visnu, and Siva—has his consort, and these goddesses can appear in a variety of forms and with various names. They are also seen as aspects of one "Great Goddess," known as Devi or Mahadevi.

ASPECTS OF THE GODDESS

The Great Goddess is widely worshipped in her various forms, the diverse characters of which attract worship for different reasons. One of the most popular forms of the goddess is the benign Laksmi, consort of Visnu and goddess of good fortune.

Laksmi is a deity who is known for her generosity; she also values social order and cleanliness, so devotees clean their houses diligently before celebrating her festivals. She is notable because she can change her identity according to her husband's different avatars—when he is Rama, she is Sita, for example. Brahma's consort

The deity Laksmi, known for her generosity, is one of the most popular forms taken by the Great Goddess.

is Saraswati, the goddess of the arts, who is said to be able to make anything that her husband thinks of. She is also goddess of learning and was attributed with the invention of the Sanskrit language, so there are shrines to her in schools and libraries. Siva's consort takes several forms, from the gentle, loving Parvati, often portrayed side by side with her husband, to the more warlike Kali and Durga. Kali is known as a slayer of demons and Durga is prized for her ability to destroy evil, but is also a fertility goddess, worshipped at harvest time and beloved of those who grow plants and herbs.

All these aspects of the Great Goddess are popular. They are widely worshipped in southern India and in rural communities elsewhere, and many of their devotees are women.

Saraswati is the goddess of wisdom and knowledge. This statue shows her holding a stylized musical instrument, as a mark of her mastery of the arts.

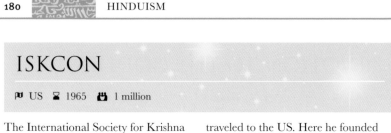

ISKCON

US   1965   1 million

The International Society for Krishna Consciousness is more widely known as the Hare Krishna movement. It is inspired by Chaitanya, a 16th-century mystic from Bengal who was said to be an incarnation of Krisna, and from the religious movement he founded, Gaudiya Vaisnavism.

In the 1920s, the leader of the Chaitanya movement in India instructed one of his followers to take his teachings to the English-speaking world. This command was fulfilled when, in 1965, the disciple, Prabhupada,

traveled to the US. Here he founded ISKCON, which attracted many non-Indians to Hinduism. Followers are devoted to Krisna, and focus their lives on him, chanting his name repeatedly, and renouncing violence, gambling, alcohol, and illicit sexual relationships.

Members of ISKCON chanting the Krishna mantra in public, an act believed to elevate consciousness.

CHURCH OF SHAIVA SIDDHANTA

US   1949   750,000

The Church of Shaiva Siddhanta (the Sacred Congregation of the Supreme God Siva's Revealed Truth) is one of a number of varieties of Hinduism centered on the god Siva. The church was founded by US master Satguru Shivaya Subramuniyaswami, known as Gurudeva, who had learned about Siva in Sri Lanka and was told by his teacher to spread devotion to the god to the US.

Gurudeva became widely respected in the Hindu community as one of the people who did most to spread knowledge of the religion beyond India. The variety of Hinduism that he took to the US was heavily influenced by that of the Shaivites of Sri Lanka. Members of the church devote

themselves to service to the community, reverence for Siva, yoga, and meditation, hoping to draw nearer to the god and achieve *moksa* (*see pp.168–169*). Values include vegetarianism and non-violence.

Gurudeva was honored by the World Religious Parliament for his work in disseminating Hindu beliefs outside India, and founded a number of other institutions to spread Hinduism in the New World—a monastery on Hawaii, the Himalayan Academy, and the newspaper Hinduism Today.

The Church has members in many countries as well as the US—the family congregation extends to Canada, Malaysia, Singapore, Mauritius, and several European nations, as well as India and Sri Lanka.

ELAN VITAL

US   1980s   Not known

The teacher Prem Pal Singh Rawat (born 1957), known as Maharaji, is a highly charismatic religious teacher whose ideas have roots in Hinduism and in other Indian religions, particularly Sikhism. He does not preach a specific creed or particular observances, but teaches a number of techniques that, when combined, are said to lead the pupil towards an inner contentment and joy. His Divine Light Mission, teaching that *moksa* comes through knowledge, began in the 1970s and grew quickly, particularly in the US. But in the 1980s, he founded a new movement, Elan Vital, which presented his ideas in a way that was free from suggestions that they were based on other religions.

Today, Elan Vital is made up of many independent organizations around the world, each working in a way that suits the local conditions. The organizations promote Maharaji's teachings and have been especially successful in attracting followers in India.

SATYA SAI BABA SOCIETY

India   1950   10 million

Satyanarayana Rajuin (born 1926) is said to have been responsible for numerous miracles from an early age. At the age of 14, he went into a trance after being stung by a scorpion. When he came out of the trance, he said he was a reincarnation of a guru called Shirdi Sai Baba, and henceforth was known as Satya Sai Baba. His fame spread as the result of his miracles, which included apparently producing objects out of thin air, and in the 1950s he began to attract followers who now number in their millions. He set down four key principles for disciples. First, they should seek the truth, *satya*, which should lead to a deeper understanding of life. This in turn should lead them to serve the community, attracting positive *karma* and leading to a favourable rebirth. Satya Sai Baba's second principle is duty, *dharma*, but he does not, like many Hindus, attach a specific *dharma* to each social class; all are said to be equal. His third principle is peace, *shanti*, and the fourth is divine love, *prema*.

Sai Baba appears before his followers in India. His branch of Hinduism is said to be followed in 130 countries.

BUDDHISM

Since its beginnings in India some 2,500 years ago, Buddhism has become one of the world's most popular religions. Millions of people in countries that stretch far and wide are inspired by the teachings of the Buddha, finding in them answers to their problems, guidance on following a path to a good life, and hope for the future.

B uddhism originated in the middle of the first millennium BCE in northern India when a young prince, called Siddhartha Gautama, left behind his life of riches and luxury to go on a quest to find out how to overcome human suffering. His quest ended when he underwent a transcendent religious experience, after which he became known as the Buddha, "the enlightened one." From then on, he dedicated his life to teaching and guiding others.

Buddhism spread widely, especially around the countries of eastern and southeastern Asia. In some countries, such as Thailand, it is the national religion, and learning about Buddhism is part of everyone's education. More recently, it has spread to the West, too, and there are now many Buddhists in the US and Europe. As the faith has spread, it has changed and adapted, so that there are now two very different strains of Buddhism—the older Theravada tradition and the younger Mahayana Buddhism, which itself has many different forms. As a result, the Buddhism of today is highly diverse and the differences between forms can be vast. For example, Theravada Buddhism has no concept of an all-powerful god, whereas in some kinds of Mahayana Buddhism there is such a concept. Although Buddhism means different things to different people, there are many elements of belief that unite the faith. All Buddhists are inspired by the Buddha's life and follow his teachings. All see their faith as an active religion that directly affects the way people live their lives. They try to live well, reduce human suffering, and give appropriate respect to the environment. And, like adherents of other eastern religions, all Buddhists see it as vital to accumulate good *karma*, so that they will enjoy a favorable rebirth into the next life.

In the Pali canon, the sacred scripture of the Theravada branch of Buddhism, the Buddha is said to have golden skin and dark blue hair.

ORIGINS AND HISTORY

Originating in northern India in the 6th century BCE, the teachings of Siddhartha Gautama—the Buddha—quickly found followers in India and, after the Buddha's death, in other Asian countries, too. Only in the last 150 years has it found many adherents farther afield.

THE ROUTE TO ENLIGHTENMENT

When Siddhartha Gautama, prince of the Sakya tribe of Nepal, was a small child, a *brahmin* (wise man) foretold that as a grown man, Siddhartha would become an enlightened sage who would help others overcome suffering. At this time to be a sage meant to become a poor itinerant beggar, and Siddhartha's father did not want this for his son. So he protected the boy, confining him to the palace and giving him every

Some depictions of the birth of the Buddha show him emerging from a lotus flower, the symbol of Buddhist doctrine.

luxury. However, by the time he was a young man, Siddhartha wanted to see the world, and he persuaded his father to let him go on a series of journeys. For the first time, Siddhartha saw evidence of suffering—his journeys included encounters with the aged and sick, and with a dead man being carried to his cremation. Some accounts of Siddhartha's life portray these experiences as occurring on actual, physical journeys; others depict them as spiritual adventures. But the result is the same: Siddhartha understood human suffering. When he met a wandering beggar, Siddhartha decided to

THE BUDDHA'S ENLIGHTENMENT

Accounts of the life of the Buddha say that he meditated under the *bodhi* tree for at least three days and nights before attaining enlightenment—a spiritual and intellectual wakefulness, wisdom, illumination, and understanding. After enlightenment, the Buddha intended to stay where he was, in a state of *nirvana*, seeing and understanding everything. But the Hindu god Brahma persuaded him to leave and teach others how to reach enlightenment, too.

Buddhists venerate images of the *bodhi* tree. Cuttings were taken from the original, and trees from the same line are believed still to exist.

leave his family, follow the ascetic's path, and search for the truth and for ways to overcome hardship. Finally, thin and exhausted, he sat down under a *bodhi* (or *bo*) tree at Bodh Gaya, in northeast India, to meditate. Siddhartha meditated until he reached a transcendent state known as enlightenment or *nirvana*, in which he completely understood life, and became free from the fear of human suffering and the endless round of death and rebirth. He had become a Buddha, an enlightened being, who could understand the truths of existence. From this point on he was known as the Buddha.

THE BUDDHA AND HIS FOLLOWERS

Traditional versions of the Buddha's life story say that, after enlightenmenment, the Buddha meditated under the tree for several weeks, at the end of which he began to tell others about his perceptions—for example, that the best way to live was to follow a middle way between the paths of luxury and poverty. Soon, like many Indian sages, he had a group of followers, who listened intently to his ideas about the

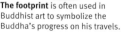

The footprint is often used in Buddhist art to symbolize the Buddha's progress on his travels.

problem of suffering and the best ways to overcome it. He preached his first sermon in a deer park at Sarnath in northeast India, where he had realized that his first five followers, known as the five ascetics, whom he had known previously, were living. This sermon marked the start of a preaching and teaching career that lasted some 40 years until the Buddha died in 483BCE, aged about 80.

Siddhartha's death came about when, visiting a smith in Kusinara (modern-day Kasia in northern India), he ate some poisoned food. Realizing that the food was going to kill him, he told his followers not to eat it, then lay down and meditated until finally he died. According to Buddhist legend, at his death the Buddha underwent a second, complete *nirvana* that took him from the world of the living forever.

By the time of the Buddha's death, his followers had memorized his teachings and they passed down their teacher's words to a growing band of disciples, who spread the ideas of Buddhism around India. These teachings became the core of the first Buddhist scriptures (*see below*). Along with the rules followed by Buddhist monks, the teachings were confirmed as genuine at several early Buddhist Councils from the 5th to the 3rd centuries BCE. Buddhist monks subsequently wrote down the scriptures.

TWO MAIN BRANCHES

The Buddha's followers spread his ideas across India and beyond. The teachings proved popular and adaptable, taking

In the 1st century CE, Buddhism worked its way north and east to China, Mongolia, and Tibet. This second strand became a distinctive branch of the faith, now known as Mahayana Buddhism (*see p.201*), or sometimes northern Buddhism. Mahayana Buddhism itself grew sub-branches and local strains, notably the tradition of Tantric Buddhism, based on Tibetan texts, and the austere branch known as Zen that developed in Japan. These

"I PREACH WITH EVER THE SAME VOICE."

Diamond Sutra

root in a variety of different places and cultures. From its base in northern India, Buddhism began to spread across the subcontinent in the 3rd century BCE, encouraged by the Indian emperor Asoka. Asoka was a member of the Mauryan dynasty of rulers, who united most of India, but who had to use violence in order to protect their borders from their enemies. According to tradition, Asoka was ashamed of the bloodshed that he had to inflict in order to secure his rule, and so turned to the non-violent faith of Buddhism to repent. Asoka built shrines in many places in India, some of which still exist, and put up Buddhist inscriptions. By the middle of the 3rd century BCE, the original strand of the faith had spread through India and south to Sri Lanka. Later, Buddhism traveled from here across the Indian Ocean to southeast Asia. This original strand is known as Theravada Buddhism (*see p.200*)

sub-branches are amazingly varied, even in terms of basic concepts such as which scriptures to follow.

THE BUDDHIST SCRIPTURES

Buddhism has no single sacred text like Judaism's Hebrew Bible or Islam's Qur'an. Theravada Buddhists use a collection of the Buddha's teachings recorded in the Indian language of Pali and known collectively as the Pali Canon (*see pp.192–193*). Later, Mahayana Buddhists developed their own versions of these teachings, which they wrote down in the texts known as the sutras, which are claimed to be genuine accounts of the Buddha's life and work. One of the most important of these is the Lotus Sutra, which was probably compiled during the 1st century CE. Written mostly in verse, this text is particularly

Bodhisattvas are enlightened beings, according to Buddhist belief. Statues of them, like this one at Po Lin Monastery in Hong Kong, are widespread.

revered among Buddhists in China and Japan, many of whom believe that they can come closer to *nirvana* by simply reciting or chanting its words.

A FAITH WITHOUT GODS

In its most basic form, Buddhism, whether Theravada or Mahayana, has no gods, because the Buddha explained that believing in and following the *dhamma* (his teaching), rather than worship, would lead to enlightenment. The Buddha himself is seen as an enlightened teacher, but not as a deity. Variants of Buddhism, especially of Mahayana Buddhism, recognize other figures—the saintlike *bodhisattvas*, or "Buddhas-to-be"—who renounce enlightenment in order to help others to reach *nirvana*.

Buddhist philosophy has been embraced by many Westerners seeking "enlightened" lifestyles.

BUDDHISM IN THE EAST

Over time, the influence of Buddhism declined in India itself, especially after the country was taken over by Muslim rulers in the 16th century. However,

Theravada Buddhist monks worship at a monastery in Wimbledon, England. Buddhism has increasing numbers of followers throughout the Western world.

Buddhism has been a vital force for hundreds of years in the lives of millions of people in the rest of Asia. Japan has proved a special stronghold for both Zen Buddhism (*see p.202*) and Nichiren Buddhism (*see p.203*), which is based on the teachings of Nichiren, a 13th-century spiritual leader who started his working life as a fisherman. This branch of Buddhism has spread rapidly and widely, and a number of faith movements based on Nichiren's teachings now exist outside Japan.

Buddhism has a long history in China, too. As well as having its ideas absorbed into China's popular religion (*see pp.188–189*), a distinctive form of the faith, known as Pure Land (*see p.203*), developed there. Followers have special reverence for the *bodhisattva* Amitabha (*see p.311*) and hope to be reborn into the heavenlike region of the Pure Land when they die.

THE SPREAD OF BUDDHISM

Buddhism has been remarkable among the eastern religions for the way it has adapted to local ideas and conditions while maintaining the Buddha's essential teaching. After a slow start in India, the faith spread through much of eastern and southeastern Asia, where it is still hugely influential. During the last century, increasing numbers of people in the Western world have also adopted the faith.

THE THERAVADA TRADITION

At the same time as the Emperor Asoka was promoting Buddhism (*see p.186*), merchants opened up trade routes through southern India. Some of these merchants were Buddhist and took their religion with them to new places. Then, Buddhist monks followed in their footsteps. Eventually, Buddhism crossed the sea to Sri Lanka, and from there to Burma, Cambodia, Thailand, and Laos. The original Theravada form (*see p.200*) is still practiced widely in these countries today. In Thailand it is the national religion, and in Burma monks and nuns who devote their lives to Theravada Buddhism are greatly respected.

Buddhist sutras (prayers), accompanied by illustrations, fill the pages of this ancient Chinese document.

THE MAHAYANA TRADITION

While Theravada Buddhism was spreading across the oceans, a completely new branch, Mahayana Buddhism, had begun to develop (*see p.201*). During the 1st century CE, this new form spread initially across Tibet, Mongolia, and China.

Mahayana Buddhism, with its many gods and *bodhisattvas*, was particularly at home in Chinese culture. Soon the Chinese were worshipping the *bodhisattvas* side by

side with the deities of Chinese popular religion and the spirits and immortals of Daoism. From China, Mahayana Buddhism soon reached Vietnam and Korea—and also Japan, where the Chinese branch known as Ch'an Buddhism became what we know today as Zen.

Ananda, the Buddha's attendant, helped to spread Buddhist practice after his mentor's death.

Although Buddhism lost its footing in India, it has remained a strong spiritual force in most of these other Asian countries, and now also has a firm foothold in the West.

BUDDHISM IN THE WEST

In the 19th and 20th centuries, Buddhism spread to the rest of the world, especially to Europe and the United States. The first Western conversions to the Theravada tradition, which was seen as the "pure" form of the faith, took place around 1880. In the 20th century, groups such as the Buddhist Society of Great Britain won many converts to Theravada Buddhism, but branches of the Mahayana tradition also attracted attention. Many people became interested in Zen Buddhism after reading works by D. T. Suzuki and the British scholar Christmas Humphreys, as well as books such as Robert Pirsig's *Zen and the Art of Motorcycle Maintenance*, first published in 1974. Tantric Buddhism (*see pp.204–205*) has now attracted many Western followers, too.

The Temple of the Tooth in Sri Lanka is said to house the Buddha's tooth, making it a popular place of Buddhist pilgrimage.

CORE BELIEFS

The Buddha set out his core doctrines very clearly in the form of two lists: the Four Noble Truths about suffering, and the Noble Eightfold Path, which explains how we can avoid suffering and live a better life. All the later ideas of Buddhism are founded on these essential beliefs.

THE FOUR NOBLE TRUTHS

The foundation of all the Buddha's teachings are the Four Noble Truths, which deal with suffering. The first Truth is that all life is suffering—meaning not simply physical pain, but also disharmonies and problems in all life's spheres, from personal, physical, and mental to economic and social. The second Truth is that the cause of suffering is desire, because humans always want what they do not have. The third Truth is that suffering will end when we are free from desire, and the fourth is that release from desire and suffering will occur as a result of following the Noble Eightfold Path.

THE BUDDHA'S NOBLE EIGHTFOLD PATH

A collection of the Buddha's teachings, the Noble Eightfold Path makes up a guide for virtuous living. It is not eight consecutive steps on a journey to perfection, but eight elements that the Buddhist should aim to practice all at once. Each element of the path deals

A wall relief shows the Buddha teaching gods in heaven after his death. The cultivation of spiritual wisdom is a key goal for Buddhist worshippers.

with a specific human activity. The first, "Right understanding," means that a Buddhist must grasp the Four Noble Truths and understand the nature of existence. The second, "Right intention" (or "Right thought"), indicates that the person must want to change, and in doing so must rid their mind of negative thoughts and feelings, especially desire. The third element of the path, "Right speech," involves telling the truth and not boasting or using coarse language. "Right conduct," the fourth element, means that a person's actions must try to be without ego or thought for the self, and they must be good and moral in order to defeat evil. The fifth part, "Right occupation," means choosing a job that is useful and does not involve such things as bloodshed, arms-dealing, slavery, or people-trafficking. The final three

THE WHEEL OF LAW

The Buddha's first sermon following his enlightenment is known as "The Discourse on Setting in Motion the Wheel of the Law." A long-established symbol of Buddhism, this wheel is usually shown with eight spokes, each of which represents a part of the Noble Eightfold Path (*see above*). And, as the wheel is circular, and so has no beginning or end, it is seen to possess the same eternal properties as the Buddha's teachings.

elements are "Right effort," cultivating self-knowledge and self-discipline; "Right mindfulness," avoiding extremes and banishing vices such as sloth, malevolence, doubt, and worry; and "Right concentration," which is concerned with meditation.

GUIDING PRINCIPLES

There are several key principles behind the Eightfold Path. One is that the Buddha asked people to avoid extremes and follow a middle way. On a personal level, he wanted to leave behind both the luxury of his upbringing (*see p.184*) and the ascetic's way of poverty and find a balance between them. Another key idea was that people should leave behind their ego to reach a state of *anatta* ("no-self") to better attend to the needs of others and better follow certain elements of the Eightfold Path, such as "Right intention" and "Right conduct." There is also another reason to achieve *anatta*. Buddhism recognizes *samsara*, the eternal round of death and rebirth, and the law of *karma* —that a person's deeds in one life affect their rebirth into the next. If there is no self, *karma* has nothing to attach itself to, and so the person comes closer to avoiding *samsara*, and to reaching the ultimate goal of the state of enlightenment, or *nirvana*.

Dragons or serpents are symbolic guardians at the gates of Buddhist temples. This example is from Thailand.

THE PALI CANON

The Buddha's teachings, originally handed down by word of mouth from one generation of monks to the next, are preserved in a series of documents in Pali, an ancient Indian literary language. Monks of the Theravada tradition (*see p.200*) wrote these scriptures down several hundred years after the Buddha died, and most of their teachings are also accepted by Mahayana Buddhists (*see p.201*).

VINAYA PITAKA

The Pali scriptures are gathered together in three collections, known as the three baskets (*ti-pitaka* in Pali). Monasticism plays a key part in Theravada Buddhism, so the first collection of scriptures, the Vinaya Pitaka, contains rules for monks and nuns. Many Theravada Buddhists join a monastery—sometimes for a short period, sometimes for life. The monastic community is important for lay people too, because they can acquire merit by making donations of food to the monks or nuns. Monastic guidelines therefore have a key importance in Buddhism. The section covering the monastic rules is called the Patimokkha, a word carrying the meaning of "things that should be made binding." The number of rules varies in the different versions of the text, but there are always more than 200 rules, and they cover practical aspects of monastic life, such as food, clothing, and housing, as well as ethical issues. The Vinaya Pitaka also includes guidelines for settling disputes and procedures for dealing with monks or nuns who have broken monastic rules.

A Buddhist monk reads from the Pali Canon, which is traditionally printed on dried palm leaves.

The collection also contains stories about the Buddha's life and historical accounts of the early communities of monks. Other branches of Buddhism have produced their own versions of these texts, which exist in the Chinese and Tibetan languages.

SUTTA PITAKA

This collection contains a series of teachings and discourses based on the recollections of the Buddha's own words memorized by his closest follower, Ananda. It is a large collection, and contains several different kinds of texts, from lengthy dialogues to shorter stories and sayings. Some of its most interesting sections are the Jatakas, narratives of the previous lives of the Buddha, which tell of the selfless deeds of the being—sometimes human, sometimes animal in form—who would later be born as the Buddha. These stories, which read like traditional fables, all have morals, and are highly entertaining. They also form valuable historical sources about life in India at the time of the Buddha.

The other important section of the Sutta Pitaka is called the Dhammapada. It is a collection of 423 verses that together explain how to live a life that will lead to enlightenment. Its key messages— living a good life, avoiding evil, cultivating a pure mind—are still important to Buddhists everywhere, and the Dhammapada is one of the most popular and most quoted of all Buddhist scriptures.

The Sutta Pitaka as a whole, with its vivid stories and inspiring teachings, is the part of the Pali canon that appeals most widely

to lay Buddhists. There are also Chinese versions of the collection, but the Pali version is the most complete.

ABHIDHAMMA PITAKA

The name of this part of the Pali Canon means "higher doctrine" and

A stone tablet from a series of 729 that together contain the entire text of the Buddhist canon. The scriptures are still the subject of intense study.

its analytical, interpretative content appeals mainly to monks and scholars. It is made up of a number of analyses of the Buddha's teachings and has itself been the subject of extensive analysis by Buddhist scholars— commentaries have been written on each of its seven books along with works examining the whole collection.

ETHICS, MORALITY, AND LAW

Buddhists are encouraged to help those in need, to be considerate, to avoid violence, and to refrain from activities that harm others. They follow an ancient set of moral precepts, the *pancha sila*, which are as relevant today as when they were drawn up many centuries ago.

GOOD AND EVIL

As in the other religions of India, such as Hinduism and Jainism, Buddhism adheres to the law of moral cause and effect, or *karma*. According to this law, human beings accrue merit or demerit (good or bad *karma*) as a result of their behavior. At death, the final balance of this good and bad *karma* determines whether the person's rebirth is favorable (such as being reborn as a human again, rather than as an animal), or not. Buddhists hope eventually to break free from the cycle of death and rebirth by reaching enlightenment (*see p.185*), but they realize that for most people this will take a very long time. In the meantime, they hope to build up merit by following the ethical precepts laid down when

A Buddhist monk cares for a tiger that lives among the monks at Wat Pa Luangta, Thailand. Kindness to all living things is a key Buddhist precept.

Buddhism began. There are eight main moral precepts, although three apply principally to monks and nuns.

CODE OF CONDUCT

The basic guidelines of Buddhist morality are laid down in the Eightfold Path (*see pp.190–191*), which forms one of the core doctrines of Buddhism. Among other things, the Eightfold Path encourages Buddhists to act with "Right speech," "Right conduct," and also "Right occupation." But Buddhism has added a number of more specific ethical instructions to guide followers, too. Chief among these are the *pancha*

THE JAKATA STORIES

Buddhist literature contains a body of some 550 tales of the Buddha's former lives. Most of these tales relate how the Buddha-to-be performed an act of virtue, bravery, or self-sacrifice in order to help others. In one story, he is a stag who offers his own life to huntsmen in place of a doe that is nursing her fawn; in another he is a monkey who injures himself when he stretches his body between two trees to form a bridge so that his tribe can escape pursuers. These stories relate a level of selflessness that followers of the Buddha are encouraged to adopt in their own lives.

sila ("five moral precepts"), a group of widely accepted rules that dates back to the beginnings of the faith.

The first precept is not to harm living things, a rule influenced by the Indian ideal of *ahimsa* (non-violence). For many Buddhists this rule, as well as prohibiting harm to humans, places a ban on harming animals—most Buddhists do not take part in blood sports and are vegetarian. However, some take a pragmatic course: they prefer not to kill animals themselves but will eat those killed by others. The second precept is not to take what has not been given. This rules out stealing, and also means that monks may accept charitable gifts but they may not beg, as the gifts must be given willingly. The third precept places a ban on misconduct involving the senses—in other words on sexual misconduct. The fourth is to abstain from false speech,

Several of the Buddha's hand gestures have specific meaning. The right hand raised to shoulder height, palm outward, is a gesture of loving kindness.

so Buddhists should not lie, nor should they make offensive remarks or gestures. The fifth and final precept bans the use of drugs or alcohol, which affect the mind, thus making it impossible to make proper moral choices.

MONASTIC PRECEPTS

The stricter life of the Buddhist monk or nun requires three further moral precepts. These were drawn up in the early history of Buddhism, and they show an austerity in monastic life that exists even today. First, Buddhist monks and nuns should avoid eating at the wrong time (traditionally, meals are taken before midday). Second, they should avoid "secular" behavior, such as going to the theater or dancing. Finally, they should not use high chairs or beds, which represent the comfortable furniture owned by the wealthy.

PRACTICES AND FESTIVALS

Buddhism is about absorbing the teachings of the Buddha and living a life inspired by them, which means that it does not have to be a ritualistic faith. Nevertheless, Buddhism does have several practices of regular devotion, and festivals that mark key points in the year.

THE TRIPLE REFUGE

Buddhists revere the Buddha, and, although he is not a god, their religious practices reflect the enormous respect that he inspires. At the heart of Buddhist ritual practice is the recitation of the Triple Refuge: "I go to the Buddha for my refuge. I go to the *dhamma* for my refuge. I go to the *sangha* for my refuge." This is a way for Buddhist followers to voice their commitment to the Buddha as an authoritative, even infallible, teacher; to affirm their faith in his teaching (*dhamma*), especially the Noble Truths and Eightfold Path (*see pp.190–191*); and to openly declare their trust in the Buddhist monastic community (*sangha*),

which includes the Buddha's first five companions (the first Buddhist monks) and the wider community of Buddhist monks and nuns.

BECOMING A MONK

Monasticism plays an important role in Buddhist practice, especially in the practice of Theravada Buddhism (*see p.200*). In this form of Buddhism many young people become monks or nuns, and still more boys join a monastery as novices for a short period as part of their education. Buddhist monks and nuns must obey a series of rules that regulate every aspect of their lives. They renounce property, money, sexual relations, and luxury, living a simple life, wearing plain robes, and shaving their heads. They spend much time meditating, and some live in remote country monasteries. However, they do not cut themselves off from the wider community. They teach others about the *dhamma*, they care for the needy, and they help the lay people who give them their food to acquire merit (good *karma*).

THE CYCLE OF LIFE

Buddhism has two very important life-cycle rituals. The first of these is an initiation ceremony, which introduces a child or adolescent into adult society and prepares the young person to spend time in a monastery. Those being initiated may be given rich clothes to wear, like those that Siddhartha put on when he went on his journeys to discover the truth about suffering, or

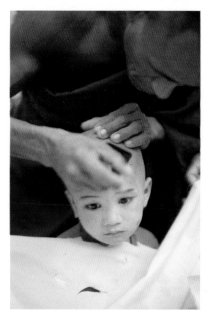

A boy has his head shaved before entering a Buddhist monastery. The shaved head represents a monk's commitment to his faith.

they may be given their monastic robes. The second is a funeral ceremony. When a person dies, the body is taken to the temple where the monks make chants or recitations that dwell on the process of death and rebirth. The prospect of rebirth helps to make Buddhist funerals hopeful occasions, in spite of their inevitable sadness. Cremation is common, especially in Theravada Buddhism, but some Mahayana Buddhists (*see p.201*) also practice burial.

Incense is burned in pots during formal Buddhist ceremonies and worship.

BUDDHIST FESTIVALS

Because Buddhism spread through many countries (*see pp.188–189*), it has a rich tradition of festivals, many of them joyous celebrations of the Buddha or the spread of Buddhism. The Buddha's birthday is particularly widely celebrated. In the Theravada tradition, his birthday is usually marked as part of the festival called Vesak, which celebrates not only the great teacher's birth, but also his enlightenment (*see p.185*) and death. Followers clean temples, make offerings, and light lanterns to symbolize the Buddha's enlightenment.

In Japan, Mahayana Buddhists hold the flower festival Hana Matsuri to mark the Buddha's birthday. Other notable festivals include New Year (famous for its water-sprinkling rites, symbolizing cleanliness), Asala Puja, a major festival in Sri Lanka that celebrates the Buddha's first sermon, and Parinibbana, a festival belonging to the Mahayana tradition that commemorates the Buddha's death and second and final *nirvana*.

A monk prostrates himself while he recites the "Triple Refuge," a declaration that he takes refuge in three aspects of Buddhist faith.

New Year in Thailand is a time for celebration and merry-making. Water plays an important part in the festivities: images of the Buddha are washed, eminent Buddhists are offered bowls of cool water, and everyone has fun spraying and throwing water over everyone else.

BRANCHES OF BUDDHISM

Buddhism has two main branches, Theravada and Mahayana, but also several others. Although their practices and sometimes beliefs vary, all forms of Buddhism share a commitment to the Buddha's teachings, to live selflessly, and to follow the Eightfold Path.

THERAVADA BUDDHISM

📍 Northern India   ⏳ 6th century BCE   👥 More than 100 million

Practiced in Thailand, Laos, Cambodia, and Burma, Theravada Buddhism is generally the form of Buddhism closest to the Buddha's original teachings, known as the *dhamma*, and highlights the importance of the *sangha*, or community of monks.

Theravada monks (and nuns, although they have a lesser status) live in basic monastic accommodation with few possessions. They follow the five precepts (*see p.194*) and every day leave the monastery to travel among lay people, who give them food in order to accrue merit (good *karma*). Monks teach the *dhamma* and the scriptures of the Pali Canon, but most importantly they meditate—to empty their minds of selfhood and come closer to *nirvana*.

Sometimes lay Buddhists will also enter the monasteries, accept the monastic lifestyle, and benefit from the monks' teaching. Outside the monastery, lay people regularly practice meditation, valuing the way it empties the mind, and hoping that this practice, as well as following the Eightfold Path (*see pp.190–191*), will enable them to live well and have a favorable rebirth.

Theravada monks may practice scholarship and engage in social work, but they spend a great deal of their time in deep meditation.

MAHAYANA BUDDHISM

📍 Northwestern India   ⚱ 3rd–2nd century BCE   ⛩ More than 250 million

The other principal branch of Buddhism (along with Theravada), Mahayana Buddhism developed after the Buddha's death and is now practiced in large areas of Asia from China to Korea. Compared with Theravada, it has a more complex view of Buddhahood, recognizes additional scriptures, and extends the Buddhist concept of the *sangha* to include the lay as well as the monastic population.

MANY BUDDHAS

In Theravada Buddhism (*see facing page*), the Buddha ceased to exist when he reached his final *nirvana*, leaving behind only his teachings, the *dhamma*. Mahayana Buddhists believe that the Buddha survives, and that they should worship him. They also believe that other beings can become Buddhas, too. When a person loses selfhood, what is left is a kind of inner essence called Buddha-nature. Mahayana Buddhists recognize a collection of beings who have attained Buddhahood and are worthy of worship.

ENLIGHTENED BEINGS

Two of the most important values in Mahayana Buddhism are wisdom and compassion, characteristics that every Buddhist aspires to. People who,

One of a series of wooden pillars on Hong Kong's Lantau Island carved with the Heart Sutra—one of the world's best-known Buddhist sutras (prayers).

through their character and their religious practice, banish selfhood are then able to approach the state of *nirvana*. But to Mahayana Buddhists, *nirvana* has no purpose unless it is used to assist others along their spiritual path. So, those who come close to *nirvana* normally remain in the world as saintly beings who are enlightened but living. They are known as *bodhisattvas* (and sometimes Buddhas) and demonstrate six perfections: generosity, morality, patience, vigor, meditation, and wisdom.

The *bodhisattvas* also attract devotion, and in many cultures are believed to respond to appeals from the needy. Popular *bodhisattvas*, such as Amitabha, the Buddha of Infinite Light, and Avalokitesvara, the Lord Who Looks Down (with compassion), are seen as gods in China and elsewhere.

The Diamond Sutra of Mahayana Buddhism is a key text for some Chinese Buddhists. The oldest-known printed book is a copy of this sutra from 868CE.

ZEN BUDDHISM

📛 Japan   ⏳ 12th century CE   ⛪ 5 million

In the 12th century a form of Chinese Buddhism called Ch'an took root in Japan, where it became known as Zen.

According to Zen, everyone is a Buddha—but not everyone has realized their potential Buddhahood or awoken to it. In addition, we all have a single identity that unites not only everyone, but also everything. We are identical with the cosmos and share our identity with all that is in it—from the tallest mountain to the tiniest grain of sand. Zen pervades every aspect of life and Zen Buddhists bring their beliefs to bear on each activity that they perform—both work and play, both physical and spiritual exercise. Activities that are especially expressive in Zen Buddhism include creating minimalist gardens and

A painting symbolizing the importance of serene meditation in the Zen branch of Buddhism.

composing poetry, often in the short, 14-syllable form known as the *haiku*.

SCHOOLS OF ZEN

The best-known schools of Zen Buddhism are Rinzai and Soto. Founded by the monk Eisai (1141–1215), who brought Buddhism to Japan from China, Rinzai challenges conventional ways of thinking. Rinzai masters may act in surprising ways, sometimes shouting at or hitting their pupils. The purpose is to shock pupils into new ways of thought so that they may have the intuitions that lead to *nirvana*. Soto Zen, which came to Japan via a pupil of Esai's called Dogen (1200–1253), is quieter and more contemplative. Dogen encouraged his followers to meditate for long stretches. Known as *zazen* or "sitting in meditation," this activity is designed to bring tranquillity to the mind, enabling the person to realize his or her Buddha-nature.

Every aspect of this tranquil and orderly Zen garden in Japan is created with mindfulness—complete absorption in the act of creation.

PURE LAND BUDDHISM

PU China   **⌛** 7th century CE   **✦** 20 million

Originating in China, Pure Land Buddhism now consists of several sects based in both China and Japan. All are centered on the Buddha known in Sanskrit as Amitabha (The Buddha of Infinite Light) or, in Japanese, as Amida. Amitabha is said to be the ruler of a kind of heaven known as the Pure Land, where he sits on a lotus, glowing with golden light. By believing in Amitabha, or by appealing to him at the instant of death, Pure Land Buddhists aim to avoid the round of death and rebirth, and go to dwell with Amitabha in the Pure Land, where everyone achieves *nirvana*. The main text of Pure Land Buddhism is the Lotus Sutra, which states that devotion to Amitabha is the one true way.

The Great Buddha (Daibutsu) at Kamakura, Japan, is a giant bronze statue of the Amitabha Buddha that stands more than 42 ft (13 m) high.

NICHIREN BUDDHISM

PU Japan   **⌛** 13th century CE   **✦** 2 million

The monk Nichiren (1222–1282) founded his school of Buddhism in Japan in the 13th century. After studying various different forms of Buddhism, Nichiren was attracted to the Japanese Tendai school, which is devoted to the Lotus Sutra, a collection of Buddhist teachings from around the 1st century CE that are not included in the Pali Canon (*see pp.192–193*). Nichiren studied the Sutra carefully and preached the importance of its contents, and especially of chanting part of the text and of repeating the mantra: "I take refuge in the Lotus of the Wonderful Law Sutra." Nichiren was so focused on this teaching, and believed so fervently

that only the study of the Lotus Sutra could lead to Buddhahood, that he eventually condemned all other forms of Buddhism as false. Because he threatened to oppose any Japanese ruler whose government did not support the monks who taught the Lotus Sutra, he spent two periods exiled from Japan, finally being freed and cleared in 1274.

After Nichiren's death, many different sects adopted his ideas, as well as the notion that Nichiren was one of the few people to achieve Buddhahood. There are still many Nichiren Buddhist sects flourishing in Japan, as well as numerous new religious movements based on this monk's teachings.

TIBETAN AND TANTRIC BUDDHISM

📍 Tibet   ⌛ 7th and 8th centuries CE   👥 6 million

According to some accounts, Buddhism came to Tibet in the first half of the 7th century CE during the rule of King Songsten Gampo. This king had two wives: one from China and the other from Nepal. Both were Buddhists, and brought their faith with them.

THE SPREAD OF THE FAITH

King Gampo built Buddhist temples and, according to some accounts, ordered the invention of a special Tibetan alphabet so that scholars could translate Indian Buddhist texts into Tibetan script. Not much is known about Gampo's faith, but his 8th-century successor, Trisong Detsen, was a committed Buddhist who invited missionaries from India and built a monastery for Buddhist monks.

From the 11th century onward, Tibetan Buddhism developed in a way that was different from the Buddhism of other countries. Tibetan Buddhism has its own orders of monks and its own religious practices. Some of these practices involve the use of *mandalas*, symbolic diagrams believed to represent the body, teachings, and mind of a Buddha. They are said to exist on several levels—as literal drawings, as devices to provide a focus for meditation, and as manifestations of the qualities of enlightenment.

MONKS AND LAMAS

One feature that Tibetan Buddhism shares with other strains of Buddhism is the importance of the monastic life. Four Tibetan orders of monks (the

Tibetan Buddhism accords special respect to Padmasambhava, an early pioneer of the faith.

Gelugpa, Nyingmapa, Kargyupa, and Skya) survive today. These monks are highly respected scholars and teachers. Most revered of all are those monks given the title of lama—a spiritual teacher who has undergone a rigorous training. Several lamas are "high incarnate," people who are believed to have been spiritual leaders in a previous life. When a lama nears the end of his life, he gives a series of clues as to the identity of his next incarnation. His followers then search until they find the child who best matches the clues, after which the child begins training as a spiritual teacher, too. The lama with the highest

PRAYER FLAGS AND PRAYER WHEELS

Tibetan Buddhists believe that it is possible to "activate" prayers or mantras by allowing their texts to move physically. One way to achieve this is to write the texts on flags, and then to hang the flags on cords to flutter in the wind. Prayer wheels achieve a similar effect. Each prayer wheel consists of a metal container filled with sheets of paper printed with prayers. Turning the wheel, which is usually small and hand-held, moves the sheets, activating the prayers.

Prayer wheels in a Buddhist monastery in Tibet. Written mantras are placed inside the wheels, which are then spun counterclockwise.

international profile is the Dalai Lama, who is head of the Gelugpa monks and a worldwide ambassador for the faith.

THE TANTRAS

One distinctive feature of Tibetan Buddhism is the use of texts known as Tantras, which describe ways in which a person can realize their Buddha-nature more quickly than in other forms of Buddhism. These ways include specific rituals, meditation, the use of *mandalas*, and even magic. The Tantras seek to reconcile all states and emotions, recognizing that all are part of the essential Buddha-nature. Tantric Buddhists revere many *bodhisattvas*—including Amitabha, the Buddha of Infinite Light—seeing each as a manifestation of Buddha-nature.

A Tibetan monk producing a *mandala* made of grains of colored sand. After completion, it will be swept away—to symbolize the transience of all things.

THERAVADA FOREST TRADITION

Northern India   **6th century BCE**   **More than 100 million**

The term Theravada Forest Tradition is used to describe the Buddhism practiced by many people in southeast Asia and, increasingly, in the West.

Founded on the traditional Theravada Buddhism (*see p.200*) that is the oldest form of the faith, it draws closely on the Buddha's teachings and places a high value on the members of the *sangha* or community of monks. Charismatic individual monks in this tradition can be inspiring spiritual leaders, heading orders of monks and giving spiritual guidance to lay people. To pursue a

disciplined life away from the world, many monks in this tradition spend at least some of their time in remote forest monasteries. Such locations give the monks not only the opportunity to follow a highly disciplined path, but also to meditate in quiet and tranquil surroundings. But Theravada Forest Tradition monasteries do not have to be remote. There are now many in Western cities where local people can learn about the faith, either staying and accepting the monastic way of life for a short period or becoming ordained.

SERENE REFLECTION MEDITATION

California   **1970**   **8 million (Soto Zen)**

The term Serene Reflection Meditation is used by the Order of Buddhist Contemplatives for their form of Soto Zen (*see p.202*). This form of Zen Buddhism is followed by many in the English speaking world—there is a US group at Shasta Abbey in California, and a UK group, based at Throssel Hole Abbey in Northumberland, England.

People may follow the path of Serene Reflection Meditation as a lay person or by choosing the monastic life. Both lay people and monks learn the practice of meditation, adhere to the moral precepts of Buddhism, and believe in the doctrine that all beings have Buddha-nature. They also believe in expressing compassion through selfless pursuits.

Meditation is at the heart of this branch of Buddhism. It is seen as a way of discovering the truth and learning how to accept the world as it is, while discovering the true nature of one's own being. Practiced diligently, it should lead to spiritual transformation.

Monks in ceremonial robes worship at the Throssel Hole Buddhist abbey and meditation retreat in the north of England.

SOKA GAKKAI

Japan   1937–1945   20 million

Makiguchi Tsunesaburo and Toda Josei were educational reformers who wanted to create a system of education that was based more on value and less on learning by rote. They were attracted to Nichiren Buddhism (see p.203) because of its stress on peace and the value of human life, and in 1937 founded an education society based partly on its principles.

Makiguchi Tsunesaburo died in 1944, but after World War II, Toda Josei refounded the organization, broadening its scope, turning it into a religious organization, and renaming it Soka Gakkai. This new branch of Buddhism was based on the ideas of Nichiren Buddhism, with a heavy stress on

the Lotus Sutra and on the ritual of chanting the words of its title. Soka Gakkai has attracted many converts, at first in Japan and later elsewhere in the world, partly as a result of very determined preaching and recruiting, and remains a major presence in Japan.

Dancers at a Soka Gakkai international annual meeting at the Royal Albert Hall in London.

FWBO

London   1967   1,000 (confirmed members)

An English-born Buddhist monk, Sangharakshita studied in India before returning home to promote Buddhism and explain how its basic teachings can be applied to modern life in the West, by forming the Friends of the Western Buddhist Order organization (FWBO).

Members of the Order are ordained, after which they become known by the title "follower of the Dharma," but they may live a monastic or a lay lifestyle, according to choice. They commit themselves to a number of core principles: taking the "Triple Refuge"

in the Buddha, the *dharma*, and the *sangha* (see p.196–197); commitment to the ideal of Buddhahood; and belief in other teachings drawn from the rest of the Buddhist tradition. These are teachings that combine a balance of moral precepts, study, and devotion.

The FWBO has also evolved new ways of building a Buddhist lifestyle in the modern world. For example, it has built ethical, Buddhist businesses that bring members together in "right livelihood," and it has developed structures for communal living.

SIKHISM

The Sikh religion was founded in the late 15th century in northern India by Guru Nanak, the first guru (teacher). Guru Nanak was followed by a succession of nine other gurus, who guided Sikhism between the 16th and early 18th centuries. Sikhs undertake to work hard, to serve others, and to meditate regularly upon the name of God.

Sikhism came into being because Guru Nanak rejected the philosophies and beliefs of Hinduism and Islam to create his own religion. Sikhs believe in one God, follow the guidance of the Ten Gurus who led the Sikhs in the early years of their religion, adhere to the teachings of the Sikh sacred book, the Guru Granth Sahib, and follow no other religion. Like the adherents of other Indian religions, Sikhs believe in the concept of *karma*, the law of moral cause and effect that means that living a good life will lead to a favorable reincarnation after death. Sikhs aim to progress upward through a series of moral states, from wrongdoer to *gurmukh*—a being totally devoted to God. Finally, they hope to reach a state of spiritual bliss that places them beyond the cycle of death and rebirth. God helps them to strive toward this state of perfection, but although this is an unworldly state, they must not try to reach it by renouncing the concerns of the world. On the contrary, a well-lived everyday life is essential in Sikhism and Sikhs are encouraged to help others whenever they can. Central to this commitment to others is the Khalsa, the community of Sikhs that was founded by Guru Gobind Singh, the Tenth Guru, in the 17th century. Sikhs strive to serve their community, and the importance of this is reflected in regular worship at the *gurdwara*, or temple, where, in addition to singing hymns, the community provides a free communal meal. This meal shows that Sikh hospitality extends beyond the Khalsa, because food is offered to anyone, irrespective of their race or even their religion. So, although the Sikhs began by rejecting the other faiths of India in order to create their own religion, and although they form a distinct community, they are notable in their generosity and openness toward followers of other faiths.

A Sikh carries the Guru Granth Sahib, Sikhism's sacred book, over his head during a religious procession in Amritsar, northwestern India.

ORIGINS AND HISTORY

Sikhism originates from one part of south Asia: the Punjab in
northwestern India, which is home to its most sacred places.
The history of the faith is closely tied to its founding fathers—
the "Ten Gurus"—and to the story of the Indian subcontinent.

GURU NANAK

In 1499, Sikhism's founding guru,
Guru Nanak, heard his spiritual calling.
Nanak was a government official who
had been born in Talwandi, west of
Lahore. He had always shown an
interest in spiritual matters, but in 1499,
when he was 30, he had
a mystical experience.
After bathing in the
Bein River, he was struck
silent for a day, and then
he made the following
pronouncement: "There
is neither Hindu nor
Muslim, so whose path
shall I follow? I shall
follow God's path."

Nanak's assertion that
there is neither Hindu
nor Muslim can be
interpreted in two ways.
On the one hand, it can

Guru Nanak preached a message
of tolerance and respect, viewing
all races and creeds as equal.

mean that most of the Hindus or
Muslims of Nanak's time were not true
to their faith. On the other hand, it can
mean that God is greater than religion.
The practical effect of the statement for
Nanak was that he became the teacher
and leader of a new faith that focused
closely on God. Nanak traveled widely,
explaining his new religious message to
communities all over India and beyond
—some accounts say that he even
traveled to Mecca, in modern-day
Saudi Arabia, to preach. But in 1521 he
settled down and founded a Sikh village
at Kartarpur, in the Punjab, and
established a pattern of
meditation and regular
worship. This village
became the heart of a
Sikh community that
flourished and began to
expand throughout the
rest of Nanak's life.

GURU NANAK'S SUCCESSORS

Just before he died in
1539, Nanak named one
of his followers, called
Lahina, to succeed him
as Guru and leader of the
Sikhs. He gave Lahina a new name,
Angad (which means "limb" or "part of
me"), and Angad became the first of
nine successor Gurus who were to lead
the Sikh community until the beginning
of the 18th century. The Gurus
displayed both spiritual vision and
bravery. For example, one of their

number, Guru Tegh Bahadur (the Ninth Guru), was martyred for his valiant defense of *brahmins* (wise men) who were resisting conversion to Islam; his son, Guru Gobind Singh (the Tenth Guru), also stood up against oppression by both Muslim and Hindu opponents.

Each of the Ten Gurus added something to the Sikh tradition. Among their achievements was the foundation of the sacred city of Amritsar, in northern Punjab, by Guru Ram Das (the Fourth Guru) and the collection of Sikh hymns to form the Sikh sacred book, the Granth Sahib, made by Guru Arjan (the Fifth Guru).

THE LAST HUMAN GURU

Guru Gobind Singh became leader of the Sikhs in 1675. After Guru Nanak he was perhaps the most important of all the Gurus. His first great achievement was the foundation of the Khalsa, the brotherhood of male Sikhs, in 1699. This provided the Sikhs with an elite group who led the way in moral standards, and gave them the status of a caste (*see p.173*) in India.

Before his death in 1708, Guru Gobind Singh made the dramatic announcement that he would be the last human Guru. He declared that,

Sikhs have great respect for their holy book, the Guru Granth Sahib, which was declared by Guru Gobind Singh to be the religion's True Guru.

from then on, the holy book, the Granth Sahib, would be the True Guru. These two pivotal acts by Gobind Singh gave the Sikhs a new direction. No longer led by one man, their faith now had a double focus. First and foremost the Sikhs were the people of the book, which was given the title of Guru and so became known as the Guru Granth Sahib. They were also people of the community of pure ones—men who would show dedicated moral leadership, but who would also be prepared to fight to defend their fellow Sikhs from attack. In the following decades, the Sikhs became grateful that Guru

The eroded, arid landscape of northern Punjab was divided by the partition of India and Pakistan in 1947, disappointing hopes for an independent Sikh state in this heartland of the faith.

Gobind Singh had prepared them so well for adversity, as their faith was to endure troubled times.

The Golden Temple in Amritsar is the spiritual heart of the Sikh religion. It was built in the 16th century, under the watchful eye of Guru Arjan (the Fifth Guru).

UNDER OPPRESSION

Not long after Gobind Singh's death, Sikhism's problems began. The Mughal rulers of India, who were Muslim-led and violently opposed to the challenge posed by the Sikhs, crushed Sikh power in 1716. The Sikhs were driven united Sikh kingdom in the Punjab, but it did not survive his death in 1839. The kingdom broke up and, after two brief wars, was taken over by the British, who then ruled India until 1947.

In the first decades of the 20th century, the period when the nationalist movement in India was gathering

"THE LORD, THE PRIMAL BEING, IS IMMACULATE..."

Guru Granth Sahib, Raag Aassaa 4

into the hills, but in the ensuing years, Mughal power declined and the Sikhs re-emerged, establishing a number of small states in the Punjab that were eventually united under a powerful leader, Ranjit Singh, who declared himself Maharaja of the Punjab in 1801. By1820 Singh had secured a strength, the Sikhs campaigned for control of their homeland and, especially, their places of worship. Protests culminated at the first Amritsar Massacre in 1919, when British troops were ordered to fire without warning on around 10,000 Sikhs—about 400 were killed and 1,000 wounded. Although the British commander who had ordered the shooting, General E. H. Dyer, was forced to retire, a shadow had passed over British rule.

THE CHALLENGE OF PARTITION

In 1947, when India was granted independence from Britain and also partitioned to form Pakistan, there was great hope for a peaceful, successful subcontinent. However, partition brought problems for the Sikhs. Many of them lived in the border country between India and the new nation of Pakistan. These Sikhs wanted their own state, but there were too few of them to overcome Pakistan's claim to the Punjab. Neither would India grant them nationhood. Eventually, in 1966, the boundaries of the Punjab were redrawn to create an Indian state with a Sikh majority, but the Sikhs were still denied nationhood and resented the way India had dictated terms to them. As a result, the Sikhs felt marginalized by their Indian neighbors, which led to years of regional friction and violence.

THE SECOND MASSACRE

In 1984, after Sikh leaders had taken refuge in the Golden Temple at Amritsar, one of Sikhism's most sacred

Guru Gobind Singh was the Tenth (and last) of the Sikh Gurus. He decreed that no human Guru would follow him.

sites, Indian troops opened fire on the building. Many were killed, and the Indian Prime Minister Indira Gandhi was blamed for the attack and assassinated. After that, violence continued to erupt between Sikhs and Muslims.

This violence led to many deaths on both sides, and the Sikh differences with the Indian government dominated Sikh history until the late 1990s.

But then, in 1999, the year of the 300th anniversary of the foundation of the Khalsa, a new direction was taken. The positive attitude shown by the people of India to the anniversary, which was echoed in the world's media, persuaded the Sikhs that they were finally accepted as a mature political and religious group on the world stage, and the violence of the previous years died down.

HOPES FOR PEACE

In recent times, the Punjab has been a peaceful state. During this more tranquil period, the Sikhs have continued to win respect in India and beyond—both for standing up for their political principles and for continuing to focus on their religion.

At the same time, the Sikh community has expanded. Although the Punjab is still the center of the religion, many Sikhs moved to the West—especially to Britain, where there are now many Sikh communities and *gurdwaras* (places of Sikh worship). With this spread has come a wider understanding of the Sikhs and their faith, and a broader appreciation of the contribution that Sikhism has made to the history of humanity and particularly to the history of the world's religions.

THE *KHANDA*

The symbol of Sikhism is called the *khanda*. It is made up of three separate parts. Rising up the center is a two-edged sword representing freedom and justice. On either side are a pair of curved swords or *kirpans*, one of which represents the religious concerns of the Sikh, the other his worldly concerns. The third element is a circle, a symbol of unity (the oneness of God and of humanity) and balance.

CORE BELIEFS

The One God is at the center of all Sikh belief. Sikhs aim not only to worship God, but also to achieve a close, personal experience of God by such means as meditation, the repetition of God's Name, and full absorption in the teachings of the Gurus.

THE ONE GOD

Sikhs believe that the one God is the eternal creator of the universe. They see God as Sat Guru ("the true teacher"), but God is also the Absolute, formless, and impossible to describe. Sikhs therefore follow the human Gurus, the ten original leaders of the Sikhs (*see pp.210–211*), and the "Eleventh Guru," the sacred book known as the Guru Granth Sahib (or sometimes the Adi Granth) as those who have revealed God's nature and teachings.

The Guru Granth Sahib does not contain a systematic explanation of Sikh teachings. It is a book of poetry and praise rather than one of moral instruction. But knowledge of its content is vital to Sikhs as a way to move closer to an understanding and love of God. In the Guru Granth Sahib,

The Sikh *kangha* comb is one of the distinguishing items of the faith that Sikhs carry at all times (*see p.219*).

God is depicted as an immortal being, without fear or hatred, who is the embodiment of truth. In this way, Sikhs see God not only as the creator but also as the being on whom all depend. It is therefore important that Sikhs not only understand the nature of God but also achieve a personal, direct experience of Him.

THE NAME OF GOD

According to Guru Nanak, one way to have a personal experience of God is to keep God's Name in your heart. The Name of God is important to Sikhs as it encapsulates God's being and shows how the formless and Absolute God is present in the world. The Name is so important that Guru Nanak actually referred to God as Nam, or Name. To meditate on the Name is one of three promises that a devotee makes on entering the Sikh community, so Sikhs spend much time meditating on the Name to bring God into their own being. The other promises are to work hard and honestly, and to give alms.

CYCLE OF REBIRTH

The law of *karma* is the process of moral cause and effect that influences how we are reborn after death. The Sikh view of the process of death and rebirth sees five stages of existence, each on a higher moral plane than the

Sikhs form a guard of honor during a Sikh festival. The use of arms in defense of the innocent is permitted by Sikh holy texts.

previous one. A person may lead one life as a *manmukh* ("wrongdoer") but, through a series of rebirths, may reach the focus on God known as *gurmukh* and the fifth and final stage of *sachkand* ("bliss"), the state beyond rebirth.

In Sikh belief, living a good life is important in the process of favorable rebirth, but how we are reborn cannot be entirely in our own hands. God is so great that it is only through his will that a person can achieve a positive rebirth

Guru Nanak in the company of Mardana, a Muslim, and Bala, a Hindu, both of whom followed Nanak as he traveled. Both were noted musicians, so it is unclear which is the player in this scene.

those who come to the truth through their own religions. So, although Sikhs do believe fervently in the rightness of their faith, and have actively sought the conversion of others to Sikhism in the past, they are essentially tolerant. Sikhism is very unusual among world religions in that it includes the writings

"ENSHRINE THE LORD'S NAME WITHIN YOUR HEART."

Guru Amar Das, Maru

or reach the state of bliss. This fact makes focusing on God and his Name all the more central to Sikhism.

SIKHS AND OTHER FAITHS

An important aspect of Sikh belief is that all people are equal since, whether man or woman, Sikh or non-Sikh, they were all created by God. Sikhs respect

of people from outside the faith in its scriptures. The Guru Granth Sahib contains teachings by several Muslim and Hindu holy men, known to Sikhs as Bhagats. This fundamental display of religious tolerance is fully consistent with the centrally important Sikh belief that all religious people ultimately worship the same God.

THE GURU GRANTH SAHIB

The Sikh scriptures are collected in a volume called the Guru Granth Sahib or Adi Granth (meaning "Primal Book"). The book is central to the Sikh faith, enshrining the message that belief in the sacred Name of God is at the heart of their religion, and its words form part of all Sikh worship. The Sikh place of worship, the *gurdwara*, is defined as a place in which a copy of the Guru Granth Sahib is kept.

THE HISTORY OF THE BOOK

The idea for an authentic collection of the Sikh scriptures came from the fifth Guru, Arjan Dev (1563–1606). To lay to rest concerns over whether or not certain texts were genuinely the work of the early Gurus, Arjan began to gather the true manuscripts. Over the course of several years, he sent his trusted companions to locate original manuscripts and then he and his follower Bhai Gurdas copied them into one volume. In 1604 the volume was finished, and Guru Arjan taught his followers to revere the book as the divinely inspired work of the early Gurus. Around 100 years later, the Tenth Guru, Gobind Singh, revised the book, adding the hymns of the Ninth Guru, Tegh Bahadur, and, modestly, just one of his own. The book also contains works by a number of respected spiritual leaders and saints from other faiths (*see p.215*). After Gobind Singh declared that the book would be the Sikhs' final Guru (*see p.211*), it became known as the Guru Granth Sahib.

THE CONTENT OF THE SCRIPTURES

This sacred book contains thousands of hymns, written in Gurmukhi, a Sikh script. The hymns are arranged in 31 sections following traditional Indian musical forms called *ragas*. Within each section, the hymns are grouped according to the Guru who wrote them, with those by non-Gurus coming at the end. Together the texts of the hymns set out and celebrate the basic beliefs of Sikhism—that God is the One, universal creator and that all the world's peoples are equal. They also indicate the moral and ethical goals of the faith, from eliminating evil to living in humility and compassion. Most Sikhs read

Sikhs always carry the Guru Granth Sahib above their heads to symbolize the sacred book's importance and show their reverence.

A Sikh elder reading from the Guru Granth Sahib. Complete, uninterrupted readings may last for up to two days.

certain key passages in daily prayer at home. Another way to use the book is to read the entire text in a continuous reading called an *akhand path*—reading the scripture out in this way this usually takes around 48 hours and often forms part of Sikh festivals. Occasions on which such a reading may take place include important family events and festivals that commemorate the birth or death of one of the Gurus.

RESPECT FOR THE BOOK

Sikhs must house the Guru Granth Sahib properly and treat it with respect. The volume is kept in the *gurdwara* on a small throne topped by a canopy close to the ceiling. It is covered with cloths that Sikhs should keep clean and change daily, and it is laid to rest ceremonially at night.

Those who read from the book adopt special rituals to show their reverence for its contents. In the presence of the book, people must be barefoot and must cover their heads. Sikhs bow before the book to show their reverence for God. And the reader or a volunteer (called a *sewadar*) waves a sacred whisk, known as a *chauri*, over the book as a sign of respect while the reading takes place. If someone needs to carry the book, for example during a festival procession, he or she bears it aloft on their head—this is a sign of the book's elevated status.

ETHICS, MORALITY, AND LAW

Sikh ethics are grounded firmly in the need to do good in the world. There are many ways to do good, but two stand out as particularly important: to help others through a practical ethic of service, and to embrace the high moral standards of the Khalsa, or Sikh community.

VIRTUES AND VICES

The ethics of Sikhism are guided by the Sikh awareness of five key virtues and five cardinal vices. The five virtues are truth, contentment, service, patience, and humility. By upholding these virtues, Sikhs hope to obey the will of God and to grow nearer to him. The five vices are lust, anger, greed, worldliness, and pride. Giving in to these vices is seen as turning away from God, and turning instead to an attitude of ego or selfishness and a tendency to be attached to the worldly side of life. Sikhs see the vices as a constant threat and temptation, and hope to avoid them by focusing on God's Name (*see p.214*) and by selflessly upholding the virtues. In doing all these things they aim to attract God's grace.

SERVICE AND EQUALITY

For Sikhs, an important way to serve God is by adhering to the concept of *seva*, meaning "service." In effect, this means serving or looking after other people. *Seva* is learned both in the family, where children are brought up to obey and respect their parents, and in the *gurdwara*, where members of the congregation help one another.

The *gurdwara* is also the setting for the most public display of the Sikh belief in service for all. At the end of Sikh worship, the *gurdwara* offers a communal meal (known as the Langar) to the community. This meal usually consists of pulses, rice, vegetables, and bread. Although Sikhs may eat meat, the Langar is usually a vegetarian meal, because Sikhs extend their hospitality beyond those of their own religion to followers of other faiths, too.

A Sikh ties a turban for his two-year-old son. The turban enables a Sikh man to cover his head and tie up his hair, which must never be cut.

By keeping the meal vegetarian, members of the *gurdwara* can be certain that the food is suitable for all.

Sikhs are expected to help the needy, whether they are followers of Sikhism or not. This caring service may take the form of charitable work inside or outside the *gurdwara*, but it also influences many Sikhs in their choice of a job. Sikhs often enter the caring professions, many becoming doctors and nurses.

Extending the ethic of service to the whole of humanity is one example of an important principle in Sikh morality. Sikhs believe that all of humanity was created by God and therefore that all of humanity is equal. Even though Sikhs have lived—and in many cases continue to live—in societies in which specific roles are assigned to women or to members of a particular social class, Sikhs value equally people of all races, castes, and social status, and they do not support discrimination. Also, men and women are regarded as equals in Sikh culture.

THE ETHICS OF THE KHALSA

The community of adult-initiated Sikhs is called the Khalsa (*see p.211*). Although the original Khalsa members were men who were prepared to take a military role in defending their people and their faith, Sikhism now permits both sexes to be admitted to this special community. Women members are referred to as Ardhangi ("the better half"). All members are admitted to the Khalsa in a special initiation ceremony at which men take the surname Singh ("Lion"), and women Kaur ("Princess").

Guru Gobind Singh laid down an ethical code for the Khalsa. Members must not commit adultery, worship Hindu deities, or use alcohol, tobacco, or narcotics. They must rise early, read the prescribed scriptures, and meditate on God's Name. They must also keep their heads covered—men with a turban, women with either a turban or scarf. Finally, they must wear the symbolic "Five Ks." These are the *kesh*

> ### THE AKALI MOVEMENT
>
> Guru Gobind Singh gave the title Akali (from Akal, God the Timeless One) to those who would die for their faith. In the 19th and 20th centuries, the Akali successfully campaigned for the reform of *gurdwaras* that were being controlled by corrupt priests, who were embezzling funds and introducing inappropriate forms of worship. The Akalis remained dominant in Sikh affairs after the formation of a political party, the Akali Dal, in 1929. In later decades they were active in the Sikhs' campaign for a Punjabi-speaking state, which came to fruition in 1966.

(the Sikh's long, uncut hair), the *kangha* (a comb to keep the hair in place), the *kaccha* (shorts worn as undergarments), the *kara* (a bracelet), and the *kirpan* (a short sword). Today, members of the Khalsa still aspire to set the highest standard of religious observance and moral conduct for Sikhs everywhere.

Sikhs cook rotis (breads) for Langar, the Sikh practice of providing a communal meal for all who attend the *gurdwara*.

A Sikh bride wears the traditional wedding adornments—rings, bracelets, and bright, glittering garments. A wedding in Sikh culture is both a solemn occasion, marking the joining together of two families, and a joyous one, looking forward to the couple's future together.

PRACTICES AND FESTIVALS

The worship and other religious practices of the Sikhs focus closely on the Guru Granth Sahib. Singing hymns from this sacred book makes up a major part of worship at the *gurdwara*, while life-cycle rituals and annual festivals also find their focus in its words.

REGULAR WORSHIP

A communal service in the *gurdwara* comprises three main parts, known as Kirtan, Anand, and Langar. Kirtan consists of singing hymns from the Guru Granth Sahib, accompanied by musical instruments such as the harmonium and tablas (small drums). In some sections of the service, the musicians sing the hymns alone, while sometimes the whole congregation takes part. Kirtan is the main part of the service and may last for several hours. Its focus on the hymns of the Guru Granth Sahib shows the centrality of the book in the Sikh faith. The second element of the service, Anand, includes further hymns, and then the recital of the Mool Mantar (*see box, opposite*). This prayer, contained

A Sikh elder meditates, hoping to achieve a sacred state of awareness and compassion for others.

in the Guru Granth Sahib, is said to comprise the first recorded saying by Guru Nanak after his enlightenment. Then comes a short sermon, and the distribution of *karah parshad*, a sacred sweet food made of flour, water, sugar, and ghee (clarified butter), to the congregation. A communal prayer called Ardas ends this part of the worship. The last section of the service, Langar, is a communal meal (*see p.218*).

THE CYCLE OF LIFE

Sikhism marks all the stages of life with special ceremonies. Two of the most characteristic are held for the naming of infants and the initiation of new members into the Khalsa.

Shortly after a baby is born to a Sikh family, the child is taken to the *gurdwara* for its naming ceremony. The child may be given a little *amrit*, a nectarlike drink made of sugar crystals and water, which represents the

A Sikh kneels in formal prayer at the altar of his local *gurdwara*. Sikh religious services stress community and sharing.

ambrosial nature of God's Name. The Guru Granth Sahib is opened at random and the *granthi*, who officiates, reads the hymn on the left-hand side of the page. It is entrusted to God that this reading is appropriate for that particular day. Parents then select a name for the child that begins with the first letter of the first word on the left of the opened page. Once the ceremony is over, the congregation gives a celebratory cheer.

For initiation into the Khalsa, five existing Khalsa members (recalling the original five members initiated by Guru Gobind Singh in 1699) perform the initiation ceremony. The five take turns to stir *amrit* in an iron bowl, while reciting verses from the Guru Granth Sahib. The five drink some of the *amrit* and the initiates drink what is left. Then the five say the Mool Mantar and the intiates repeat it five times. After this, the initiates are told their Khalsa duties, from praying daily to wearing the "Five Ks" (*see p.219*). A reading, and sharing of *karah parshad*, ends the ritual.

SIKH FESTIVALS

Because Sikhism originated in the Indian subcontinent, the Sikhs adopted many of the traditional Hindu festivals, giving them meanings appropriate to their own faith. These festivals, known as *melas*, include Diwali, the festival of lights,

which for Sikhs recalls the release from prison of the Sixth Guru, Hargobind, in the 17th century, when people lit their houses with candles to welcome him home. Hola Mohalla is the Sikh equivalent of the Hindu Holi. "Hola Mohalla" means "Attack and place of attack" and commemorates the training of the early Khalsa members in martial arts.

In addition to the festivals adopted from Hinduism, Sikhism has its own festivals called *gurpurbs*. These mark key events in the faith's history and the lives of the Gurus. They are celebrated with processions in which devotees carry the Guru Granth Sahib through the streets. A key part of many *gurpurbs* is often a complete reading of the book, which takes about 48 hours. Adherents also sing hymns and give readings connected with the particular Guru whom they are commemorating. The most important and most holy of the *gurpurbs* is the one that celebrates the birthday of Guru Nanak. Two other major *gurpurbs* mark the birthday of Guru Gobind Singh (the Tenth Guru) and the martyrdom of the Ninth Guru, Tegh Bahadur.

THE MOOL MANTAR

The Mool Mantar appears at the beginning of the Guru Granth Sahib and distils the essence of Sikhism. The creed of the religion, it was composed by Guru Nanak. Its words are so important that Sikhs believe that they cannot be properly translated. The Mool Mantar speaks of the Oneness of God and his eternal existence, and his role as creator and sustainer of all things. He is said to be beyond time, birth, and death. People know him through the grace of the Guru—which means through himself, because Nanak always refers to God himself as "the Guru."

JAINISM

Although it has the fewest adherents of the ancient religions of India, Jainism has proved to be highly influential among people from all cultures and backgrounds. Its overriding ethic of self-help and, especially, its philosophy of non-violence have inspired campaigners against violence and oppression throughout the world.

J ainism is one of the longest-established religions of India. It has no single founder, but its followers believe that their faith has been revealed to a number of leaders, known as *tirthankaras* or *jinas*. The most familiar of these is Mahavira, who lived in the 6th century BCE and is said to have been the most recent of 24 enlightened teachers who laid down the tenets of the religion. The words of Mahavira formed the basis of Jain scriptures. Monks and nuns memorized these scriptures because they were not permitted to have physical possessions, such as books. Over time, some of Mahavira's words were lost, especially in the mid-4th century BCE when a number of monks died in a famine. Later, the texts were written down and monks were allowed to keep books, so the rest of the scriptures survive.

Jains differ as to whether these scriptures contain the actual words of Mahavira, but they revere them because of the truths they enshrine about Jain belief. For Jains, life is a continuous cycle of death and reincarnation, from which faith offers a route to liberation. They do not recognize any deity, and have no priests to help them on their religious path. Jainism is, therefore, a religion that places the emphasis on the believer's own actions. By living in the right way—adopting the correct kind of belief, knowledge, and conduct—followers can move toward liberation. One principle above all others defines Jainism and sets it apart—the principle of *ahimsa*, or non-violence. Jains believe that every living thing has a soul, so all followers avoid causing unnecessary harm to even the lowliest of creatures, and they are also strict vegetarians.

Today in India there are more than four million Jains, but the religion's austere lifestyle has meant that it has not spread widely beyond the subcontinent.

The festival of Mahamastakabhisheka ("anointing of the head") takes place every 12 years at the 56 ft (17 m) statue of Gomateswara, a Jain holy man.

ORIGINS AND HISTORY

Although its followers see Jainism as having a history stretching back to the earliest times, the religion as it is practiced today was in fact born in India in the sixth century BCE. Most of its followers still live in India, where they lead a life that centers on causing no harm to others.

MAHAVIRA

Jainism really began with the mission of Mahavira in the 6th century BCE. The most recent of 24 spiritual teachers, known as *tirthankaras* or *jinas*, Mahavira was born to the warrior class in the Ganges Basin area of India. At 30, he adopted the life of a wandering ascetic and, after 12 years, attained enlightenment. He had 12 disciples who used his teachings as the basis of the Jain scriptures. The new faith spread around India, but growth was slow as Jainism is an austere religion that demands total nonviolence and presents the complete self-denial of the ascetic as its most exalted form.

TWO KINDS OF JAINISM

During the 4th century CE, a major split occurred within Jainism. One group argued that all possessions presented barriers to liberation and wanted to achieve total self-denial. Even clothes,

The Jain temple at Ranakpur in India was built more than 500 years ago and is one of the faith's key sites.

they believed, implied ideas of modesty irrelevant to those who were detached from the world; people also risked killing living things when they washed their clothes in the river. This group of Jains abandoned all their possessions and became the Digambaras, or "sky-clad" ascetics. The remaining group, who held that purity was more to do with the mind than clothing, became the Shvetambaras. Despite this schism the early medieval period was the time

Documented descriptions of Jainism's precepts and history eventually replaced the early, fragile oral tradition of the faith—as in this antique holy text.

of Jainism's greatest flowering, although its spread was eventually to be halted by a resurgence of Hinduism in sects devoted to Siva and Visnu.

JAINISM IN MODERN TIMES

Today, most Jains live in western and central India. The influence of the Shvetambaras is particularly strong in

"TO THE PURE ONE BELONG FAITH AND KNOWLEDGE."

Pravachansara, 274

Rajasthan and Gujarat, while the Digambaras have most of their followers in the area around Mysore.

Jainism has principally influenced the modern world via its doctrine of *ahimsa*, or nonviolence. For example, in the 20th century, the Jain teacher Raychandbhai Mehta helped Mahatma Gandhi to see the strength in the Jain ethic of nonviolence. The history of India, with the Nationalists' nonviolent resistance to British rule—which eventually led to independence—might have been different, and more bloody, without the Jain influence on Gandhi.

CORE BELIEFS

The aim of Jainism is to live as pure and disciplined a life as possible in order to move closer to the ultimate spiritual goal of enlightenment. Jains realize that enlightenment is a highly exalted state that most people will be unable to attain—but still all Jains aspire to it.

GODS, BODY, AND SOUL

Jains do not believe in a supreme creator god, and while they may recognize gods that exist in the universe, they do not see them as objects of worship nor as powers that can help in the quest for enlightenment. Jainism does, however, recognize five levels of supreme beings who can help believers along their spiritual path and whom they revere (*see box, below*).

In Jainism, a living thing is seen as being made up of two parts, a body and a soul. The body is essentially a physical container—it is the soul (known as the *jiva*) that really matters. The *jiva* is eternal and provides us with our moral responsibility. Like the followers of other Indian religions, Jains believe that life is a series of deaths and rebirths, and that a person's actions throughout life attract *karma* (a spiritual credit and debit system), which influences the way in which a person is reborn after death.

Enlightened beings known as *tirthankaras* are venerated as spiritual guides in Jainism.

Jainism's unique take on this process is that the *karma* that a person's actions attracts is seen as a kind of physical substance that attaches to the soul. To break out of the endless round of death and rebirth, *karma* has to be removed. To achieve this, a person has to undergo a process of purification and discipline described in the teachings of the spiritual guides, the *tirthankaras*.

THE SPIRITUAL PATH

In particular, Jains try to follow the path of the Three Jewels—Right knowledge, Right faith, and Right conduct. For those who follow the most demanding spiritual path—becoming a monk or nun and adopting a life of almost total renunciation—Jains add a fourth Jewel,

---

THE FIVE SUPREME BEINGS

At the top of the Jain spiritual hierarchy are the *jinas* or *tirthankaras*, the figures from whom the original teachings of Jainism stem and who attained enlightenment. Next come the *siddhas*, liberated souls who dwell in Heaven. Then come the senior religious teachers who lead the Jain monastic orders; followed by the teachers who, although they do not lead their own orders, play a vital role in instructing the monks and nuns about the scriptures. Fifth are the monks themselves.

The Jain "cosmic wheel" incorporates the Five Supreme Beings in its design and illustrates the spiritual hierarchy of the faith.

that of Asceticism (sometimes called Right penance). Monks and nuns take five "Great Vows" of nonviolence, speaking the truth, sexual abstinence, not taking what is not given, and detachment from people, places, and things. Lay people take similar but less restrictive vows—for example, unlike monks and nuns, they are not expected to renounce relationships with other people. Lay Jains do, however, renounce

Jain priests lay out offerings in the form of a *mandala*—a geometric representation of the universe according to Jain cosmology.

religions, are just as important to Jains as the lives of other species, including humans. Nevertheless, lay Jains aim to get as close to the ideal as they can, and in so doing they hope to make progress along a path of spiritual advancement. One Jain text lays out 14 stages on this path, beginning with a kind of

"DO NOT KILL ANY LIVING BEINGS."

Mahavira, in Acaranga 4:23

violence, eat only vegetarian food, and do work that does not involve the deliberate destruction of life. Even these strictures can be difficult to follow. For example, those who grow things in the soil can easily destroy unintentionally the lives of insects or other creatures— and these lives, overlooked in most

spiritual sleep and ending with total freedom from attachment to the physical world. Most people hope to rise through these levels of spiritual progress, but accept that they will not get anywhere near the last few stages, which are reserved for liberated souls and *tirthankaras* alone.

ETHICS, MORALITY, AND LAW

Jain ethics are derived from a series of vows that ban sins, attachment
to worldly things, and, above all, violence to living beings. The vows
have different levels of severity, according to how far the individual is
able to approach the ascetic ideal represented by Jain monks and nuns.

VOWS OF RIGHT CONDUCT

The Jain attitude to morality and
behavior springs from the Three Jewels
known as Right knowledge, Right faith,
and Right conduct (*see p.228*). Jains
believe that the first two Jewels—
knowing the principles of Jainism
and believing in them—are nothing
without the third, actually following
them. So lay people take a series of
vows that guide them along the correct
moral path.

The first five vows are less restrictive
versions of those taken by monks and
nuns (*see p.227*) to renounce violence, to
tell the truth, not to steal, to be sexually
restrained, and to avoid attachment to
material things. Next comes a series of
"assistant" vows designed to help the
devotee keep the first five. These cover
sins such as covetousness; discourage
violence by banning the keeping of
weapons; and restrict the area in which
sin might take place by limiting travel.
A third set of vows focuses on religious
observance. Jains promise to spend at
least 48 minutes, (one-thirtieth of the
day) meditating every day. They also
promise to spend occasional 24-hour
periods living in a monastic community.
And they promise to help the
monasteries, which they can do by
donating items that the monks are
allowed to accept—food, water, clothes,
furniture, pots, and blankets.

European Jain students learn the moral and ethical
values underpinning the religion during an open-air
evening class in the UK.

Jains believe that by following all these moral precepts they will benefit physically, for such a life will build a healthy body, and spiritually, because it will reduce harmful *karma*. Some Jains choose to follow an even more exacting path, making eleven further moral promises that almost emulate the lifestyle of the monk. These eleven vows include fasting between sunset and sunrise, avoiding sexual relations completely, eating only leftovers, living as a monk for six periods each month, and at all times striving to live an ascetic life.

A Jain symbol of the "liberated" soul, representing the ultimate goal of ethical living.

NONVIOLENCE

The one principle that sets Jain ethics apart from all others is that of *ahimsa*, or nonviolence. This principle is taken much further than in other faiths because Jainism has a deep respect for lower forms of life as well as higher, and because it considers even substances such as earth, air, and metal to be living things that can be hurt by human activity.

Jain ethics recognize that if all these things are alive, it is impossible for human beings to live without doing harm to them. But they believe that they must limit this harm. All Jains are vegetarian, and most eat only fruit, nuts, and milk, which are seen as by-products of living beings rather than actual living things. Jainism bans many occupations—for example, farming, because cultivation results in harm to creatures in the soil and even to the soil itself. Even carpentry is an unacceptable occupation for a Jain because sawing timber injures it. Acceptable jobs are limited to trade, finance, and fields such as teaching and art.

Nonviolence pervades monastic life still more deeply. Monks carry a small brush to sweep insects from their path as they walk; they strain drinking water to avoid swallowing tiny organisms; and they do not use lamps so that moths do not perish in their flames. In these details, monasticism takes the Jain respect for life to its logical conclusion.

THE OPEN PALM

The Jains adopted the symbol of the open palm in 1975, when the 2,500th anniversary of Mahavira's enlightenment was said to have occurred. The symbol is seen to denote the command to stop violence (the hand often has the word *ahimsa* written on it). In other words, it is an icon of peace. The symbol is seen carved on the walls of Jain temples, as well as appearing in publications devoted to the Jains.

PRACTICES AND FESTIVALS

Although Jains do not recognize a supreme god, they do have temples and shrines containing statues of the *tirthankaras*, which they use for worship. Jains believe that by honoring the *tirthankaras*, but not by appealing to their mercy, they can move closer to enlightenment.

REGULAR WORSHIP

Each Jain temple is presided over by one of the *tirthankaras*, the early teachers of the faith. Inside the temple there is a statue of the relevant *tirthankara* and, for most Jains, this image is central to their worship.

The simplest form of Jain worship is called *darshan*. This ritual, which is also used in Hinduism, involves making eye contact with the image of the *tirthankara*, often while reciting a *mantra* (a sacred sound or verse). Jains believe that *darshan* brings the worshipper into contact with the *tirthankara* and his teachings, which in turn takes the devotee further down the spiritual path.

Another form of worship intended to bring the worshipper closer to the supreme beings involves cleaning the image of the *tirthankara*, anointing it with substances such as saffron, and decorating it with flowers. Some adherents insist that Jains should use only flowers or petals that have already fallen from the plant in order to comply with the ethic of nonviolence. Finally,

Concentrating on images of enlightened beings, such as this statue, forms an important part of Jain worship.

worshippers may also make offerings to the *tirthankara*. As well as the communal temples and shrines, many Jain houses contain small shrines to enable the inhabitants to perform rituals of worship at home. These home shrines can be carved quite elaborately in a style similar to the temples, and they may contain statues not only of the *tirthankaras*, but also of their attendants.

Image-related worship, whether in communal temples and shrines or shrines in the home, is common among most Jains. However, there are two Jain sects, the Sthanakvasis and Terapanthis, that reject image-worship and instead practice devotion to senior monks.

DAILY RITUALS

Lay Jains usually try to practice as many of their faith's daily rituals as possible. These include time spent in prayer and meditation, including a 48-minute meditation when the devotee should aim to be at peace with the world; visits to a temple or shrine, ideally in the morning and evening; and reading from the scriptures. Jains

Home shrines and altars are common features of Jain worship, giving space to the private worship of *tirthankaras*.

also like to make a habit of helping those in need, caring for others, and giving regularly to the monks and nuns.

Prayer is offered by a Jain community in India. The cloth masks worn over the mouth and nose are to prevent accidental inhalation of insects.

THE CYCLE OF LIFE

Jains celebrate the rites of passage for lay people in similar ways to those of Hinduism. Marriage ceremonies, for example, can be elaborate, including the couple's declaration to marry, giving gifts to the bride-to-be, exchanging vows, and other rituals. The main ceremony is usually conducted by a Jain priest or by a senior, respected member of the community. Jainism stresses that

of Paryusana Parva. This lasts eight days during the monsoon season (usually in August). Most Jains stop work, fast, and spend time at the temples and monasteries—the most devout Jains spend at least 24 hours in a monastery, following the same routine as the monks or nuns. The festival ends with an act of reconciliation—people ask the forgiveness of others and everyone vows not to carry any grudges they may bear into the New Year. Jains

"TRUTH ALONE IS THE ESSENCE IN THE WORLD."

Mahavira, in Prasnavyakarna 2:2

adherents should not waste time and money on ceremony, but that they should perform the rituals with the seriousness appropriate to a celebration that takes place once in a lifetime.

FASTING AND FESTIVALS

An austere religion, Jainism places a strong emphasis on fasting at key points in the calendar—in particular, at the end of the Jain year during the festival

fast on other days, too, such as the full moon each month, and during festivals that commemorate the birth and death of Mahavira.

Some of the Jain festivals are adapted from Hinduism. The most popular is Diwali, the festival of lights. Whereas Hindus focus on the goddess Laksmi during Diwali (*see pp.174–175*), Jains see the festival as celebrating the enlightenment of Mahavira.

EASTERN RELIGIONS

T HE RELIGIONS of China and Japan have a multitude of gods and spirits, and, in China especially, different traditions are mixed together. But several eastern belief systems, notably Confucianism, Daoism, and Shinto, stand out from the mix. Although Shinto is largely limited to Japan, the ideas of Confucius and the Daoists have proved influential all over the world.

For hundreds of years, writers on Chinese religion have talked about *San-chiao* (the three ways), by which they mean Confucianism, Daoism, and Buddhism. These three religions have shaped the way that people in China think about life, death, and the cosmos for more than 2,000 years. Confucianism and Daoism originated in China itself, whereas Buddhism (*see pp.182–207*) came to China from India around 2,000 years ago.

BLEND OF BELIEFS

For much of this period, the three ways have existed peacefully side by side. Many Chinese people have not felt the need to choose one faith and reject the others. Rather, people take what is best or most suited to them from the

A Japanese *inro*, or decorated case for small objects, depicting the Buddha, Confucius, and Laozi.

three. From the philosophy of the great sage Confucius (*see p.313*), they have learned the importance of an ethical code based on respect for others and the maintaining of the correct relationships between father and child, husband and wife, ruler and ruled. In this respect, Confucianism was also an important tool for maintaining the power of the Chinese royal family in imperial times—emperors worshipped Heaven and believed that this gave them their mandate to rule; but they employed Confucian scholars to run their civil service.

In Daoism, the Chinese have found a very different philosophy, one that seeks to follow a way, the Dao, which involves sensitivity to the patterns of

"PRESERVE YOUR PURITY."

Red Writings and Jade Mysteries (Daoist text)

the universe, and the nurturing of the natural flow of energy through the body. Buddhism brought a way of understanding the suffering in the world and a way of leaving it behind. The Chinese adopted Mahayana Buddhism, with its many *bodhisattvas*, and some schools of Chinese Buddhism are based on devotion to these saintly beings.

All of the three ways have been combined and developed in Chinese popular religion, in which people seek the help of the gods (who may be *bodhisattvas*, Daoist immortals, or deified figures such as Confucius), especially during troubled or challenging times.

JAPANESE FAITHS

Religion in Japan is also the result of a 2,000-year evolution. During this time, most of the religious traditions of China have

entered the country and been given a distinctively Japanese twist—such as the Zen and Nichiren strands of Buddhism, for example (*see pp.202–203*).

But the uniquely Japanese religion is Shinto, a faith that is known as "*kami no michi*," "the way in accordance with the *kami*," or simply "the way of the *kami*." The *kami* are a vast pantheon of divine beings: the spirits of animals, birds, trees, mountains, and other natural phenomena, plus the immortal gods and goddesses who live in Heaven and control our lives. Shinto is still widely practiced, and its followers not only believe in the importance of worshipping the *kami* correctly, but also have special prayers that they offer to the *kami* when they confront a challenge, such as taking an examination, or face danger.

A Daoist pilgrimage temple on the north peak of Hua Shan, one of five sacred mountains in China.

CONFUCIANISM

The writings attributed to the great Chinese sage
Kong Fuzi (Confucius) are read all over the world. They are
admired for their humane qualities, their wisdom, and their
direct language. In China Confucius became so revered,
and his teachings so identified with religious ideas, that
Confucianism is now considered a religion in its own right.

Confucius was born in 552 BCE in the small state of Lu (part of modern Shandong Province). He held mostly lowly jobs at the Lu court, but as he grew older he devoted most of his time to moral teaching, acquiring a circle of disciples. His reputation grew after his death in 479 BCE, and he became China's most respected moral teacher. Confucius taught people about the concept of *jen* – goodness, humanity, or benevolence – and insisted that this was a quality that could be learned; it did not belong, as many people then thought, to the upper classes. Through his teachings, Confucius encouraged his followers to love and respect others, to do good works, and to respect tradition. He insisted that his message was a religious as well as a moral one – his ideas came from Heaven, he said. After his death,

Confucius's pupils spread his ideas across China with the aid of a number of books, known together as the Classics, which were attributed to the master.

The religious message in these books, as well as emphasizing the value of *jen*, tells people to cultivate moderation in their lives and emotions in order to reach a state of mental and spiritual harmony. In addition, Confucius's ideas about respect for tradition bolstered an older religious movement in China – veneration of ancestors combined with worship of Heaven. Confucius himself was revered for his insights, and his teachings were incredibly influential, especially at the Chinese imperial court, where the emperors believed that their right to rule came from Heaven itself.

The disciples of Confucius did not claim that he was a god. He was such a great and venerated teacher, however, that followers of other Chinese belief systems, such as the popular religion of the roadside temples (*see pp.256–257*), added him to their pantheon.

During the 1st century BCE Confucianism became China's state religion. It remained so until the middle of the 20th century.

ORIGINS AND HISTORY

The core values of Confucianism—harmony, education, and respect
for the ancestors—have been upheld in China since time immemorial.
Today, these values, now labeled as Confucian, continue to influence
the culture in China, and the wider world, too.

EARLY BEGINNINGS

The roots of Confucianism date back
hundreds of years before the birth of
Confucius in 552BCE. Many of the
values later championed by Confucius
were already espoused in China
during the Shang dynasty (ca.1766–
ca.1050BCE), especially at the imperial
court. The emperors valued particularly
highly members of their entourage who
were well educated, trained in the
correct rituals, and motivated by virtue.
These core values came to the fore
again in the time of the Zhou
dynasty (1050–771BCE), but in
the sixth century BCE, the power
of the Zhou emperors began to
break down. Various scholars
put forward ideas about how
best to rebuild order. One of

these scholars was Confucius and his
ideas gained the most support. What
we call Confucianism was taking shape.

CONFUCIAN TEXTS

As Confucianism gained ground,
a series of books known as the Five
Classics (see p.244) were compiled. Each
of the books—Changes, History, Poetry,
Rites, and the Annals—promotes the
key Confucian concept of harmony in
all things. The books were attributed to
Confucius, but we do not know for
certain who compiled them.
Nevertheless, along with other
works such as the Analects,
which summarize Confucius's
teachings about order and
harmony, they have always
been viewed as the works

Yongle, the third emperor of
the Ming dynasty (1368–1644),
was one of many rulers to
adopt Confucian ideas.

Part of a Tang dynasty (618–907CE) manuscript of the Analects of Confucius, which provide scholars with a summary of Confucius's ideas.

that sum up his ideas. These writings were supplemented with the works of other writers, including the Chinese philosopher Xunzi (who flourished *ca.*298–*ca.*238BCE). Xunzi put forward the idea that humans needed to be disciplined by laws.

THE FAITH AND THE STATE

Under the Han dynasty (206BCE–220CE), the imperial court took up Confucian beliefs wholeheartedly. Imperial scholars combined the ideas of Confucius and Xunzi to create a belief system that survived at the heart of Chinese culture for some 1,700 years. The Han rulers gave Confucianism an organizational structure, founding a university, having the Classics re-edited, and setting up a system of competitive examinations for the civil service based on Confucian principles. Soon, the faith spread to Vietnam and Korea, too.

During the Song period (960–1279CE), the Neo-Confucianism movement elaborated on Confucian ideas. Its focus was on the role of the individual, who could use Confucius's philosophy to follow a path toward self-development and enlightenment.

THE MODERN WORLD

Confucian values remained at the heart of Chinese life until the end of the imperial period in the early 20th century. When China turned to communism, the state was no longer focused on Confucian ideals. However, the Chinese people still valued the virtues of harmony, respect, and balance—some saw them as fundamental to the Chinese character and just as applicable in a communist state as in an imperial one. In the late 20th century, new scholars showed how the people could still apply the ancient philosopher's values to modern times. Some have even suggested that Confucianism has underpinned China's recent economic success.

THE CONFUCIAN SAGES

The writings of Confucius provided the Chinese with advice about many aspects of life, from family relations to diplomatic protocol. Devotees therefore viewed Confucius as a sage with profound insights, and regarded later Confucian scholars in a similar way. Some scholars taught in schools, passing their wisdom to the next generation. The state funded academies of advanced study where scholars discussed Confucius's teachings in order to themselves become high officials, imperial aides, and sages.

Confucius was the founder of a long line of sages and scholars who interpreted and elaborated on his original political and spiritual teachings.

CORE BELIEFS

At the center of Confucian belief is the concept of harmony at every level—from the individual person to the entire cosmos. This fundamental concept pervades the Confucian discussion of personal morality, government, natural phenomena, history, and even the gods.

THE GODS

Confucianism involves two different concepts of god. First, there is an ultimate reality, known as *Taiji*. This is an unknowable absolute force that orders the universe. Since the time of the Neo-Confucians (*see p.241*), many people have believed that through scholarship, contemplation, meditation, and other mental disciplines, it is possible to achieve a kind of unity with *Taiji*, which can lift the mind to another plane. More accessible to ordinary people, though, are the host of lesser gods—the deities, spirits, and immortalized ancestors who live in Heaven. These are seen as inhabiting a Heaven similar in social structure to imperial China, with a ruling immortal called the Jade Emperor and ranks of godly civil servants administering his realm. This hierarchy was especially important to the Chinese emperors, who saw the correct worship of these deities as a

> ### YIN AND YANG
>
> In traditional Chinese thought, all things are made up of two essential aspects, known as *yin* and *yang*. Yin describes things that are dark, moist, soft, cold, and feminine; *yang* refers to things that are light, dry, hard, warm, and masculine. Everything in the universe, from the functioning of the state to individual human relationships and a person's health, has *yin* and *yang* qualities in varying proportions. The goal is to keep these two aspects of existence in balance so that harmony can prevail.

way to validate their own rule on Earth, a system they referred to as the Heavenly Mandate.

ORDER AND HARMONY

According to Confucius, underpinning both the godly and the human worlds is a cosmos made up of two fundamental principles, called *yin* and *yang* (*see box, above*). Confucianism also expresses the vital cosmic forces in terms of the "Five phases"—fire, wood, metal, water, and earth. Each of these "phases," or elements, is understood on a spiritual as well as a physical level. One dominates the cosmos at any one time, and the balance between them influences the harmony of life.

Balance features in some of Confucianism's other key principles, too. Among the most famous is Confucius's most succinct moral formula, which is his version of the golden rule of Christianity: "What you

Confucius placed special emphasis on the need for harmonious life within the family unit, believing it to be the foundation for the rest of society.

Associated with both *yang* and *yin*, and thus with both the male emperor and female empress, the phoenix was an auspicious symbol in imperial times.

do not want done to you, do not do to others." This moral precept is clearly part of the Confucian ideal of balance.

STUDYING THE CLASSICS
Confucius believed that the books we now know as the Five Classics (*see p.244*) held the most important teachings. In

behavior. The second book, the Mencius, contains the teachings of the Chinese philosopher Mencius or Mengzi (*ca.*372–*ca.*289BCE) and emphasizes the goodness of people and the power of education to bring about both intellectual and moral improvements. The third volume, the Great Learning, shows how the development of the individual is the key to a wider harmony in society.

"DESIRE WHAT IS GOOD AND THE PEOPLE WILL BE GOOD."

Confucius, Analects 12:19

addition, later Confucians ranked four more works, now known as the Four Books, as similarly important. The first, known as the Analects, contains Confucius's own teachings and shows how following the rites of the early emperors correctly provides a model for ideal human and governmental

The fourth, the Doctrine of the Mean, shows how to attain the unity of the cosmos and humankind.

Confucians study all of these texts, learning from each how they can balance *yin* and *yang* to foster and maintain harmony within themselves, their environment, and the cosmos.

ETHICS, MORALITY, AND LAW

The moral values of Confucianism focus on ways to achieve harmony at a personal level and at the levels of the state and government. Adherents are expected to act in cultivated and humane ways and to observe modes of behavior that reflect those laid down by Confucius.

LI AND REN

In Confucianism, adherents can achieve harmony by two means: *li* (ritual or protocol) and *ren* (humane conduct). *Li* is epitomized by the behavior of the ancient sages in the Five Classics (*see box, below*), and involves a correct mixture of ritual, manners, and ceremony. A person can achieve *li* by studying past examples of correct conduct and by personal development. Confucianism encourages its followers to study the arts, because the ancient sages were accomplished poets and musicians. These skills help to make a person more refined, and better developed morally.

Ren encompasses a number of virtues, such as goodness, love, humanity, and generosity. Confucianism urges its followers to be guided by *ren* in all their dealings with other people, above all taking on board the wants and

Confucius shown teaching his insights on creating a harmonious society to his first disciples.

needs of other individuals, rather than thinking only of the self.

FAMILY VALUES

Confucianism has a number of family-centered values designed to bring harmony to family relationships. Confucius laid out the nature of correct relationships between parents and children, husband and wife, elder and younger brother, friend and friend, and ruler and subject. Filial piety is vital above all; Confucianism insists that children should respect and honor their parents and always obey their elders. The state has been known to take these ideals to extremes—in some periods children were not allowed to testify against their parents in court cases, but could serve a penal sentence on their

---

THE FIVE CLASSICS

Confucius used books known as the Five Classics to teach his students. The first, the Book of Changes, covers the metaphysics of the cosmos and humanity's relationship with the universe. The Book of History gives examples of ideal government. The Book of Poetry is a treasury of early Chinese verse on all aspects of life. The Record of Rites is a handbook of correct actions. Finally, the Spring and Autumn Annals is made up of a series of judgments about good leadership.

Confucian scholars carried forward the original teachings of Confucius after his death and applied them to society over the centuries.

behalf. Fundamentally, though, Confucius intended family values to be reciprocal—children should obey their parents, and parents should support their children.

NATIONAL VALUES

According to Confucius, harmonious families built a harmonious state. The ideal of respect for family elders was according to *li* and *ren*, and be refined and cultured. Members of society were expected to make their contribution to the well-being of the state, too—especially farmers, who needed to work hard because the Chinese relied upon them for their food supply.

Although these state ethics applied particularly under imperial rule, modern-day China has inherited many

"VIRTUE IS NOT LEFT TO STAND ALONE."

Confucius, Analects 4:25

echoed in his ideas on the correct relationships between citizens and government. Rulers need to respect the gods, and those who are ruled should respect their rulers. During imperial times especially, rulers were expected to see that their subjects worshipped Heaven and carried out religious rites, so that the royal family could continue to govern with the Mandate of Heaven. Rulers were also expected to live of the values. The new constitution of 1913 placed Confucian ethics at its heart, and they also remain influential in states such as Singapore. Values such as religious tolerance, putting the community first, and awareness of the key role of the family in moral life still inspire many in Asia and beyond.

A Chinese woman laboring in a rice paddy in China. Willingness to work and respect for social hierarchy are important Confucian ethics.

Dragons adorn the roof of a mausoleum for
Confucius. Although powerful, dragons were
seen in China as good-natured, just, and honest
creatures whom people petitioned for favors.
The use of dragons as a Confucian emblem
spread to Japan, where this building is located.

PRACTICES AND FESTIVALS

In its early days, Confucianism involved a number of ritual practices, many of which were celebrated by the emperor himself. Today, those who follow Confucian beliefs are more likely to do so for the practical ethics of the teachings, rather than for the rituals and ceremonies.

CHINESE RITUALS

Chinese religion has always been a synthesis of different traditions, blending Confucian, Daoist, and Buddhist ideas. The Chinese year is punctuated by many festivals, but these events are not specifically Confucian. Indeed, the content of many of the festivals that have developed in the world's Chinese communities comes largely from the practices of Daoism (see pp.250–261). Confucianism is primarily a belief system that focuses on ethics and behavior, and rituals are not now as important as they were in Confucius's time, when it was seen as essential to preserve the correct rites.

IMPERIAL WORSHIP

In traditional Confucianism, the essential religious observances were those carried out by the emperor and his officials. These involved the emperor making certain offerings to maintain his harmonious relationship with Heaven and to confirm his mandate for government. The rituals could involve sacrifices not only to the emperor's own ancestors, but also to the ancestors of other emperors and to the gods or culture heroes, such as Fu Xi, who were said to have founded China in the far-distant past. It was the emperor's

Worshippers gather to recite prayers at Lung Shan Temple, Taiwan. The importance of Confucian ritual has declined in recent times.

The spirits of the dead reside in carved wooden ancestor tablets, according to followers of the Confucian faith.

shrines in the home. These shrines – usually in the main living room of the house – comprised an altar supporting several spirit tablets, where ancestor spirits were said to dwell.

The most important Confucian rite of passage is marriage, because it signals the creation of a new family unit in which to foster harmony and to hope for children. Marriage in Confucianism involves a complex series of rituals, with correct procedures that govern the proposal, engagement, giving of a dowry and bride-price, and exchange of vows. At the heart of the traditional marriage ceremony itself is the point when the groom takes his bride to his family's ancestor tablets, and the couple bow to them. This action effectively introduces the bride to the ancestors of her new family, and enables the ancestors to bless the union.

The other important life-cycle rituals of Confucianism take place when someone dies and joins the ancestors. Family members wear mourning clothes of coarse material, and mourners arrive at the funeral with gifts of money and incense as their contribution to its cost. The body of the deceased is placed in a coffin, along with offerings such as food and treasured possessions. A willow branch, which signifies the deceased's soul, is carried with the coffin to the burial-place. After the burial has been completed, the branch is taken to the family's home altar, where it is used in a ritual that installs the soul at the family's shrine.

responsibility to carry out these acts of worship, especially those that took place on important dates in the calendar, such as the solstices—the longest and shortest days of the year. (A department of the imperial civil service dealing with astronomy took charge of working out when these dates would occur.) To practice this worship was to maintain the harmony between Heaven and Earth. These imperial ceremonies ended with the fall of the empire, but some of their sacred sites, such as the Temple of Heaven in Beijing, survive.

CYCLE OF LIFE

Reverence for the ancestors was the personal equivalent of state-driven imperial worship. Again, it was a way to maintain harmony between the world of the Earth and the realm of the immortals. It also had a moral point, as honoring one's ancestors was an activity that reminded people of the importance of respect for elders and filial piety, which are among the key values of Confucianism (*see pp.244–245*). Chinese people would go to their parents' graves to make offerings—this was particularly the duty of sons. Ancestors were also honored at

Fearsome stone guardians stand over tombs in China, highlighting the value of ancestry in Confucian society.

DAOISM

The Chinese religion of Daoism began with the work of two philosophers. The first, Laozi, thought by some to be legendary, probably lived during the 6th century BCE; the second, Zhuangzi, lived 300 years later. Both wrote key texts that helped to create a mystical religion that has continuously renewed itself for thousands of years.

D aoism takes two principal forms, philosophical Daoism (*daojia*) and religious Daoism (*daojiao*). The original form, *daojia*, began with the teachings of Laozi, who was said to have been a contemporary of Confucius. Laozi is said to be the author of the Daode jing, a book that was probably in fact written in the 4th or 3rd century BCE. This book reveals a deeply mystical and inward-looking philosophy, but Laozi was also a practical teacher, who taught people how to reach spiritual fulfilment. He encouraged people to look within themselves to find what kind of person they should be. In doing so, they would find the Dao ("way"), which was both the source of order in the cosmos and the path they should follow in the world. Laozi's followers aimed to live according to the Dao.

The Daode jing and other philosophical writings, such as the Zhuangzi (named after its author), are still widely read for their insights and spiritual guidance. *Daojiao* or religious Daoism, however, takes these philosophical ideas much further. The Dao is seen as a path toward immortality, and this path is followed by channeling the forces of nature within one's own body. Religious Daoism, therefore, places strong emphasis on matters such as diet, exercise, and breathing, as well as the kinds of moral behavior that enable one to live in harmony with the Dao.

Daoism has also become associated with the popular religion of China (*see pp.256–257*), a fascinating belief system involving many deities. These deities are seen as immortals—men and women of outstanding virtue or wisdom who have gained everlasting life. Many are said to control specific aspects of life on Earth, and followers of the popular religion make offerings to one of them when they have a specific problem or issue.

A woman prays at an altar in the Man Mo Temple in Hong Kong. The coils of incense and soft lamplight are typical of Daoist places of worship.

ORIGINS AND HISTORY

Many of the philosophical ideas that are central to Daoism predate
the early writers who are attributed with the faith's foundation.
However, by adding their own ideas to the core principles, these
learned men created a new, distinctive belief system.

EARLY BEGINNINGS

Among the founding ideas of Daoism
are those of the two primal forces *yin*
and *yang* (*see box, p.242*) and of the vital
energy or life-force known as *qi*, as well
as the idea that the cosmos is populated
by myriad deities. The most prominent
writer to add to these ideas was Laozi
(or Lao-tzu), who wrote the Daode jing
(or Tao Te Ching). Daoism's other
pioneering texts are the Zhuangzi and
Huainanzi, written between the 4th and
2nd centuries BCE. These texts explore
the ideal of following a path, or Dao,
that is in tune with the cosmos, the
relationship between people and the
universe, and meditation practices.

The Chinese philosopher Laozi (who lived during
the 6th century BCE) is usually credited as the
principal founder of Daoism.

RELIGIOUS DAOISM

During the Han dynasty (206BCE–
220CE), the Daoist philosophical ideas
of the early texts became a religion.
Laozi was seen as a god and those
skilled in his teachings were regarded
as adepts who could guide followers
toward immortality. In the ensuing
centuries, Daoism adapted, evolving
new sects and rituals, developing
medical and magical practices designed
to prolong life, and
promoting meditation.
By the time of the
Tang emperors (618–
907CE), Daoism was
popular at the court,

with state-sponsored temples and the use of the Daode jing as a set text for students of the civil service.

Support for the religion continued during the Song and Yuan dynasties (960–1368). The Quanzhen school of Daoism (13th century) saw the importance of the three main Chinese religions—Daoism, Confucianism, and Buddhism —and encouraged people to read the texts of all of them. This open attitude to other faiths proved influential in a culture that absorbs outside influences and makes them its own. Like the other prominent school of Daoism from this period, the Zhengyi, Quanzhen attracted followers. Indeed, Daoism generally continued to be influential until the early 20th century.

RECENT DEVELOPMENTS

With the rise of communism in China, the fortunes of Daoism changed. The communists condemned rival belief systems as superstitious. The most aggressive assaults on Daoism came during the Cultural Revolution of the 1960s and 1970s, when the state demolished temples and burned Daoist books. Since then the climate has become more tolerant. In Chinese communities outside mainland China, such as in Taiwan, Daoism is popular. Daoism's attention to meditation techniques and its concern for finding a path in tune with nature have brought interest both from Westerners seeking alternative spiritual paths and from those who are anxious about the environment.

Mountains and rivers are regarded as sacred in Daoism, which looks to the harmony and serenity of the natural world as a model for spiritual balance.

THE DAODE JING

Said to contain the teachings of Laozi, the Daode jing probably combines the words of many early spiritual teachers. The text explains the principle of the Dao, which guides everything in the universe, sustains all things, and remains unchanged while all else flows around it. The Daode jing also emphasizes feminine, yielding qualities, which, it says, are like water—at once soft and strong.

Daoist sages believed that by following the Dao diligently and rigorously they could achieve immortality.

CORE BELIEFS

At the heart of Daoist belief is the concept of the Dao, or the Way. The Dao is the eternal, unfaltering principle that underpins the universe. By following the Dao, believers can expect a long and healthy life, and the possibility of joining the immortals in Heaven.

THE WAY

As Laozi pointed out: "The ways of men are conditioned by those of Heaven, the ways of Heaven by those of the Dao, and the Dao came into being by itself." A mysterious phenomenon, the Dao is said to be on one level inactive, while at the same time never leaving anything undone.

Followers of Daoism try to live in a manner that is in tune with the Dao. This aspiration was especially important for rulers, both because of their power to influence the lives of others and because their subjects would look to them as examples of correct behavior. So Daoism promotes the way of the wise ruler, who cultivates detachment, scorns material luxuries, and does not pursue domination for its own sake. Others, too, aim to live up to these ideals.

The Eight Immortals are among the most prominent Daoist deities, and symbolize prosperity and longevity.

THE OUTER AND INNER WAYS

Daoists believe that the world will be healthy and things will go well when *yin* and *yang* are in balance, and when people live in harmony with one another and with the cosmos. The founders of the philosophy rejected the Confucian ideals of duty to one's elders and superiors because they believed that these were manmade rather than heavenly concepts.

Daoists are more interested in what they see as a spiritual harmony, and they also aim for an inner balance, which brings health of body and mind. The way they approach this inner balance involves a complex set of beliefs about the human body. Daoists believe that the body contains many invisible channels along which the vital life-energy *qi* flows. In Traditional Chinese

---

LIFE-ENERGY

For a person to be healthy, energy or *qi* must flow steadily along a series of meridians (channels) in the body. When disease blocks this flow, various forms of Chinese medicine can help to release it. In acupuncture and reflexology, for example, the practitioner presses certain points on the body to restore the free-flow of *qi* along the meridians. Getting this flow right—that is, free and in balance—fosters both physical and mental well-being, and promotes longevity.

A medical figurine showing the meridians in the human body. There are 12 key meridians through which the vital energy *qi* flows.

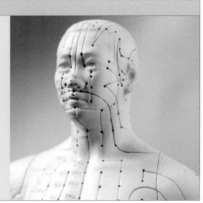

Medicine, practitioners aim to restore a person's internal harmony so that energy flows freely—the key to health.

THE IMMORTALS

Balancing *yin* and *yang* by following the Dao and using its techniques to achieve health and satisfaction are seen as worthwhile in themselves, but there is an ultimate goal beyond this—immortality. In philosophical Daoism there is a spiritual notion of immortality: a person who achieves spiritual balance reaches a plane above the mundane and beyond material things, and so becomes immortal in a conceptual way. But religious Daoism has developed a whole mythology of Heaven and the immortals, and followers of the Dao hope to join these deities when they die. For many Chinese, these immortals are figures that they should worship and appeal to for help in times of difficulty (*see pp.256–257*). But the immortals also convey a profound message. Many of the inhabitants of Heaven are seen as people who lived on Earth and achieved immortality through outstanding deeds or single-minded following of the Dao. Their stories are often colorful and full of incident, but their message is clear: devotion to the Way will result in immortality.

T'ai chi is one practice that helps the vital energy *qi* to flow freely through the body.

CHINESE POPULAR RELIGION

The term Chinese popular religion is used for the blend of Daoism, Confucianism, and Buddhism practiced by many people in Chinese communities around the world, and is associated especially with Taiwan, Hong Kong, Malaysia, and Singapore. This synthesis of faiths emphasizes the immortals, the festivals that bring together the community, and a host of other religious observances.

THE HIERARCHY IN HEAVEN

At the heart of Chinese popular religion are the many thousands of "immortals," who range from exalted but mysterious, shadowy beings to familiar figures whose images are seen in many Chinese homes. At the top of the heavenly hierarchy are the Jade Emperor and his consort the empress, followed by the court of gods who act as their servants and officials. These heavenly bureaucrats parallel the enormous earthly civil service that existed in imperial China.

The Jade Emperor, and many of the courtiers, are too exalted to deal directly with mortals on Earth, so there are lesser messenger deities who act as intermediaries between devotees and Heaven. The most popular of these are the Kitchen God and his wife, who are said to produce an annual report of every person's deeds and deliver it to the Jade Emperor. In many Chinese homes a print that includes portraits of the Kitchen God and his consort is displayed above the stove in the kitchen. At the end of the year, homeowners smear honey on the god's mouth to make his report "sweet" and full of good words, and

Kuan Yin—the goddess of mercy—is one of the most popular deities in the Chinese pantheon.

then take the print down from the wall and burn it in the stove. The smoke from the fire is said to carry the god's report to Heaven.

APPEALING TO THE GODS

Chinese popular religion is highly pragmatic. Devotees call on the gods to help them when they face difficulties, encounter stress, or confront some new challenge in their lives. The many deities have different roles. There are gods who preside over health, others who are said to help those who are taking examinations or starting new business ventures, and still others who look after new mothers. In addition, there are deities who are popular because they play more general roles. Among these are the three gods of good fortune, Fu Hsing (god of happiness), Lu Hsing (god of wealth), and Shou Hsing (god of longevity). Of these, Shou Hsing is especially popular, because long life is valued highly in Chinese culture, coming only through having a good balance of *yin* and *yang*. He is also linked with the south, the most auspicious of the cardinal directions.

A Chinese family firing crackers in honor of the Kitchen God, who was regarded as a protector of the home in Chinese popular religion.

Another very popular deity is the goddess of compassion, Kuan Yin, one of the *bodhisattvas* of Mahayana Buddhism (*see p.201*). She is said to be infinitely merciful, and always to answer her worshippers' prayers.

Devotees pray to all these gods, using the smoke from burning incense to send their messages to Heaven. These offerings take place at popular religion temples. One temple may contain several altars, each with statues of a different deity at which worshippers can make offerings and appeal for help and support. People will select a deity according to their problem, but may also pray to a favorite deity, such as Kuan Yin.

Followers of Chinese popular religion light incense sticks so that the smoke from the sticks can carry their prayers to Heaven.

ETHICS, MORALITY, AND LAW

Like many Eastern religions, Daoism is seen as a path that offers a way to live an ethical life. Although it may seem passive to Western eyes to follow a faith that accepts the world as it is, Daoism also has many moral precepts that show people how to respect others and live well.

THE PATH TO GOODNESS

The one overriding ethical principle of Daoism is *wu-wei*, the concept of non-interference, or going with the flow. Nature and the Dao show no favorites, and the follower of the Dao should show a similar impartiality. Sages of philosophical Daoism were therefore encouraged to be detached from the world, and to live in tune with nature. Religious Daoism kept these ideals but with a new interpretation: the Dao and the sage should favor the good. Adherents were taught to follow *wu-wei*, to try to be "supple" in their responses to the world, to be humble, and to cultivate their feminine side. At the same time, Daoists should avoid vices such as cursing and bad language, insulting others, greed, fornication, theft, gossip, promise-breaking, anger, and hard-heartedness.

THE "THREE WAYS"

In China, the ethical goals of Daoism were often combined with those of Confucianism and Buddhism. Daoists embraced Confucian virtues such as respect for order, along with Buddhist ideals of self-cultivation

"IT IS THE WAY OF THE DAO TO ACT WITHOUT ACTING."

Daode jing 63

A Chinese herbalist prepares treatments for ailments. Daoists believe that good conduct does as much to promote health as medicine and a good diet.

and following a moral path. They realized that each of the "Three Ways" offered mutually compatible spiritual and ethical learning. Soon, the teachings became codified into lists of moral precepts. Some of these lists formed the basis of vows taken by adepts when they committed to a moral life (like the vows taken by Buddhist monks). They promised such things as to avoid evil or cruel thoughts, to cultivate humaneness and love, to avoid excess in all things, and to accept the teachings of the Daoist sages.

GOOD BEHAVIOR

In Daoism, quite simply, if you follow the ethical path diligently, you will live longer. Some early sages recommended that people take alchemical preparations to prolong life, but these were said to work only if those administering and taking the elixirs lived according to Daoist moral principles. Today, the rituals that Daoist priests perform to foster health and prolong life are said to be effective if the celebrant lives a good life. If people are benevolent, the world becomes a better place; but if there is an excess of sin, some Daoist writings predict that there will be a cataclysm, followed by the appearance of Lord Lao (Laozi in his immortal form), who will renew the world both morally and spiritually. Daoists do not passively wait for this to happen, but do their best to cultivate benevolence in their lives, for their own good and for the good of others.

The Black Dragon Pool near Kunming, China, is associated with a moral parable of an evil dragon forced to convert to a life of benevolence.

PRACTICES AND FESTIVALS

Daoists take part in many religious practices, not all of which are related to the Dao. These rites include temple offerings, participating in festivals to balance *yin* and *yang*, and performing the correct funeral rites to fulfil the deceased's hope of joining the immortals in Heaven.

RELIGIOUS OBSERVANCE

Daoist observances take various forms involving both self-development through practices such as meditation, and offerings at temples, where images of Daoist deities may stand side by side with other Chinese gods and goddesses (*see pp.256–257*). Daoism places much importance on sacred sites, including springs, caves, and above all mountains, and for this reason pilgrimage is another important practice. Sacred mountains such as Tai Shan in eastern China, which has hundreds of shrines, are popular pilgrimage places.

A Daoist priest meditates in a forest glade. Meditation and living a harmonious, balanced life are important in Daoism.

CYCLE OF LIFE

In China, family and family life are highly regarded institutions. As a result, some of the most important rituals and customs in Chinese life surround marriage. Astrology plays an important part in the traditional preparations for a marriage. An astrologer casts the horoscopes of both bride and groom to check their compatibility, and helps the two families to choose the most auspicious day for the ceremony. There are a number of rituals of betrothal before those of marriage. These attend to the balance of *yin* and *yang* in the individuals, with the aim of bringing harmony to the relationship. An auspicious wedding begins a new

A woman kneels to offer a prayer at Hong Kong's Wong Tai Sin temple. Visiting sacred sites, such as temples and mountains, is important for Daoists.

family that will underpin social stability and bring more people into the world to follow the Dao. So, the participants in the marriage rites carefully observe the correct physical placing of guests, with the groom's family to the east (*yang*) and the bride's to the west (*yin*).

The last rites carried out when a person dies are just as carefully considered. Mourners express the relationships of *yin* and *yang* by again adopting pre-ordained positions— men to the east, women to the west— as well as the correct orientation of the deceased's body, with the head toward the south. At the deceased's home, the family altar is covered with white cloths (white is the color of *yin* and mourning).

Coins are used to make predictions of future events in some Daoist oracular systems.

Mourners may also burn money and symbolic paper artefacts to ease the soul's journey Heavenward. For similar reasons, after the funeral mourners may go to subterranean chambers under temples and present sacrifices that are designed to ensure that the soul passes as quickly as possible through the afterlife's process of judgment.

FESTIVALS

The Chinese year has many festivals, but one specifically Daoist festival is the *jiao* ceremony that takes place on or near the winter solstice and marks the renewal of the heavenly, masculine *yang* force at this point in the calendar. The ceremony is celebrated by Daoist priests who have undergone purification rituals and who wear lavish vestments, while the overall *jiao* festival is commemorated with notable music, dancing, and giant effigies of the gods that are intended to frighten away malevolent spirits.

Other Chinese calendar festivals, of which there are many, are not specifically Daoist, but may be led by Daoist priests. They begin with the New Year festival, a time of house-cleaning and the settling of old debts. This is another celebration of the renewal of *yang*, and decorations are usually in *yang* colors such as red, orange, and gold.

New Year is followed by the Lantern Festival, with its many offerings to the gods; and also by Qingming, a time to remember the dead and to celebrate the coming of spring. The midsummer festival, the Double Fifth, marks the peak of *yang* force, and aims to protect people from too much *yang* by the use of five "poisons" (centipede, scorpion, snake, toad, and lizard) —which are seen in designs on clothes and in the form of amulets— and five colors (blue, red, yellow, white, and black). The Feast of the Hungry Ghosts marks a time when the gates of Hell are said to open, letting out malevolent spirits. Priests hold ceremonies to encourage the spirits to repent—or to return to Hell.

SHINTO

Shinto is the indigenous religion of Japan. An ancient religion, with its roots in practices and beliefs that date back to prehistoric times, Shinto continues to attract and retain many adherents. Somewhat unusually for such a living faith, Shinto remains largely the preserve of Japanese people who live in their native land.

The term *shinto*, usually translated as "the way of the gods," was first given to Japan's native religion in 720CE, a few decades after Buddhism arrived in the country. The Japanese used the name Shinto to distinguish the local Japanese beliefs from the new way of the Buddha. The beliefs of Shinto had probably existed for thousands of years before this time. They would have been rooted in animism, with its notion that natural phenomena, such as mountains, trees, and animals, were invested with divine power.

Shinto is concerned with a variety of divine beings known in Japanese as *kami*. There are said to be an infinite number of *kami*, and they include all kinds of natural forces and entities, along with a host of spirits, life-giving deities, and other phenomena—anything

in fact that displays impressive power or life-force can be considered a *kami*. Followers of Shinto worship these countless *kami* both in the home and at thousands of shrines all over Japan. Some *kami* are prominent deities, such as the sun goddess Amaterasu or the rice god Inari; others are ancestor spirits; still others are deities known only in particular Japanese regions. Regardless of the importance of individual deities such as Amaterasu, there is no hierarchy of *kami*—all are imbued with spiritual power.

Although Buddhism became important in Japanese spirituality after it was introduced to the country, Shinto remains an essential, defining part of Japanese life, culture, and belief. The religion underwent a major revival in the second half of the 19th century and today the faith is still strong. Many people visit shrines to make a request to the *kami*, ask Shinto priests to lead life-cycle ceremonies such as weddings, and celebrate the Shinto calendar festivals.

Shrine maidens perform a *kagura,* or ritual Shinto dance, at the Meiji Shrine in Tokyo. The dance forms part of a traditional rite of purification.

ORIGINS AND HISTORY

The influence of Shinto on Japan's identity became clear in the 19th and early 20th centuries, when the faith was closely linked with the Japanese state. Since then, Shinto has been cut loose from government, and now holds its own among Japan's other religions.

EARLY SHINTO

Shinto-like practices first appear to have emerged during Japan's Yayoi period (*ca.*300BCE–*ca.*300CE), when the Japanese people established rice cultivation and so held sowing and harvesting rituals. By the time Mahayana Buddhism (*see p.201*), with its many Buddhas or *bodhisattvas*, arrived in Japan in the 6th century CE, worship of the *kami* (*see pp.266–267*) was an

took control of Japan and promoted rival belief systems, including Daoism and Confucianism, which drastically reduced Shinto's influence.

THE SHINTO REVIVAL

During the 18th century, scholars revisited the Shinto texts; then, in 1868, the Shinto revival was complete when the Meiji emperor took back the reins of power from the Shoguns and made

"AS MANY SPIRITS AS BLADES OF GRASS"

Anonymous Japanese poem

established part of the country's culture. Many people saw the incoming Buddhas as rivals to the *kami*, and two clans vied for power in Japan at this time: one worshipped the *kami*, the other the Buddhas. The Buddhists won, and erected many temples, eclipsing the local *kami*. In spite of this, *kami* worship continued, and soon became known as Shinto. The two faiths coexisted until the Tokugawa Shoguns (1603–1867)

Shinto an official state religion. The Japanese imperial family claimed to be descended from the sun goddess Amaterasu, who had sent her grandson, Ninigi, to rule Japan. Larger shrines, such as that at Ise, began to take precedence over smaller, local shrines. Once devoted to local *kami*, these now focused on the imperial cult, which was known as "State Shinto" and was used to promote nationalism. Buddhist sites were destroyed and people who objected to State Shinto were punished.

MODERN SHINTO

In the aftermath of World War II, everything changed. Japan's new

Shintoists believe that Izanagi and Izanami (symbolized by these "wedded rocks") created Japan and were the parents of the sun goddess Amaterasu.

THE EMPERORS AND THE SUN GODDESS

Japan's close identity with the sun, from the symbol on its national flag to its popular name as the "Land of the Rising Sun," helped to strengthen claims that the royal family was descended from the sun goddess Amaterasu, the most significant of all *kami*. The emperors worshipped Amaterasu at the shrine at Ise, the headquarters of State Shinto. Eventually, in 1946, the emperor publicly renounced his divine lineage, to become merely a constitutional figurehead.

This Japanese maritime flag shows the rising Sun with its radiating rays. The country's national flag shows just the red disc of the rising sun.

constitution removed Shinto's status as a state-sponsored religion and gave the people of Japan the freedom to worship how they wished. Cut loose from the state, Shinto reorganized itself, forming Jinja Honcho, a new association of shrines that could organize the religion and promote it as a national, but not nationalistic, faith. The influence of Shinto appears in other aspects of Japanese life, too—even the traditional sport of Sumo wrestling is based on Shinto rituals. In fact, this ancient faith is still an important part of Japan's entire national identity, despite the country's forward-thinking attitude.

A procession of Shinto priests makes its way toward a temple. Processions form an integral part of Shinto practice.

CORE BELIEFS

Shinto belief centers on myriad deities called *kami*, who range from powerful beings, such as the sun goddess Amaterasu, to little-known local spirits. Maintaining the correct relationships between human beings and the pantheon of *kami* is fundamental to Shinto belief.

The *kami* are a vast population of spirits that influence human life and everything else that happens on Earth. They are described in several Japanese sacred texts, including the Kojiki ("Record of Ancient Matters"), which was written in 712CE by Ono Yasamaro, and the Nihonshoki, compiled a few years later by a group of Shinto scholars. These texts describe an infinite number of *kami* with widely varying characters. Some are deities that relate to a specific family or clan; others are the spirits of natural phenomena, from waterfalls to mountains; still others are specific to particular neighborhood shrines, where local legends tell their stories. Some *kami* are benevolent spirits, while others are evil—for example, some of the most dreaded are ghosts or *obake*.

The rising Sun is presided over by the goddess Amaterasu, according to Shinto belief.

Among the most famous *kami* are the gods and goddesses at the center of Japanese mythology. At their head are the primal couple Izanagi and Izanami. Their children are the sun goddess Amaterasu and the storm god Susano. Of the two siblings, Amaterasu is the Shinto deity who has attracted most veneration, both as the ancestor of the imperial line (*see box, p.265*) and as a gentle goddess whose Sun warms the Earth. There are a number of other *kami* who are worshipped widely. One is the rice god Inari. Traditionally worshipped by farmers who wanted to ensure a good rice crop, Inari now attracts the devotion of all, especially those in business, as he offers hope of prosperity. Another ancient deity whose cult has developed is the warrior god Hachiman. This god provides an

Shinto pilgrims visit a temple high on the slopes of Mount Fuji in Japan. The mountain is one of the most sacred sites in Shinto.

A Shinto shrine in the midst of a volcanic landscape in Nagano, Japan. The spirits in all natural things, known as *kami*, are central to Shinto beliefs.

example of a deity who is worshipped in both Buddhist and Shinto temples. To followers of Shinto, both civilian and military, he is Japan's protector; Buddhists see him as a reincarnation of the Buddha Amida (*see p.203*).

ANCESTOR SPIRITS

Followers of Shinto believe that, when a person dies, their soul joins the ranks of the *kami*, making ancestor spirits an important spiritual class. Most ancestral *kami* are not well known outside their immediate family, who worship them at small family shrines. But one or two, including those of former emperors, have developed major cults.

Japan's war-dead have also been revered as *kami*, and Shintoists worship them at a shrine in Tokyo called Yasukuni. This shrine is controversial, especially when politicians worship there, as, although the Japanese state officially gave up its religious involvement in 1945, many identify Yasukuni with the extreme nationalism of the pre-1945 era.

RITUAL AND LIFE

When they worship the *kami* using the correct rituals (*see p.270*), devotees believe that they are helping to purify the world. The *kami*, presiding as they do over different aspects of the world, from the sun to a local cave or stream, are responsible for looking after it. But they are capricious and unpredictable spirits, as well as beings with great power. Followers of Shinto believe that by observing the appropriate rituals of devotion they can help to ensure that the *kami* continue to act in benevolent ways and keep the world running smoothly.

"I FULFIL HIS PRAISES WITH THE HEAVENLY RITUAL."

Yengishiki, Fire Ritual

ETHICS, MORALITY, AND LAW

Shinto is not a dogmatic religion and does not have complex legal codes, lists of cardinal virtues, or inventories of deadly sins like many other faiths. Instead it relies on a number of key moral concepts that guide people and act as a focus for their values.

HARMONY

Probably the most important moral concept in Shinto is harmony. Japanese ethics derive from a blend of influences, because—as well as Shinto—Daoist, Confucian, and above all Buddhist belief systems have all had a major influence in Japan. All these religions value both cosmic and personal harmony. One of the specifically Shinto contributions is the concept of *wa*, a kind of positive harmony that devotees should foster both in human affairs and in the wider world. Shinto encourages thoughts, actions, and emotions that preserve and nurture *wa*, and discourages everything that disrupts or destroys it. So, in essence, Shinto upholds all conventional and moral behavior that preserves family relationships, holds society together, and protects the natural environmental balance. This means that, while Shinto tends to encourage social conformity, it also supports efforts to conserve the environment and takes the lead in such initiatives as anti-pollution campaigns.

Shinto ritual is another way to foster harmony. Customs such as regular bathing are seen not only as acts of purification, but also of preserving the world's harmony by ensuring that people are ritually pure. Other Shinto practices, from the ritual cleansing of the devotee at the shrine to the periodic reconstruction of the shrines themselves, may also bring harmony.

THE IMPORTANCE OF "FACE"

Another important Shinto ethical concept is *tatemae*, or "face." People who step outside social norms, do wrong, or let the rest of society down in some way,

THE TORII

Most shrines have a *torii* or ceremonial gateway, which takes the form of a pair of sloping posts supporting two cross-pieces, and may be made of wood, stone, or even metal. Usually painted vermilion, the *torii*, through which worshippers must enter, acts as the marker between the outside world and the sacred space inside the shrine. Some large shrines, especially those dedicated to the god of rice and prosperity, Inari, have many *torii*. This is because business people donate them to the shrine in thanks to Inari when he has helped them to achieve success.

During the festivals known as *matsuri*, Shinto shrines may be carried through the streets—here of Japan's capital city, Tokyo—by worshippers in traditional dress.

sin affected the lives of others—was expected to commit suicide.

FAMILY AND SOCIETY

In Shinto ethics, the group is usually more important than the individual. Historically, individuals belonged to a clan, each with its own *kami* whom clan members were obliged to worship. People felt that society would dissolve if they did not honor the clan. Today, people are loyal to the *ie*, a term that embraces a kind of extended family, including both *kami* and living members.

Followers of Shinto also owe a wider loyalty to society. In State Shinto (*see p.264*), this meant that the religion laid a heavy emphasis on loyalty to the ruler and on keeping him in power—a secure emperor meant a stable society. Today, the aim is to promote the well-being and stability of society as a whole.

lose face and are left to confront shame. For many, the fear of shame acts as a brake on immoral behavior. But those who do wrong are expected to atone. For a minor offense, this might mean a public apology; while for a more serious wrongdoing, it may involve offering a compensatory gift. Followers are meant to perform such acts of atonement not in order to attract good *karma* (*see p.168*) nor to ensure a place in the next world, but because to perform them is right and helps to preserve the structure of society. Traditional Shinto values maintained that a person who had sinned gravely—especially if the

A floating *torii* gate at sunset. *Torii* provide Japan with some of its most striking pieces of Shinto architecture.

PRACTICES AND FESTIVALS

The focus of Shinto religious practices is to maintain a harmonious relationship between people and *kami*. At day-to-day shrines, devotees ask for the help of the *kami* in their lives. At festivals, celebrants come together to show the spirits their reverence and devotion.

SHINTO WORSHIP

Many Shinto religious practices are based on need. A person will carry out an act of worship if they have a specific problem or challenge in their life and want to ask the *kami* for help. To do this, he or she visits a shrine and makes an offering of some kind. There are several forms of offering. One of the most popular is a sacred object, such as a votive tablet known as an *ema*, that bears a message to the *kami*. Purchased at the shrine, the *ema* may bear the shrine's symbol or an image that represents the person's hopes—for

example, an *ema* bought by a student in hope of exam success might bear the image of a great scholar such as the 9th-century patron of education Sugawara no Michizane. The petitioner buys the *ema*, writes a message to the *kami* on it, and hangs it up at the shrine. After it has been displayed for some time, the *ema* is burned as an offering to the *kami*. Alternatively, a person can buy protective amulets called *omamori*. These usually take the form of small bags that the devotee carries around. In the bag is a piece of paper on which the person writes their prayer. A *fuda*, a wooden plaque with an inscription, has a similar effect, but the devotee places it in a

Bathing in iced water while praying is believed to ensure the participants' good health in the New Year.

One of many seasonal festivals, the spring "peach festival" gives thanks for the health of daughters; peach blossom is a symbol of feminine beauty.

prominent position in the home, preferably in the household shrine. Most people do not believe literally in the magical power of these objects—rather, *ema*, *omamori*, and *fuda* provide symbols of the person's commitment to living in harmony with the *kami*.

CYCLE OF LIFE

Shinto has a number of traditional life-cycle rituals intended to create and reinforce a person's relationship with the *kami* and the *kami's* shrine. The first, called *hatsumiyamairi*, takes place some 30 days after a baby is born. The child, usually carried by its grandmother, is taken to a shrine and blessed, after which it is protected by that shrine's *kami*. Children are reintroduced to the *kami* at a ritual called *shichigosan*, which is held on November 15 each year. On this day, parents take girls aged seven and three, and boys aged five, to their local shrine where they are blessed once more. On January 15 each year,

A traditional pink *omamori kami* offering, which devotees can purchase at most Shinto shrines.

men and women who have reached official adulthood (20 years old) visit the shrine to give thanks in the festival of *seijinshiki*; while the festival of *yakudoshi* provides an opportunity for people who have reached ages that are considered to be inauspicious (typically 33 for women and 42 for men) to make special shrine visits and acquire amulets that protect them from the problems that are said to occur in these years. Some shrines specialize in this service of protection from bad luck.

SHINTO FESTIVALS

Known as *matsuri*, a word that conveys many meanings, including ritual, celebration, veneration, and prayer, all Shinto festivals aim to honor and give thanks to the *kami* so that they will provide support for Japan and its people. They tend to be times of cheerful celebration, with music, dancing, processions, and special foods; statues of the *kami* are often ceremoniously taken to dedicated temporary shrines where they are given special devotion during the *matsuri* period. The biggest *matsuri* of all is the New Year festival, when people eat a celebratory meal and then visit shrines to ask the *kami* to support them in the coming year. Even at Japan's smaller shrines there is a festive atmosphere and the feeling that all over the country people are performing the same celebrations.

Numerous other festivals follow throughout the year, many of them linked to important events in the agricultural cycle. For example, numerous festivals mark rice-planting in April; summer festivals protect growing crops from extreme weather conditions; and autumn celebrations include harvest festivals.

New religious movements

T HE 19TH AND 20TH CENTURIES saw an explosion of new religious movements across the world, from new branches of existing faiths to the completely original movements described in this chapter. Most of these began with one person's unique belief or powerful religious experience, and the personality and charisma of these founders is often what gives them their character.

In the 19th century the world was becoming increasingly secular. The pressures of modern life, and the need to reconcile scientific developments with certain aspects of existing belief, meant that members of some religions began to reinterpret their faith. Movements such as Humanistic and Reconstructionist Judaism are typical of such reinterpretations.

Modern pressures could have an opposite effect, taking people back to religious basics or a more literal reading of scripture. The many varieties of Pentecostal Christianity are an example. Movements such as ISKCON in Hinduism (*see p.180*), found new aspects

to the existing religion; while still others added new visions and approaches to the established faith, for example in the way that the Salvationists imposed a military model on their Christianity (*see p.117*). The core beliefs of all these branches of religion are, however, recognizably those of the original faith.

BEGINNING ANEW

New religions, on the other hand, have few, if any, ties to what went before, instead coming directly from their founders' vision. One group, labeled "World-denying" movements—for example, the Children of God— emphasizes the need for their followers

The standing Stones of Callanish on the Isle of Lewis in Scotland are among the ancient pagan sites now visited by followers of New Age religions.

The Matrimandir in Auroville, India, is a center for followers of Sri Aurobindo.

to live on a different level from the rest of society, often cutting themselves off completely from their neighboring communities. They can be authoritarian and demanding—values that have sometimes brought them into controversy.

By contrast, many other new religious movements embrace the world. In converting large numbers to their way of thinking, these movements aim to bring about a wide transformation that makes the world a more spiritually aware place. On an individual level, they aim to transform their adherents by leading them along a spiritual path that will encourage self-realization and personal growth. These movements are less concerned with distinctions between the sacred and profane than other religions, and focus more on the spiritual health of their followers. Movements such as Transcendental Meditation (*see p.281*) place a high value on the personal experience of adherents and usually have an egalitarian outlook —salvation or spiritual growth is open to everyone who accepts the movement's ideas. One or two religions, including the Baha'i Faith (*see p.280*), are still more ambitious, aiming to bring about world unity by fostering tolerance of all peoples and all faiths.

"THE GODS ARE EVERYWHERE YOU LOOK."

Temple keeper, Hong Kong

NEW RELIGIOUS MOVEMENTS

Religion is constantly evolving. Conceived out of the unique visions of inspirational modern thinkers, and drawing on the wisdom and beliefs of the ancients, several new religious movements stand out for their far-reaching spiritual influence.

OMOTO

Japan   1892   150,000

In 1892, a Japanese woman called Deguchi Nao became possessed by the folk deity Ushitora-no-Konjin. As a result, she and her son-in-law Deguchi Onisaburo founded Omoto, which centered on this god. Omoto attracted many converts, but at the time Shinto was Japan's national religion, and the authorities saw Omoto as a challenge to both Shinto and the emperor. In 1921 the government suppressed Omoto, but in 1945, when the Japanese were given religious freedom, the faith reformed, concentrating on charitable work, cultural activities, and campaigns for religious tolerance. Adherents read Deguchi Nao's *Fudesaki* ("From the Tip of the Writing Brush"), which describes her revelations, as well as texts by Deguchi Onisaburo and other leaders.

The group encourages the Japanese arts, such as Noh theater and the tea ceremony, and sponsors a volunteer organization that does aid work, campaigns for peace, and promotes international understanding through the universal language of Esperanto.

The Japanese tea ceremony is a notable ritual in Zen Buddhism and in Shinto. Omoto has adopted it as part of its own practice.

MAHIKARI

Japan | 1959; 1978 | 800,000

Mahikari is the name for two Japanese religions. The first, Sekai Mahikari Bunmai Kyodan ("World Religious Organization of True Light Civilization"), was founded by Okada Kotama following a godly command to save people from the end of the world.

The second group, Sukyo Mahikari ("True Light Supra-Religion"), was founded after Okada's death. The two groups share many ideas and practices, some of which derive from Shinto. In addition, followers claim that climate change heralds the dawn of a new age, and that people should shed material values to prepare for the renewed world. They believe in a purification ritual in which, by the laying on of hands, divine light moves through the giver and pervades the receiver.

The Mahikari World Shrine, in Takayama, Japan, is the headquarters of the Sukyo Mahikari religious movement.

AGONSHU

Japan | 1978 | More than 300,000

In the 1950s Kiriyama Seiyu had a religious revelation: he believed that he had been saved by the *bodhisattva* Kannon (*see p.314*). Kiriyama became an ascetic for a number of years and then had a further revelation: that he had become free from *karma*—the spiritual credit system—and should now teach others how to follow the same spiritual route. He saw himself as creating a new kind of Buddhism, although actually his faith blends Buddhist ideas with Japanese notions such as ancestor-worship and spiritual healing. Kiriyama taught that good works, and specific practices such as meditation, can eliminate harmful *karma* and that they can also address the problem of the wider world's spiritual malaise. Followers of Agonshu believe that worldwide discord has occurred because people have been allowed to die before eliminating their negative *karma* or without the correct funerary rites. These acts have created an accumulated world spiritual crisis that we can remedy by diligently following Agonshu.

Kannon is a female Buddha worshipped by members of the Agonshu faith.

TENRIKYO

Japan   1838; 1970   1 million

In 1838, Nakayama Miki, a farmer's wife, reported that she was possessed by the spirit Tenri-o-no-Mikoto ("Lord of Heavenly Reason") and she began to develop healing powers. She soon had a number of followers, and the religion that developed around her beliefs became known as Tenrikyo, which breaks down as *ten* ("heavens"), *ri* ("truth" or "reason"), and *kyo* ("teach").

Tenrikyo's headquarters in Tenri City, Japan. The faith has centers in many countries outside Japan, including the US, Britain, and Australia.

THE DEVELOPMENT OF TENRIKYO
To begin with, the Tenrikyo belief system involved many spirits, but as the religion developed it concentrated on one god, most often referred to as Oyagami ("God the Parent").

Nakayama Miki composed two sacred books, the Mikagurauta, a core text chanted at every Tenrikyo service, and the Ofudesaki. These books deal with the basic ideas of Tenrikyo, including living a good life.

HOKORI
According to Tenrikyo, selfish or sinful acts cause a substance called *hokori*, or spiritual dust, to settle on a person's

mind and soul. The vices of greed, meanness, partiality, hatred, animosity, covetousness, and anger all cause different kinds of *hokori*. This dust obstructs happiness, but people are able to prevent the dust settling by trying to live well and in harmony with others and nature; by spending time in reflection on thoughts and actions; and by receiving divine grace.

When they are free from *hokori*, people everywhere will achieve their goal of leading a joyous life and the world will be transformed.

The Tenrikyo faith places special emphasis on the sacred nature of motherhood. The religion's founder, Nakayama Miki, is known as "Honored Mother."

CAO DAI

Vietnam 1929 8 million

From its small beginnings in Vietnam, Cao Dai aims to unify all the world's religions—not by amalgamating them into a single, "gray" whole, but by recognizing their various qualities and promoting tolerance. The Cao Dai faith views all people as brothers and sisters who derive from a common divine source and who, if we can recognize the fact, can progress toward a unified divine destiny of inner and outer peace. Cao Dai initially found many followers in Vietnam, but in 1975 Vietnam was taken over by the communists, who suppressed Cao Dai there, although encouraging its spread around the world.

A large congregation attends a religious service that draws on many religious traditions at a Cao Dai temple in Vietnam.

THE SPIRIT OF CAO DAI

Cao Dai's founder, Ngo Van Chieu, worked as an official for Vietnam's French government. Interested in spiritualism, he attended seances and at one of these said that he had received messages from a spirit called Cao Dai, a name that translates as "High Tower" and that Daoists (see pp.250–261) use for the Supreme Deity. In his messages to Ngo Van Chieu, Cao Dai outlined various teachings, including vegetarianism and the need for a universal outlook in religion. At the time there was something of a religious vacuum in French-ruled Vietnam—Buddhism was in decline, and many people were looking for new spiritual leadership. As a result, Cao Dai's teachings soon found many followers around the world and a new faith was born.

From the beginning, the Cao Dai faith absorbed ideas from many different religions. It drew on Confucian ideas about society, Daoism for its name and some of its rites, and Buddhism and the Indian religions for its ideas about rebirth. It also drew on the experiences that Ngo Van Chieu and his friends had had with spiritualism (see p.289). Further seances revealed more messages from Cao Dai himself.

Like many other new religious movements, such as Theosophy, Omoto (see p.276), and the Baha'i Faith (see p.280), Cao Dai seeks to unify Eastern and Western religions.

RELIGIOUS SYNTHESIS

Two basic principles unify the apparent diversity of the ideas that have inspired the Cao Dai faith. The first is that all religions have the same origin, in other words that God, Allah, the Dao, and so on, are all the same. The second is that all people should follow a morality based on love and justice in order to unite with God. This focus on the essential unity of creation is summarized in an important Cao Dai aphorism: "The sky, the earth, and ten thousand things are of one same constitution." The faith's teachings are recorded in its sacred text, the Thanh Ngon Hiep Tuyen.

In 1975, with communist rule in Vietnam, Cao Dai's headquarters moved to Canada, where there are now many believers. There are also followers in exiled Vietnamese communities in other countries around the world.

BAHA'I FAITH

Persia (modern Iran) 1844 5–7 million

The teachings of the Baha'i Faith began in 1844 with the mission of a merchant's son called Siyyid 'Ali-Muhammad, who became known as the Bab ("Gate"). The Bab looked forward to the coming of a great prophet, who would be called Baha'u'llah ("The Glory of God") and who would show humanity how to live in peace. In 1853 Mirza Husayn-'Ali, a Persian nobleman and a follower of the Bab, had a religious revelation that he was "He Who God Shall Make Manifest." After this he was accepted as Baha'u'llah. He produced a vast body of writings that cover everything from spirituality to government, and these texts, known as Tablets, form the Baha'i Faith's main scriptures.

The Baha'i Faith has three main principles. First, there is one God, and all faiths worship the same God, whatever they call him. Second, there is one religion. All the world's faiths draw on the same basic spiritual truths, and all have been founded by one of the line of "Manifestations of God," who

Baha'i places of worship, such as the Lotus of Bahapur temple in Delhi, India, have nine sides and a central dome to signify world unity.

include Moses, Jesus, Muhammad, the Buddha, and others—and Baha'u'llah. Third, there is one humanity. We are all created by God and are members of one worldwide family, and the Baha'i Faith aims to unite this family, overcome the differences that divide us, and so bring salvation both for individuals and for the world.

Today, the Baha'i headquarters are at the Baha'i World Center near Haifa, Israel, although the faith has followers in many countries.

The gold-domed shrine of the Bab lies among beautiful gardens in Haifa, Israel. The Bab was laid to rest here after his death in 1950.

THE CHURCH UNIVERSAL AND TRIUMPHANT

US   1958 (as Summit Lighthouse); 1974 (as CUT)   30,000

The Church Universal and Triumphant (CUT) is a small, American-based movement rooted in some of the ideas of the late-19th-century Theosophy movement. Theosophy recognized a series of divinely inspired beings, including the Buddha, Jesus, and the leaders of Theosophy, as spiritual Masters, leading the world toward a new era of truth. In the CUT, as in other new religious movements, this new era is called the Age of Aquarius.

In the 1950s a man named Mark Prophet claimed to be a messenger of the ascended spiritual Masters and he set up a religious group known as Summit Lighthouse. In 1974, following Prophet's death, his widow Elizabeth reorganized the group as the CUT. Elizabeth Prophet receives messages, or "dictations," from the ascended Masters, just as her husband once did.

The church believes that spiritual light manifests itself as seven rays. The seventh ray—a violet flame—descends into the believer's heart to engender mercy, forgiveness, justice, freedom, and transmutation. Members of the CUT study the sayings of the Masters as recorded by the Prophets before becoming full communicants of the church. Rituals include mantras and prayers for wisdom and the transmutation of *karma*.

TRANSCENDENTAL MEDITATION

India   1957   3 million

Indian scientist and teacher Maharishi Mahesh Yogi developed the techniques of Transcendental Meditation (TM) in the 1950s as a modern form of the teachings of the ancient Yoga Sutra. In the 1960s the movement attracted the interest of the Beatles and other celebrities, which boosted its popularity. Those who teach TM regard it not as a religion but as a meditation practice that enables a person to settle the mind to a point of total mental stillness (and for some, to states of enlightenment or bliss).

The body becomes still, too, but the meditator does not go to sleep. Those who want to learn how to practice TM attend a short series of lectures and personal sessions with a teacher. Once they have learned the technique, they meditate for about 20 minutes a day.

Maharishi Mahesh Yogi, the founder of Transcendental Meditation, who died in 2008.

Voodoo believers bathe in muddy waters as part of rituals conducted at a Voodoo temple in Souvenance, Haiti, on Good Friday. This temple is the only Haitian center for the Dahomey branch of Voodoo belief, which traces its roots back to West African tribal religion.

RASTAFARIANISM

Jamaica   1930   700,000

Rastafarianism began as a belief system specific to the oppressed black people of the Caribbean and the US. Now a global movement, it is popular for both its teachings and its cultural manifestations, such as reggae music. Rastafarians believe in God, known as Jah, and that the Ethiopian emperor Haile Selassie I (1892–1975) was an incarnation of God.

MARCUS GARVEY

Jamaican Marcus Garvey (1887–1940) devoted his life to black emancipation. In 1914, he founded the Universal Negro Improvement Association and he proposed that black people from the New World should settle in Liberia and build a new black state. He had many supporters, but the Liberian government turned down his plans. His fortunes then fell into decline—but his vision continues to inspire.

THE AFRICAN WAY

Rejecting modern civilization, which it calls "Babylon," Rastafarianism embraces a vision of an ideal African society, known as "Zion." The movement originally proved popular among supporters of the "back to Africa" movement, which aimed to resettle black people in the continent of their ancestors. It sees the African way of life as more true to nature than modern civilization. Adherents' distinctive dreadlocked hair symbolizes this belief in being true to nature. Rastafarians also point out that the first humans came from Africa and they link themselves with African symbols such as the pan-African colors of red, green, yellow, and black.

WORSHIP AND PRACTICE

Rastafarians view Haile Selassie I, whose titles include "Lion of Judah" and "King of Kings," as a messianic savior whose coming is predicted in the Christian Bible. Indeed, some members consider themselves to be Christians—although most hold Christianity at a distance. As a rule, Rastafarianism rejects the intellectualization of Biblical scholarship and instead sets much greater store by personal perceptions and the intuitions of the self. A personal relationship with Jah is vital, and believers also see the divine as something internal, as part of the individual self.

To come to correct judgments about life, Rastafarians meditate and take part in group religious discussions known as "groundings." The result of these practices is claimed to be knowledge of God rather than simply belief in him.

This Rastafarian man wears red, green, black, and yellow—colors that symbolize African unity.

VOODOO, SANTERÍA, AND CANDOMBLÉ

 Haiti, Cuba, Brazil   18th–19th centuries   65 million

With their roots in the New World, these three religions are derived mainly from African beliefs brought across the Atlantic by slaves and immigrants and then combined with Christianity. These religions use rituals such as drumming, singing, and dancing so that believers may communicate with deities and call upon them for help.

VOODOO

Also called Vodou (although both are terms used by outsiders), Voodoo is a religion of Haiti that combines African religion with elements of Roman Catholicism. It is now also recognized as an indigenous religion in Benin. Followers believe in spirits called *loa*, who represent ancestors or African gods from Nigeria, Benin, and Zaire, and also a remote high God, called Bondye. Voodoo uses spirit possession to enable people to communicate with the *loa* and to enable the *loa* to take part in religious celebrations.

SANTERÍA AND CANDOMBLÉ

Santería is a Cuban religion that blends African Yoruba beliefs with Spanish Catholicism and, in particular, identifies the Catholic saints with Yoruba deities. For example, the Catholic St. Barbara becomes the Yoruba thunder god Chango. Cuban Santeríans recognize 16 of these deities, whereas American followers acknowledge only seven.

Candomblé began in Brazil and represents another importation of Yoruba deities into a country where foreign rulers had imposed Catholicism. Deities offer advice and support to their worshippers through mediums and in exchange for offerings.

Haitian women dance in the streets of Souvenance in Haiti during the annual Voodoo ceremony for Easter—a crossover from Christian tradition.

NEW AGE SPIRITUALITIES

The phrase "New Age" is a term used to describe a number of belief systems and practices that came to prominence in the second half of the 20th century. Originating in the Western world but drawing heavily on Indian and other religions, New Age ideas have proved to be influential in a whole range of aspects of human life—from personal spirituality to global ecology.

KEY BELIEFS

A variety of beliefs and activities, from astrology to yoga, have been labeled "New Age" to indicate that the Earth is at the dawning of a new era of spiritual awareness, and that certain ideas have been reinterpreted from ancient belief systems. Although the various New Age movements may seem to have little in common, many share the idea that spiritual insight comes from several sources—not only gurus or spiritual masters, but also from the deceased or extra-terrestrial beings, or even from within. Another common belief is in our ability to heal ourselves— many "New Agers" look to therapies, such as reiki and shiatsu, for physical and mental well-being. Finally, New Age religions are not generally concerned with sin —problems are seen as examples of negativity to overcome. Many New

Astrological divination, predicting the future by observing celestial phenomena, is a New Age practice.

The Goetheanum, at Dornach in Switzerland, is the home of Rudolf Steiner's school of spirituality, which he established in the 1920s.

Age beliefs focus closely on the individual, but New Age philosophy looks beyond this, with the belief that if enough people change for the better, society and the entire planet will change, too.

LEVELS OF BELIEF
The most literal New Agers believe that we are at the dawn of a new era that will bring a major change in the

world's spirituality. However, many more focus their beliefs on personal action. These New Age followers are likely to be "spiritual seekers," looking for a solution to their own crisis of belief. They might do this by taking up meditation or yoga, studying shamanism, or by following a new religious movement.

Still other people see the New Age as offering answers to society's problems. These followers may be involved in the ecology movement, pacifist and philanthropic groups, or "alternative" medicine, but are still often aware of the spiritual benefits of what they pursue.

GEORGE GURDJIEFF

George Ivanovich Gurdjieff was born around 1866 and grew up in Kars, on the border of Russia and Turkey. Believing that humans had lost the ability to function in a harmonious way, he practiced healing in St. Petersburg until the Russian Revolution, when he fled to France. At Fontainebleau, he set up the Institute for the Harmonious Development of Man, and his teachings, which helped people to "know themselves" and to regain their inner harmony, are influential on many in New Age movements.

Stonehenge, in Wiltshire, England, is an ancient center for pagan worshippers, from the Druids to followers of modern New Age beliefs.

PSYCHEDELIC SPIRITUALITY

Britain and North America   1930s and 1950s   Not known

The term "psychedelic," which means "mind- or soul-manifesting" was coined to describe the perceived effects of certain mind-altering drugs. Some people believe that the ways in which drugs alter our sense-perceptions can open up new levels of insight, as with certain mystical religious experiences.

The author Aldous Huxley was an early commentator on the effects of psychedelic drugs.

The use of drugs to trigger religious experience has a long history. There is evidence for it in prehistoric societies, and Hindu writings praise the hallucinogenic plant *soma*. But the modern use of psychedelic substances dates from the 1930s, with the development of LSD, and the 1950s, when British writer Aldous Huxley wrote about his mystical experiences with the drug mescaline. Huxley saw mescaline as a way to open up a new, more vivid perception of the world. When he wrote about this in *The Doors of Perception* (1954), a number of

people took up his ideas. In the 1960s many artists and musicians devoted themselves to producing work that would trigger or enhance psychedelic experiences.

POTENTIAL FOR HARM
Adherents of Psychedelic Spirituality justified the use of drugs by relating them to the spiritual practices of primal cultures, and claimed that the use of natural hallucinogens such as "magic" mushrooms inspires a mysticism that is close to the Earth. However, it soon became clear that psychedelic drugs could be harmful, both physically and mentally, and mind-altering drugs are now illegal in many countries. And, although users claim spiritual insights, others criticize their chemically induced "instant" mysticism, believing that true spirituality comes only after long, devoted practice.

"Magic" mushrooms, when eaten, produce the powerful psychotropic effects that inspired leading figures in psychedelic spirituality.

SPIRITUALISM

📍 Hydesville, New York 📅 1848 👥 11 million

Common in many times and cultures, "spiritualism" centers on the idea that practitioners can contact the spirits of the dead. It began specifically as a new religious movement with the work of the Swedish philosopher Emanuel Swedenborg (1688–1772), who claimed to have talked to spirits and angels and who wrote at length about the nature and structure of the spirit world. The work of German physician and scientist Franz Anton Mesmer (1734–1815) was also influential. Mesmer developed techniques of hypnotism said to enable people to fall into trance states and contact spirit beings.

Spiritualists believe that the Ouija board can reveal messages from the spirit world during a seance.

A DEVELOPING MOVEMENT

Spiritualism became widespread in the mid-19th century, after two sisters, Kate and Margaret Fox, captured the attention of thousands when they said that they had had a conversation with a spirit in Hydesville, New York, in 1848. In the following decades, Spiritualist churches were founded and many people (particularly upper- and middle-class women in the US and Europe) took up Spiritualism at home, encouraging spirits to rap tables, speak through mediums, or spell out messages on a Ouija board (a device invented in 1869). The creation of bodies such as the Spiritualist Association of Great Britain, in 1872, and the National Spiritualist Association of the US, in 1893 (now the National Spiritualist Association of Churches), formalized the movement, which survives with many followers today.

SPIRITUALIST BELIEFS

Most Spiritualist churches list a number of key tenets of belief: the fatherhood of God; the brotherhood of humanity; communication with spirits and angels; reward or punishment after death for the life lived on Earth; personal responsibility; and some kind of path of progression. Followers especially value insights that come from the spirits, which they believe are metaphysically closer to God. Believers therefore take seriously the moral and ethical advice of the spirits, and many view the spirits as guides to both earthly and heavenly matters. Some Spiritualists see themselves as following in the Christian tradition, presenting their communication with spirits as a "third revelation" after those of the Old and New Testaments. Mainstream Christians reject this interpretation.

SPIRITUALIST PRACTICES

For many Spiritualists, though, the regular practice of Spiritualism and developing the skills of the medium are more important than concepts. Spiritualist churches hold regular services, which generally include some kind of mediumistic or clairvoyant element. They may also feature the practice of spiritual healing.

WHO'S WHO IN RELIGION

T HE WORLD'S religions are densely populated. The gods of the polytheistic faiths and the prophets and teachers of monotheistic religion are diverse, fascinating, and sometimes baffling—especially to people who come to them from other cultures or belief systems. This chapter describes key figures in the monotheistic, Indian, and Eastern religions.

The earliest religions were typically polytheistic—meaning they venerated many gods. From Ancient Greece to India, from Africa to Japan, polytheistic religions tried to explain the enigmatic forces of the cosmos. Every force—the sun and the stars, the rain and the thunder, mountains, hills, trees, and rivers—had its own deity. These gods helped to account for phenomena, such as the weather or the phases of the moon, that people did not understand.

Some deities became especially prominent—sometimes because they controlled particularly powerful forces, such as the sun or the sea; sometimes because they took part in the creation of the cosmos; sometimes for other reasons to do with their place in the celestial hierarchy. From these collections of deities grew the huge and sophisticated pantheons, or collections of gods, that still feature in several of the world's most influential religions. Hinduism, Shinto, and the religions of China all have many gods—their numbers are often in thousands. This chapter outlines the biographies and roles of a small selection of these—generally the ones that are most prominent in their pantheons, and most worshipped by people today. Their nature varies with the culture that gave birth to them. Chinese popular religion includes many deities who began life as humans and attained immortality because of their remarkable character. Shinto deities are seen as *kami*: spirits inherent in natural phenomena. The gods of Hinduism are the most diverse of all, but some can come to Earth in human form. The pages that follow are a first step to understanding this huge variety and these differences.

A 19th-century illustration of various Chinese gods, who appear amid the clouds of heaven.

MONOTHEISTIC RELIGIONS

The outlook of the monotheistic religions is very different. In Judaism, Christianity, and Islam, the One God is an infinite and absolute being, a concept so vast that it cannot be expressed in ordinary language at all. So the One God of monotheistic religion does not make an appearance in this Who's Who, except in the person of Jesus Christ, whom Christians see as the Son of God made human and who, to Muslims, is a prophet. The monotheistic faiths also recognize many prophets and teachers, whose work helps us to understand God and who map out moral instructions for the faithful. This chapter outlines the lives and teachings of the prophets of Judaism and Islam, and the prophets and great teachers of Christianity—the people whose lives were devoted to mediating between the infinite world of God and the finite world of human beings. For the faithful, their work is a window into the absolute and their lives show how to explain and stand up for one's beliefs, often in conditions that are unfavorable or hostile. Today, as in the past, they are figures who both instruct and inspire.

Hindu deities on the *gopuram* (tower) at the Sri Meenakshi temple in Madurai, India. The Hindu pantheon is a diverse one.

THE MONOTHEISTIC RELIGIONS

The three great monotheistic religions, Judaism, Christianity, and Islam, share many of the same key figures—although sometimes their roles vary from one faith to another. For example, Islam recognizes many Biblical characters, including Jesus, as prophets.

Adam

✦ Judaism, Christianity, Islam   📖 First man, prophet (in Islam)

The monotheistic faiths interpret the life of Adam in different ways, but they all see the eating of the Fruit of the Tree of Knowledge as its most important event. Adam eats the fruit after being encouraged to do so by his wife, Eve, and by the serpent, usually interpreted as Satan.

In Judaism and Christianity, Adam is the first man, created by God in his own image. God makes him from the dust of the Earth and then breathes life into him, creating humankind.

At first, Adam lives a life of ease with Eve in the Garden of Eden. When he and Eve eat the Fruit of the Tree of Knowledge, which God has forbidden them to do, they are expelled from the garden and have to work for their living. They leave behind their life of idyllic happiness and, feeling shame for their nakedness, live a hard and punishing life.

For Christians, the Fall is a disaster: it taints humankind, which needs to be redeemed through Jesus Christ (who is seen as a "second Adam").

In Judaism, although Adam is said to have lost his radiance after eating the fruit, this event is not understood as a tragedy; it brings about new knowledge and new opportunities for Adam and the rest of humanity.

In Islam, Adam is also the first man. God makes a covenant (agreement) with him, and he becomes the first prophet. The eating of the fruit is not seen as a "fall." Adam repents and Allah is merciful toward him. He then travels to Mecca to build the first *ka'aba* (*see pp. 142–143*), according to the Islamic account.

Adam and Eve have been the subjects of thousands of works of art over the centuries, their life in Eden an enduring symbol of lost innocence.

Noah

✛ Judaism, Christianity, Islam   📖 Patriarch, prophet (Islam)

In all three monotheistic religions, Noah is famous as the man who heeded God's warnings of the Great Flood, built the ark, and saved humanity from disaster.

The Book of Genesis describes how Noah saves humanity and the animals from the flood. After the waters subside, God blesses Noah and makes a covenant with him. This represents a new beginning for humanity.

The story is popular in all three monotheistic religions. Judaism and Islam, in particular, have developed the account in Genesis. Later Jewish sources emphasize Noah's righteousness. In Islam, Noah's ark carries 40 men and 40 women. When the flood subsides, they found a city called Thamanin ("The Eighty"). Their endeavor represents a new awareness of the Unity of God.

Noah is best known as the builder of the ark, but he is also seen as the inventor or "father" of wine in the Christian tradition.

Abraham

✛ Judaism, Christianity, Islam   📖 Patriarch, prophet (Islam)

For Jews and Christians, Abraham is the prime early example of a person of faith. In Islam, he is known as Ibrahim and is the first person to submit to Allah—in other words, the first Muslim.

The Bible's Book of Genesis recalls how the prophet Abraham left his home city of Ur in Mesopotamia (modern Iraq) to travel to Canaan where, God promised him, he would become the father of a great nation. Abraham had no children at this stage, and his wife, Sarah, seemed to be too old to conceive. But Abraham kept faith, and the couple had a son, Isaac. On this and other occasions, Abraham's trust in God is seen by both Jews and Christians as a prime example of the importance of faith. He is the prototype Jewish and Christian prophet.

Abraham is also an important figure in Islam. The Qur'an tells how he restored the worship of the one God at Mecca. His obedience to God, his refusal to worship idols, and the fact that he is also an ancestor of Muhammad, make him the archetypal Muslim, and Islam is sometimes referred to as the religion of Ibrahim.

Ishmael

✦ Judaism, Christianity, Islam
📖 Prophet

Ishmael was the son of Abraham and his servant, Hagar. After Abraham's wife, Sarah, gave birth to Isaac, Ishmael and Hagar were driven away from Abraham's camp into the desert. When they ran out of water, Hagar ran between two hills in panic. These hills are said to be Safa and Marwah near Mecca. Running between these hills became part of the ritual of the Hajj (*see p.139*), so Ishmael and Hagar inspired a rite of the pilgrimage.

Ishmael is also said to have built the Ka'aba in Mecca with his father.

Lot

✦ Judaism, Christianity, Islam (as Lut)
📖 Prophet

Lot was the nephew of Abraham. He settled near Sodom, one of the cities of the plain that God later destroyed because of their inhabitants' immoral behavior. Lot was allowed to escape with his family, provided that they did not look back at the cities. Lot's wife looked back and was turned into a pillar of salt, but Lot and the rest of his household were saved.

Christian and Islamic traditions praise Lot as a moral man and in Islam he has prophet status.

Lot and his daughters fled from the destruction of the cities of the plain to a refuge in the mountains.

Jacob

✦ Judaism, Christianity, Islam (as Ya'qub)   📖 Patriarch

Jacob is a pivotal figure in the early history of the Jews: he is the third patriarch, and an ancestor of the tribes of Israel. A complex character, Jacob is also known as a trickster, an ancestor, and, curiously, a wrestler.

Jacob was the grandson of Abraham and the son of Isaac and Rebekah. His elder brother was Esau. It was foretold that both brothers would be the fathers of great nations, but that the elder brother would serve the younger.

The latter part of the prophecy was fulfilled when Jacob tricked his brother Esau out of his inheritance, and deceived his father into giving him the blessing rightly accorded the firstborn of the family. Jacob was himself tricked by his uncle Laban after seeking refuge in his household. Laban made him work for 14 years before he was allowed to marry Rachael, the woman he desired.

The other part of the prophecy bore fruit because Jacob was the ancestor of the people of Israel. A key story in the Book of Genesis describes the mystical roots of this ancestry, when Jacob had a mysterious encounter with an angel, or perhaps with God himself, whom he met while journeying to the land of Canaan. Jacob wrestled with this figure; after the struggle he was given the new name of Israel and made peace with Esau once more. With his two wives and two concubines, Jacob had 12 sons who became the ancestors of the 12 tribes of Israel. Esau became the ancestor of the Edomites.

Moses

✛ Judaism, Christianity, Islam (as Musa)   📖 Prophet

The great Jewish leader Moses is famous for leading his people to the "promised land" of Canaan and for receiving the tablets of the law from God. In Islam, he is a prophet.

Moses was born in Egypt, and when an order went out to kill male Jewish babies, his parents hid him among reeds on the banks of the Nile River. Discovered there by the Egyptian king's daughter, he was taken into her care and grew up in the royal palace. When he grew up, he had a vision of God in a burning bush and was ordered to lead his people out of Egypt—although he eventually died before his people reached the promised land. At Mount Sinai, God revealed the Torah (*see pp.68–69*) to Moses, and so for the Jews, Moses is a combination of leader, prophet, lawgiver, and founder of Torah-based religion.

In Christianity he is seen as a precursor of Jesus (*see p.301*). In Islam he is, with Abraham (*see p.295*), one of the two most important prophets of monotheism before Muhammad (*see p.305*) himself.

Some translations of the name Moses interpret it as meaning "Son of the Water" in reference to his being rescued from the Nile.

Joshua

✛ Judaism, Christianity, Islam (as Yusha')
📖 Prophet, leader

Just before he died, Moses chose Joshua to replace him as leader of the Jews. Joshua led his people in the conquest of Canaan, apportioning land to his followers, the representatives of the 12 tribes of Israel. These and the other events of his life are narrated in the book of Joshua, which deals with the occupation of the promised land by the Jews, with descriptions of the land and its division, and with Joshua's speeches.

As well as being an inspired leader, Joshua was also said to be very wise, acquiring his wisdom when Moses laid his hands upon him.

Samuel

✛ Judaism, Christianity
📖 Prophet, judge

Samuel's mother, Hannah, dedicated him to God when he was born and he became a notable Jewish prophet, judge, and military leader. The Hebrew Bible portrays him as a great and highly moral leader who could criticize both kings and others when they broke the Jews' Covenant with God. Unable to defeat the Jews' enemies, the Philistines, he strengthened Israel by supporting the idea of a monarchy and anointing the first king, Saul. When Saul proved to be a poor king, Samuel promoted his successor, David. His achievements are set out in the two Books of Samuel.

David

✦ Judaism, Christianity, Islam (as Dawud)
📖 King, prophet

As a young man, David became a hero by killing the Philistine giant, Goliath. Later he became king, uniting the kingdoms of Israel and Judah and defeating many enemies. He is also said to have composed many of the Psalms. As an ideal and godly king, he holds a unique position in Jewish thought and national identity.

In Islam, he is called Dawud and is a prophet. His musicality and piety are praised and his wisdom is said to be God-given.

David's victory over his formidable adversary, Goliath, set him on the path to the throne of Israel.

Nathan

✦ Judaism, Christianity
📖 Prophet

Nathan was a prophet at the court of King David. He is said to have written a "Book of Nathan the prophet," which included accounts of the reigns of David and Solomon—this text is mentioned in the Book of Chronicles. Like the Biblical prophets who came after him, Nathan was able both to predict future events and to set moral standards. Although he criticized David for his affair with Bathsheba, he supported Solomon, the son of David and Bathsheba, helping him to become king and safeguarding the line of David.

Solomon

✦ Judaism, Christianity
📖 King, prophet

The son of David and Bathsheba, Solomon was one of the most prestigious of all the Jewish kings. He ruled a large kingdom, stretching from the Euphrates river to the border with Egypt; he promoted international trade, engaged in diplomacy, and sponsored big building projects, including a large palace for himself and, most notably, the Temple in Jerusalem. Famous for his wisdom, he was said to be the author of the Biblical Proverbs and the Song of Solomon.

King Solomon and the Queen of Sheba confer in a medieval depiction of their historic meeting.

Elijah

✦ Judaism, Christianity
📖 Prophet

Elijah was a prophet at the time of the Jewish king Ahab. The main events of his life, including his killing of the prophets of the god Baal, are narrated in the First Book of Kings.

The Book of Malachi predicts that on the Day of Judgment, Elijah will return. This prediction affords Elijah the status of a symbol of the Messiah, which gives him a special importance in Jewish belief.

This notion of Elijah as someone who will return at the time of judgment is repeated in the Gospels and so makes the prophet a key figure in Christian ideas of the Last Judgment.

Isaiah

✦ Judaism (as Sha'va), Christianity
📖 Prophet

Isaiah was a major Jewish prophet and author of the book that bears his name. He lived during the reigns of four kings of Judah (Uzziah, Jotham, Ahaz, and Hezekiah), took part in the political life of his country, and may have died a martyr. He taught the supremacy, holiness, and moral standards of God. His book includes prophecies against Israel's enemies, criticisms of the moral lapses of his people, accounts of the Jewish exile in Babylon, and hopes for the future of a "reborn" Jerusalem.

Elisha

✦ Judaism, Christianity
📖 Prophet

Chosen as the successor of Elijah, Elisha was a prophet during the reigns of Kings Jehoram, Jehu, Jehoahaz, and Joash. Although he was the prophetic heir of Elijah, he was a very different character. Whereas Elijah was a solitary figure, Elisha led guilds or companies of prophets. He became involved with the rulers of the day, advising them, taking part in their wars, and encouraging a rebellion. He also performed miracles, and Christians view him as an important forerunner of Jesus.

Jeremiah

✦ Judaism, Christianity
📖 Prophet

One of the major prophets of the Judeo-Christian tradition, Jeremiah lived at the time when the Jews were conquered by the Babylonians. Many Jews went into exile in Babylon, but Jeremiah was taken to Egypt. According to Christian tradition, he died a martyr's death by stoning. The Book of Jeremiah, as well as recounting the main events of the prophet's lifetime, contains his prophecies, sermons, and sayings. It also contains a series of passages known as Jeremiah's Confessions—expressions of sorrow at human suffering.

The theme of sorrow is continued in the Bible's next book, Lamentations, which is sometimes attributed to Jeremiah. This consists of a series of poems expressing grief and anger at the sacking of Jerusalem. These writings bring the reader closer to Jeremiah than to any other Biblical prophet, for the grief he expresses is very personal.

Ezekiel

✦ Judaism, Christianity
📖 Prophet

Ezekiel was a learned man and priest who lived at about the same time as Jeremiah; he became a prophet when he was in exile in Babylon. His prophecies are recorded in the Book of Ezekiel. His message was one of reverence at God's holiness, with thoughts about how the Temple would be rebuilt in the future; he stressed the moral responsibility of each person.

Ezekiel's prophecies included a revelation that the Jewish people would eventually have their own land, which they would inhabit after a period of exile.

John the Baptist

✦ Judaism, Christianity, Islam (as Yahya)   📖 Teacher, prophet

A contemporary of Jesus, John the Baptist preached in the Jordan Valley. He railed against immoral behavior, and encouraged people to repent their sins or risk the anger of God, paving the way for Jesus's mission.

John the Baptist was outspoken in his condemnation of sinners, including King Herod Antipas, who ruled the area around Galilee as a client king of the Romans. Herod incurred John's wrath for marrying Herodias, the wife of his brother, Philip. Mark's Gospel relates that Herod eventually had John beheaded. Josephus, a 1st-century Jewish historian, records that John was executed to prevent a potential uprising from breaking out.

John was well known as a preacher who baptized his followers in the river, and Jesus was one of those to be baptized. In fact, early Christians saw John as a precursor of Jesus—a kind of reincarnation of the Old Testament prophet Elijah (*see p.298*), who, it was said, would return to Earth to herald the coming of the Messiah.

In Islam, John is a prophet who was given wisdom by God when a child, and who was sent to confirm God's words.

Mary

✦ Judaism, Christianity, Islam   📖 Mother of Jesus

The Gospels tell how an angel visited Mary and told her that she would have a child through the intervention of the Holy Spirit. As the mother of Jesus, Mary therefore became the most revered of all the Christian saints. She has even inspired a special branch of theology, called Mariology.

The Gospels of Matthew and Luke say that Mary conceived Jesus while a virgin. After Jesus's birth she appears relatively little in the narrative of Jesus's life and mission until the end, when she is described near the cross and seen with Jesus's disciples after the Resurrection.

As Christian thought developed in the centuries after Jesus's life on Earth, Mary became more revered. The early Christians came to place a special value on celibacy, making Mary's virginity especially an object of devotion. The stress on Jesus's divinity made Mary still more special. Eventually, the doctrine of the Immaculate Conception developed, meaning that Mary was free from the taint of original sin from her birth, and she became revered by both the Orthodox and Catholic churches.

In Islam, she is described as free from sin and as one of the four best women in Paradise.

The Nativity is the celebrated story of Jesus's birth at Bethlehem in the humble setting of a cattle barn beside an inn.

Jesus

✦ Judaism, Christianity, Islam 📖 Teacher, Son of God, prophet

The four Gospels provide the only substantial early accounts of Jesus's life. The Gospels describe his birth to Mary in Bethlehem, his life and mission in the Galilee area, and his crucifixion and subsequent resurrection.

The Gospels tell how Jesus was born to Mary and Joseph, who lived in Nazareth in Galilee. Matthew and Luke say that he was conceived by Mary when she was still a virgin, through the intervention of the Holy Spirit. Very little is known about his early life, although Luke relates how he spoke learnedly with the Temple scholars when his family visited Jerusalem.

THE MISSION OF JESUS

At around the age of 30, Jesus started to preach, beginning as an associate of John the Baptist, who baptized him in the Jordan River. He preached and taught in the Galilee area, and central to his message was the kingdom of God, which he sometimes described as something that would come soon, at other times as something that already existed. He also healed the sick and was able to cause miracles, which he saw as demonstrating the power of God rather than his own power. After a few years, Jesus was arrested and tried in Jerusalem. His offense was preaching in such a way as to challenge the Temple authorities in interpretation of Jewish law, something that offended Judea's Roman rulers, as the Jewish authorities cooperated with them. He was crucified, but Matthew, Luke, and John relate how he appeared to his followers after he had died.

THE IMPORTANCE OF JESUS

For the Jews, Jesus was a notable teacher and healer with strict moral standards. For Christians, he is the Son of God and the focus of their faith. They believe that following Jesus's teachings and believing in him as their savior will lead to their salvation. For Muslims, he is a major prophet: a man who caused miracles, healed the sick, and told people to worship Allah. He is not seen as the Son of God.

The image of Jesus Christ is recognized all over the world as a symbol of compassion and mercy, and it has inspired a rich tradition of Christian art.

The Apostles

✦ Christianity   📖 Teachers, leaders, followers of Jesus

Jesus attracted many followers, but he selected an inner circle of 12 men, who helped him with his mission and carried on after him. The 12 are conventionally known either as Jesus's disciples (from the Latin verb "to learn"), or his apostles (from the Greek word for a messenger).

We first meet the disciples in the Gospels, when Jesus calls them to follow him. The first four, Andrew, James, John, and Simon (known as Peter), were fishermen whom Jesus invited to become "fishers of people". Another, Matthew, was a tax collector who collaborated with the Romans. All were told to give up their jobs and follow Jesus, helping him with his work of teaching, preaching, and healing, relying on the goodwill of others for support.

By choosing 12 apostles, Jesus was probably making a reference to the 12 tribes of Israel, and suggesting that Israel would be renewed by the group. To begin with, their role was specifically to preach to Jewish people, although after Jesus's resurrection their work was widened and they and their successors preached to non-Jewish communities too.

In many ways the apostles are seen as ideal examples for Christians to follow. They give up their livelihoods and family ties for Jesus, accept the hardships that Jesus says will come with discipleship, and are generally loyal to him. But this loyalty is flawed. They often misunderstand Jesus's teaching, and in Matthew's Gospel Jesus sometimes accuses them of having "little faith." Even Peter, who was Jesus's favorite disciple and his most enthusiastic follower, eventually denies his Lord, as Jesus predicted he would. And the disciple Judas betrays Jesus to the Romans in return for money. The disciples are complex characters, rooted in a world of tough moral choices.

Christ is often depicted flanked by the apostles, as in this Byzantine mosaic. They were later responsible for spreading the Christian faith to Europe.

Mary Magdalen

✦ Christianity   📖 Follower of Jesus

Jesus had numerous followers, many of whom were women.
Some helped Jesus in his ministry and among his most
devoted followers was Mary Magdalen, who came
from a town on the western shore of Lake Galilee.

According to Luke's Gospel, Jesus healed
Mary of seven evil spirits. This story
of exorcism no doubt encouraged later
commentators to see her as a reformed
prostitute, and to identify her with other
women called Mary in the Gospels,
notably the Mary who anoints Jesus's
feet. There is no evidence for these
identifications. More important is her
appearance in all the Gospels before and
after the crucifixion. She stayed near the
cross and played a part in the events
after the Resurrection. John's Gospel
describes how she goes to Jesus's
tomb, finds it empty, and then
meets the risen Jesus.

Mary Magdalen is traditionally
associated with penitence in the
Roman Catholic tradition.

Paul

✦ Christianity   📖 Christian missionary

Paul was born into a Jewish family in Tarsus, Cilicia, and
originally had the old Hebrew name of Saul. He began as
a strong opponent of Christianity, but was converted and
became one of the greatest Christian missionaries.

On his way to Damascus in pursuit of
some Jewish Christians, Paul had a
mystical conversion experience and
became a Christian himself.

He embarked on an ardent career of
missionary work, making three journeys
during which he traveled to Asia Minor
(Turkey) and Greece, founding many
churches, before being martyred in
Rome. His life story is told in the Book
of Acts, but we know more about his
beliefs from the letters he wrote to the
various churches he founded. These
letters (or epistles) make up many of the
later books of the New Testament.
Paul's letters to the Christians in Rome,
Corinth, and Ephesus stress that
humanity is redeemed by the grace of
God through faith in Jesus Christ. He
tackles problematic issues such as free
will and predestination, providing
theological material that has been
discussed and expanded upon by
Christian thinkers ever since.

Hud

✦ Islam
📖 Prophet

Hud was a prophet who was sent by God to the people of 'Ad, an extinct tribe probably from southern Arabia. The people of 'Ad were an important people, one of the lost Arabian tribes. They are often mentioned in the Qur'an and probably lived in a place called Iram of the Pillars.

Hud's warning to the people of 'Ad is mentioned three times in the Qur'an. Like many of the early peoples of the Arabian Peninsula, the people of 'Ad followed a polytheistic religion. Hud told them that they should worship the One God, but they refused to listen to him, and would not give up the gods that their fathers had worshipped. When they rejected Hud's message, God destroyed them. Just as Hud warned the people of 'Ad, so his story warns later people that they should worship only the One God.

Salih

✦ Islam
📖 Prophet

The prophet Salih was sent to the people of Thamud, probably the Nabatean settlement of Mada'in Salih ("the cities of Salih") in northern Arabia. He delivered the message that they should worship the One God, bringing a she-camel (symbol of endurance and submission to God) as a sign. The people did not heed his message, ham-stringing the camel rather than giving her water and accepting her as a valuable gift from God. As result, God punished the people with an earthquake.

The Muslim prophet Salih produces a camel from a rock. This miracle was caused by God, but its meaning was ignored by the people.

Seth

✦ Islam
📖 Prophet

Seth was the son of Eve (*see p.294*). He was born after the disaster that befell Adam and Eve's other two sons when Cain murdered Abel. His arrival is described in the Book of Genesis, where it is said that Eve saw him as a replacement for Abel, given by God. Although a relatively minor figure in Judaism and Christianity, Seth is seen as a prophet in Islam and among Gnostic Christians. According to the Book of Genesis, he lived to be 912 years of age, and was the father of Enosh, another figure who lived to a patriarchal age.

Shu'ayb

✦ Islam
📖 Prophet

Sometimes identified with Jethro, father-in-law of Moses, Shu'ayb was a prophet who was sent to the people of Midyan. He told them of the One God and explained to them how to lead a more moral life. His message included instruction to give the full measure when trading and not to steal or rob. But the chiefs of the Midyan were full of pride and did not listen to Shu'ayb's message, threatening to banish the prophet and his fellow-believers. Again, God sent an earthquake to destroy those who rejected his message.

Muhammad

✦ Islam   📖 Prophet

The Prophet Muhammad, the Messenger of God, was born in the year 570CE. He was the person to whom God revealed the words of the Qur'an, which form the basis of the Islamic faith. He is the last and most important in the line of Islamic prophets and the founder of the first Muslim community.

Muhammad was a member of the Quraysh tribe and was brought up by his grandfather because his own father died before he was born. He always thought deeply about spiritual matters.

As a young man, he was employed by a widow, Khadijah, to lead camel caravans to Syria. When he was 25, he and Khadijah married. Muhammad was much influenced by the Hanifs, people who followed a monotheistic faith that they traced back to Abraham (*see p.295*); his trading journeys also brought him into contact with Jews and Christians. But his own people at Mecca worshipped many gods. Muhammad spent time alone meditating on the truth and began to receive revelations after the angel Jibra'il commanded him to "Recite." These revelations produced the words of the Qur'an. When Muhammad told his family that there could be only one God, Khadijah, 'Ali (Muhammad's cousin), and his servant Zayd became believers, as did Abu Bakr. But they were not made welcome in polytheistic Mecca. Invited to Yathrib (later called Medina), Muhammad moved there in 622CE. The Muslims faced opposition from Mecca and the two communities fought—Muhammad defeated Mecca and rid the city of idols in 630CE. One of the Prophet's later experiences was the Night Journey, during which he was taken to Jerusalem and up to Heaven by a creature called Al-Buraq. Muhammad died in 632CE.

Al-Buraq, the winged steed that carried the Prophet Muhammad from Mecca to Jerusalem on the night when he ascended to the seven heavens.

THE INDIAN RELIGIONS

Among Indian religions Hinduism stands out for having thousands of deities—a few, including those featured here, are prominent. In Indian Buddhism some varieties of the faith recognize many Buddhas and *bodhisattvas*, enlightened teachers and beings.

Siva

✦ Hinduism   📖 God of the Trimurti

Along with Visnu and Brahma, Siva is one of the three principal Hindu gods, collectively called the Trimurti. Known as "the destroyer", Siva is also a powerful creative force, because he recreates what he destroys. He is generally one of the most widely worshipped of all the Hindu gods.

Siva has no fewer than 1,008 epithets, or phrases, to describe him. These show him to have a paradoxical personality—not only does Siva both destroy and create, he is also quick to judge and yet merciful; he is erratic in his movements and yet an advocate of the stillness found in meditation.

There are many portrayals of Siva in Hindu temples and shrines, and the god can be depicted in many ways. He is usually shown as a male humanoid figure—perhaps a handsome young man or a beggar. His body may be covered with ash and his hair may be matted, to indicate his detachment from the cares of the world. Siva sometimes has a moon, which represents passing time, in his hair. His face is often shown with three eyes, which stand for the sun, the moon, and the fire of Siva. This fire is a symbol of his destructive force, but it also indicates his great wisdom.

Objects linked to Siva are the hourglass, the ax, and prayer beads. A common portrayal of this god is as the dancing Siva, the deity who brings the dance of life to an end, but who also sets it going again.

Siva, the second god of the Hindu Trimurti, is often depicted with his mount, the white bull Nandi. He is also sometimes shown with his consort Devi.

Vissu

✦ Hinduism   📖 God of the Trimurti

Visnu is the first god of the Hindu Trimurti (the other two are Siva and Brahma). He is generally known as "the preserver", and to his followers he is a powerful and responsive deity who is full of goodness and kindness.

Like Siva, Visnu encompasses many opposite qualities—he is both powerful and gentle, fearsome and kind. These complementary traits befit a deity whose main purpose is to keep the balance of life on an even keel. When evil becomes too dominant in the world, Visnu is said to come to Earth to set matters right. He does this by adopting one of ten forms, or avatars. Visnu's avatars are Matsya (the fish), Kurma (the tortoise), Varaha (the boar), Narasimha (the man-lion), Vamana (the dwarf); and five who take human form—Parashurama, Rama, Krisna, the Buddha, and Kalkin (who has yet to appear). Of these avatars, two in particular are widely worshipped in their own right: Rama, the noble hero of the Ramayana (see p.171), and Krisna, the god who narrates the teachings of the Bhagavad Gita (see p.170).

Several symbols are linked to Visnu, including the discus (representing the speed of his thought) and the mace (a symbol of his power).

Brahma

✦ Hinduism   📖 God of the Trimurti

Unlike his counterparts Siva and Visnu, Brahma, the other god of the Trimurti, is a shadowy figure. The creator of the universe, his exalted position makes him somewhat remote and means that he is not widely worshipped—there are only two temples dedicated to him in India.

Brahma exists only to create—he does not have Visnu's or Siva's destructive role—and to sustain the universe. His most striking features are his four heads. According to one account, he originally had five but, during a feud, Siva cut one of them off. The remaining four, which enable Brahma to see in every direction at once, represent his all-seeing nature. The four heads stand for the four Vedas and the four Hindu castes. Brahma's name resembles that of Brahman, the absolute or ultimate reality, and he is a kind of embodiment of this primal force.

Portrayals of Brahma sometimes feature objects such as a vessel with a spout, representing the Earth that he created. He also appears with a set of prayer beads, and a book, which represents the Vedas.

Brahma is the least worshipped of the Trimurti, but Hindus believe that he is the creator and essence of all things.

Rama

✦ Hinduism
📖 Avatar of Visnu

Rama is the seventh avatar of the god Visnu (see p.307). He is, with Krisna, one of the most popular and widely worshipped of Visnu's avatars. The hero of great epic poem the Ramayana (see p.171), Rama rescues his wife Sita from the clutches of Ravana, the demon king of Lanka, and by defeating Ravana rids the world of an evil force. The Ramayama describes Rama with strikingly human qualities. His emotions, his vulnerability, and the hardships he faces when he loses Sita all make him a character with whom devotees find it easy to identify. Similiarly, his noble actions, and his loyalty and fidelity to his wife, make him a figure to look up to.

Krisna

✦ Hinduism
📖 Avatar of Visnu

The eighth avatar of Visnu, Krisna attracts wide devotion among Hindus. His character is portrayed in various ways. In the Puranas (a collection of Hindu myths), he is a mischievous but winning child. In the poem, the Bhagavad Gita (see p.170), he is a powerful and wise teacher who instructs Arjuna in the *dharma* and the power and goodness of Brahman (see p.168). In many stories he is a slayer of demons and rids the world of evil; other accounts emphasize his love for his consort Radha, which is seen as an image of the love felt between God and the human soul. Krisna is therefore worshipped in many forms—as child, lover, and wise teacher.

Ganesh

✦ Hinduism
📖 God

A son of Siva (see p.306), Ganesh is recognizable because of his elephant's head. A story tells how Siva returned from a journey to find a young man guarding the room of his wife Parvati. When the youth would not let Siva in, the god cut off his head. When he realized he had decapitated his own son, Siva ordered that Ganesh be given, as a replacement, the head of the first creature to appear – which was an elephant. To compensate, Ganesh was appointed god of good fortune, who overcomes obstacles and helps people to deal with challenge and change.

Hanuman

✦ Hinduism
📖 God

The popular monkey god Hanuman is best known as a major character in the epic poem the Ramayana, in which

he helps Rama to rescue his abducted consort Sita. The monkey god's supernatural powers include shape-changing, and distance-defying leaps that come in handy when he helps Rama to overcome the evil Ravana. An extremely active figure, Hanuman is also a model of religious devotion, spending much of his time worshipping Rama and singing hymns in his praise.

Hanuman the monkey god
mustered an army of monkeys
to assist in the rescue of Sita.

Durga

✦ Hinduism
📖 Goddess

Durga is one of the most complex incarnations of Siva's consort Devi. Like her husband, Durga is an ambivalent character. She destroys numerous demons, which is reflected in statues that show her standing on her mount, a lion, with a fearsome expression on her face. But she is also a sustaining character with a reputation for growing things, such as healing herbs. Durga is widely worshipped, especially at the festival of Navaratri.

The Hindu goddess Durga sits astride a lion in the guise of destroyer goddess.

Laksmi

✦ Hinduism
📖 Goddess

Laksmi is the consort of the god Visnu and a goddess of creation and the Earth. When Visnu appears in one of his avatars, Laksmi is beside him, so she, too, has many forms, including Radha, the consort of Krisna, and Sita, the wife of Rama. She sets high store in correct conduct, telling the truth, and domestic harmony—which includes keeping the house clean and tidy. Laksmi is a popular goddess, with a wide following, especially among women, and at the annual Festival of Lights, Diwali (*see p.174–175*).

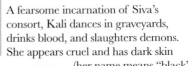

Parvati

✦ Hinduism
📖 Goddess

In her most benign form, Siva's wife is called Parvati. Her name means "daughter of the mountain" and she is said to have been born from the Himalayas. She is gentle and caring, and her role is mainly to accompany Siva and to act as a foil to him. So, when Siva is being and ascetic and cutting himself off from the world, Parvati brings him back to reality and provides the active strength for him to intervene in life. She is the symbol of the ideal wife, and is usually depicted beside her husband.

Kali

✦ Hinduism
📖 Goddess

A fearsome incarnation of Siva's consort, Kali dances in graveyards, drinks blood, and slaughters demons. She appears cruel and has dark skin (her name means "black"); her expression is terrifying, and her tongue drips blood. However, Kali is also a mother figure, and a goddess who can release people from the round of death and rebirth, teaching devotees that you have to accept death before you can achieve release from it.

Devotees sometimes make large-scale sacrifices to the terrifying and destructive deity, Kali.

Buddha

✦ Buddhism   📖 Buddha; enlightened teacher

Born Siddhartha Gautama, the Buddha was once a prince who lived a sheltered life. When finally he saw human suffering, he began to search for ways to overcome it. His teachings now inspire millions of followers.

Prince Siddhartha Gautama began his quest for the solution to suffering by leaving the luxury of his family's palace —as well as his beautiful wife—and following the life of an ascetic. However, he soon discovered that even this unworldly, contemplative existence does not liberate a person from suffering. Then, meditating under a tree, which became known as the *bodhi* tree, he finally discovered the truth about suffering and how to break free from it. With this discovery, he reached the exalted state of spiritual awareness known as enlightenment, or *nirvana*.

The Buddha spent the rest of his life (some 40 years in all) as a wandering teacher, attracting a growing band of followers to whom he explained the Four Noble Truths about suffering, and the Noble Eightfold Path that people should lead to break free from the cycle of death and rebirth. During the rainy season, the Buddha and his followers lived together as a community. This ritual is the origin of a devotional custom in Theravada Buddhism (*see p.206*) in which lay people join a monastery for at least part of their lives.

Buddhists do not see the Buddha as a god, but rather they view him as an enlightened teacher who has revealed vital truths about the suffering in the world and how they can triumph over it. However, because of the importance of his teachings and the exemplary nature of his character, Buddhists are devoted to him and honor him in rituals such as the "Triple Refuge" (*see p.197*). For all Buddhists, the Buddha is at the heart of their beliefs and his teaching guides their lives, although in some branches of Buddhism there may be other figures, such as the many *bodhisattvas*, whom Buddhists worship independently, too.

The Buddha's exploits are widely documented in both writings and artworks. His feats, such as riding on a flying horse, form part of Buddhist lore.

Amitabha

✦ Buddhism
📖 Buddha

The Buddha of Infinite Light, Amitabha is a key figure in Mahayana Buddhism, especially in Chinese communities and in Japan. In these places he is venerated as the sovereign of the Pure Land, a Buddhist Heaven said to lie in the West. Amitabha was said to have been a monk, called Dharmakara, who took a series of vows, and promised not to attain *nirvana* until he had kept all of them. He built up positive *karma* a result of these vows, which enabled him to create the paradise of the Pure Land. The 18th vow was that anyone who believed in him could reside with him in the Pure Land until they attained *nirvana*. Amitabha is often depicted on a lotus flower, with a halo of light.

Avalokiteshvara

✦ Buddhism
📖 Buddha

The most popular, accessible, and widely worshipped of all Buddhas, Avalokiteshvara is known above all for his compassion—he will always answer the call of those in need, and he helps devotees to recognize their own innate Buddha-nature. Confusingly, the sex of Avalokiteshvara varies from one culture to another—in China he becomes the goddess Kuan Yin (*see p.314*); in Tibet he is male and reincarnated in a number of compassionate kings of the region. In Pure Land Buddhism he accompanies Amitabha and welcomes souls to Paradise. Avalokiteshvara is portrayed in various ways. He may have eleven heads, symbolizing his main virtues, or 1,000 arms, representing his many powers.

Bodhidharma

✦ Buddhism
📖 *Bodhisattva*

A historical figure, Bodhidharma was a Buddhist monk said to be from southern India, who sailed to China, arriving there in about 527CE. He taught a meditative kind of Buddhism, famously telling the emperor of China that enlightenment does not come through good deeds, but through meditation. His Buddhism became known in China as Chan—and when it spread to Japan became Zen. Chan and Zen Buddhists still honor Bodhidharma as their founder. He is said to have spent nine years meditating and to have lost the use of his legs as a result. He is also seen as a smiling figure, who brings good luck and protection.

Maitreya

✦ Buddhist
📖 Buddha; *bodhisattva*

Maitreya is the "Buddha to come," a figure who waits in a special heaven, called Tusita, for the time when he will come to Earth and take up the role currently played by the Buddha himself. This will be after a long period during which Buddhism has fallen out of favor and is no longer practiced—meaning that Buddhists generally see Maitreya as a kind of Messiah figure. The name Maitreya means "the friendly one" and this *bodhisattva* is especially popular in Tibet and in China and Japan, where he takes the form of the smiling, joyful "Happy Buddha."

Followers of Maitreya believe he will one day come to Earth to renew faith in Buddhism.

THE EASTERN RELIGIONS

The deities of the Eastern religions range from the founders of faiths such as Confucianism and Daoism to the hundreds of immortals who populate the pantheon of Chinese popular religion, and the countless spirits or *kami* of Shinto.

The Jade Emperor

✦ Daoism, Chinese popular religion   📖 King of the gods

The Jade Emperor is the most exalted god in the Chinese pantheon. Because of his eminent role, he is an extremely important figure both in the mythology of Daoism and in Chinese popular religion, but he is actually a remote figure and ordinary mortals never come into contact with him.

As usual with Daoist deities, there is a story that explains how the Jade Emperor (known variously in Chinese as Yü Huang, Shang Ti, and Yü Ti) became an immortal. He was originally the son of a king and queen who, for a long time, had been childless. When the gods finally granted the king and queen their wish for a son, the child grew to be both wise and good looking. In due course he succeeded his father as king, but later gave up his throne to meditate. By doing so he achieved great knowledge and devoted the rest of his life to healing the sick. When he died, his outstanding qualities won him the role of ruler of the immortals. The emperor's wife was Hsi Wang Mu and the pair were said to rule a court in Heaven that was a mirror image of the imperial court on Earth.

The Jade Emperor was first said to be the ruler of Heaven under the Sung emperor Chen Tsung (998–1023CE).

Chen Tsung commissioned a statue of the god and had it placed in his court, where the Jade Emperor became the main imperial deity. Today, he is still seen as the most eminent Daoist deity.

The Daoist Court of Infernal Justice, in which unworthy souls are condemned to Hell, is presided over by the Jade Emperor (*top center*).

Confucius

✦ Confucianism 📖 Teacher, founder of Confucianism

Few facts are known about the life of the great Chinese sage Confucius. We do know that he was born in the mid-sixth century BCE, came from the small state of Lu, and was a minor official who devoted his life to teaching.

The conversations and opinions of Confucius are recorded in the Analects, which were written down in the 3rd century BCE. The Analects reveal that Confucius was a man with a great respect for tradition—many of his moral principles were held in China long before his birth. Nevertheless, Confucius's moral ideal was to become a humane person, and this value was the one above all that he passed on to his followers. According to Confucius, the way to attain this humane virtue was through the act of loving our fellow human beings and behaving with integrity in all things.

A great sage and teacher, Confucius attracted many followers, who spread his ideas around China. Although he received very little recognition at the court of Lu, when Confucius died the Duke of Lu built a temple to his memory. Ever since, although his role is primarily that of a philosopher and ethical teacher, Confucius has also been seen as one of the Chinese immortals.

Laozi

✦ Daoism, Chinese popular religion 📖 Teacher, founder of Daoism

Little is known about Laozi's life, although one account says that he was keeper of records at the Chou court in Loyang, which was the capital of Chou China. He may have been the author of the Daode jing, but even this is not certain.

Laozi is closely identified with the concept of the Dao (see pp.254–245) as the absolute foundation of all things. Because of his importance—and his status as a Daoist immortal—a number of remarkable legends grew up around him. According to one, Laozi was born from his mother's left side after a pregnancy that lasted eight years. Tales like this are especially important to adherents of Chinese popular religion; most Daoists are more interested in Laozi's philosophy.

In one story Laozi, shown here riding his ox, is said to have possessed white hair and a long beard from the moment of his birth.

Kuan Yin

✦ Buddhism, Daoism, Chinese popular religion   📖 *Bodhisattva*

Kuan Yin is the Chinese female form of the male Indian Buddha Avalokiteshvara (*see p.311*). As well as being a prominent figure in Eastern Buddhism, she is one of the most worshipped goddesses in Chinese popular religion.

The name Kuan Yin means "hearing the cry" and this merciful *bodhisattva* (or sometimes goddess) is renowned for her caring and compassion, and loved because she is said to take heed of the appeals of all people who are in difficulty. Kuan Yin is particularly attentive to childless couples (especially those who want a son). She is said to help women through the pain and trauma of childbirth, and she cares for children when they are sick. In addition, devotees appeal to her if they have a family crisis that involves children. Many also see her as a patron of

travelers and seafarers, and will often make an offering to Kuan Yin before embarking upon a journey.

Known as Kannon in Japan, Kuan Yin is popular throughout the East, and has many shrines and temples dedicated to her worship. She is often depicted with her head slightly bowed, looking downward, to indicate that she is watching over the world. She is also sometimes shown with many arms— a reference to the story that the Buddha Amidha gave her a thousand arms with which to dispense her mercy to the thousands who ask for her help.

Pa Hsein

✦ Daoism, Chinese popular religion   📖 Eight immortals

The Pa Hsien or Eight Immortals are a group of Daoist deities who are among the most popular and familiar in Chinese communities. Their images are common in temples, homes, and Chinese opera. As a group they encompass old and young people, rich and poor, and man and woman.

The Eight Immortals include people who were made immortal because of their good deeds, such as the selfless hermits Chung-li Ch'üan, Ts'ao Kuo-chiu, and Lan Ts'ai-ho, who lived the life of a beggar, giving away most of what people gave him. Lü Tung-pin and Li T'ieh-kuai, who learned the way of Daoism from Laozi himself, gained immortality because they were great thinkers. The others were immortals through some special

powers: the magician Chang-kuo Lao; Han Hsiang-tzu, who made flowers bloom from a clump of earth; and Ho Hsien-ku, the female immortal who could float over land.

A theatrical prop showing the Eight Immortals crossing the sea hints at the popularity of this Daoist story.

Tsao Chün

✦ Daoism, Chinese popular religion
📖 God of the hearth, kitchen god

Tsao Chün has a very specific role in Chinese popular religion. Throughout the year he observes people's behavior, then he makes an annual report on their conduct to the Jade Emperor. Families hang a print of the god's image, or a plaque bearing his name, over the stove in their kitchen. A few days before New Year, they make an offering to the god, and then burn the print so that the rising smoke takes the god and his message to the Jade Emperor. The family buys a new image or plaque to hang in the kitchen for the forthcoming year.

Zhong Kui

✦ Daoism, Chinese popular religion
📖 Destroyer of demons

With his fearsome expression and protruding eyes, his unkempt clothes and worn boots, Zhong Kui is one of the most awesome Chinese deities. This is fitting, because it is his job to help people by destroying the demons that bring trouble and disease. His legend says that, when he was mortal, he was treated unfairly in the civil service examinations and not given a high enough mark because of his ugly appearance. As a result, he committed suicide and, once immortal, devoted himself to roaming the world defeating sinister demons.

Fu Lu Shou

✦ Daoism, Chinese popular religion   📖 Three gods of happiness

Portrayed as a group of old men, the Fu Lu Shou, or "three gods of happiness," are probably the most familiar of all traditional Chinese deities. They are common in most Chinese communities, and are well known to Westerners from images in Chinese restaurants and other businesses.

The Fu Lu Shou are Fu Hsing, the god of happiness, Lu Hsing, the god of wealth, and Shou Hsing, the god of longevity. The "Hsing" element of their names is sometimes replaced with "Shen," meaning "spirit," which suggests beings who have never been mortals, in contrast to the deified humans who make up much of the Chinese pantheon. Together these gods represent the three qualities that Chinese people most want for themselves and their families. Although the trio are often portrayed as a group, the most popular is Fu Hsing. His image shows an old man, bald, with a high forehead, carrying a staff and a peach, the emblem of immortality.

The Daoist gods of happiness, good luck, and longevity represent the most sought-after attributes and virtues in Chinese culture.

Amaterasu

✦ Shinto   📖 Goddess of the sun

The sun goddess Amaterasu, daughter of Izanami and Izanagi, is one of the most important deities in Shinto. As well as controlling the life-giving force of the sun, she became the key deity in state Shinto and represented the vital link between the imperial family and the gods.

A number of stories about Amaterasu describe the problems that occur when she quarrels with her brother Susano, the storm god. In one story, Susano threw a flayed horse into the room where Amaterasu was weaving cloth. She was so annoyed that she went into exile, throwing the Earth into darkness. The other gods hatched a plan to bring her back, creating such a distraction outside the cave where she was hiding that she emerged in great curiosity.

To make sure that the Earth was peaceful in the future, the sun goddess sent Ninigi, her grandson, to rule there. He founded the imperial dynasty, giving the Japanese emperors a lineage stretching back to the gods. The claim that the imperial family was descended from the gods was finally renounced by Emperor Hirohito after World War II.

In Japan's creation myth, Amaterasu, goddess of the sun, was lured from a cave by a wild and comic dance performance by her sister, Ama-no-uzume.

Susano

✦ Shinto
📖 Storm god

When Susano was born—as a result of the creator-god Izanagi blowing his nose —he was given the sea to rule. Susano was disappointed at this because his siblings Amaterasu and Tsukiyomi had been given, respectively, the sun and the moon. So Susano caused frequent storms, upsetting the other gods and even killing one deity, Wakahirume, goddess of the dawn. As a result he was banished from Heaven. He was better behaved on Earth, bringing rain to help the crops grow, and planting strands of his hair on hills where they grew as trees.

Tsukiyomi

✦ Shinto
📖 God of the moon

The Japanese moon god was born from the water drops that fell from Izanagi's eye when he washed himself after visiting the underworld. When people observed the predictable waxing and waning of the moon, they began to see Tsukiyomi as a god who could foretell the future. Priests took detailed observations of the moon's phases and used them to predict future events. They used large bronze mirrors to look at the moon, for fear that if they looked Tsukiyomi directly in the face, the sight would drive them insane.

Izanami and Izanagi

✦ Shinto 📖 Creator deities

The goddess Izanami and the god Izanagi are the creator gods of Shinto mythology. They were commanded by the other gods and goddesses to "solidify" the Earth and to populate it with life. They also parented gods of nature.

Various accounts of the creation tell how Izanami and Izanagi stood looking down at the primal ocean from a rainbow, a celestial bridge, or the Milky Way. Izanagi took the jeweled spear of Heaven, dipped it into the water, and stirred. When he pulled out the spear, drops of salt water dripped from it and solidified to form the first island.

Next the pair of deities made love, as a result of which Izanami gave birth to the 14 islands of Japan. Izanami also gave birth to another generation of deities, who became gods of the fresh and salt water, the winds, and other natural phenomena.

The last of these deities, Kagutsuchi, was god of fire. He scorched Izanami as he was being born, ending her life, and she went down to the underworld. Izanagi wanted Izanami back, but when he journeyed to the underworld, he was so revolted by her rotting flesh that the pair became estranged, and thereafter the worlds of the living and dead were irrevocably separated.

Inari

✦ Shinto
📖 God of rice

Inari is the Shinto rice god and all-important controller of the food supply. He took over this responsibility after the death of Ukemochi. Inari is also seen as god of prosperity in Japan, because those who could grow a good rice crop would become wealthy.

His image is seen quite widely in Japanese culture. He is usually portrayed as a benevolent old man, often sitting on a full sack of rice, and sometimes giving out food to others. Portraits of Inari often show him with a pair of foxes, who act as his messengers.

Inari fox statues (kitsune) celebrate the companions of Inari, and, some believe, an earthly form taken by the rice deity.

Ukemochi

✦ Shinto
📖 Food goddess

Ukemochi was the original food goddess of Shinto. She was married to Inari, who was originally a celestial blacksmith and skilled craftsman. But one day there was a disaster. The moon god Tsukiyomi, who was the consort of Amaterasu, killed Ukemochi. This led to upset among the gods. Amaterasu and Tsukiyomi fell out and henceforward the sun and moon were forever separated and did not appear together in the sky.

Meanwhile, the supply of food on Earth was threatened because there was no longer a goddess to protect the rice harvests. Inari, distressed at the loss of Ukemochi and the threat of famine, became the rice god himself.

DIRECTORY

DIRECTORY

This section contains quick-reference information on a variety of topics, from the names and roles of major deities in the religions of the ancient world to prominent Christian saints. There are also reference charts of world faiths and new religious movements.

ANCIENT GREEK AND ROMAN DEITIES		
GREEK NAME	ROMAN NAME	ROLE
Aphrodite	Venus	Goddess of love
Apollo	Apollo	God of sun and the arts
Ares	Mars	God of war
Artemis	Diana	Goddess of hunting
Asclepius	Aesculapius	God of healing
Athena	Minerva	Goddess of wisdom
Demeter	Ceres	Goddess of the harvest
Dionysus	Bacchus	God of wine
Eos	Aurora	Goddess of the dawn
Eros	Cupid	God of love
Hephaestus	Vulcan	God of fire
Hera	Juno	Queen of the gods
Hermes	Mercury	Messenger; god of finance
Hestia	Vesta	Goddess of the hearth
Pan	Faunus	God of fields, woods, and shepherds
Poseidon	Neptune	God of the sea
Zeus	Jupiter	Sky god; ruler of the gods

The archery of Cupid was thought to inspire love, his mischievous spirit mirrored in its unpredictable nature.

ANCIENT NORSE DEITIES

NAME	ROLE
Aegir	God of the sea
Freyja	Goddess of fertility
Freyr	God of plenty and fertility
Frigg	Goddess of rain
Hel	Queen of the dead
Idun	Goddess of spring
Loki	Trickster god
Njord	God of the wind
Norns	Fates
Odin	God of war, ruler of Asgard
Thor	God of thunder
Tyr	Sky god

Thor was a formidable, hammer-wielding god in Norse lore.

ANCIENT CELTIC DEITIES

NAME	ROLE
Andraste	Goddess of victory
Belanus	God of fire and light
Cernunnos	God of fertility
Epona	Goddess of the earth
Grannus	God of springs and the sun
Mars	God of war
Nantosuelta	Consort of Sucellus
Nehalennia	Goddess of seafarers
Sucellus	King of the gods; god of fertility
Taranis	God of thunder
Triple Mother	Goddesses of plenty and motherhood

Epona

ANCIENT AMERICAN DEITIES

NAME	ROLE
MAYA	
Ah Puch	God of death
Chac	God of rain
Hun Hunahpu	God of maize
Itzamna	God of creation, day, and night
Ixchel	Goddess of fertility and childbirth
Kinich-Ahau	God of the sun
Tohil	God of fire and sacrifice
AZTEC	
Chalchiuhtlicue	Goddess of rivers, lakes, and springs
Huitzilopochtli	God of war
Mictlantecuhtli	God of death
Quetzalcoatl	God of life and the wind
Tezcatlipoca	God of creation
Xipe Totec	God of spring
Xolotl	God of the ball game
INCA	
Ilyap'a	God of the thunder
Inti	God of the sun
Mama Cocha	Goddess of water and rain
Mama Kilya	Goddess of the moon
Pacha Mama	Goddess of the earth
Viracocha	God of creation

Chichen Itza, a Maya sacred site in Yucatan, Mexico. The pyramid is named the *Castillo*.

BRANCHES OF BUDDHISM

The diagram shows the two main strands of Buddhism: the older Theravada strand, and the more diverse Mahayana, which embraces many different beliefs and is the main source of branches as diverse as Tibetan and Zen Buddhism.

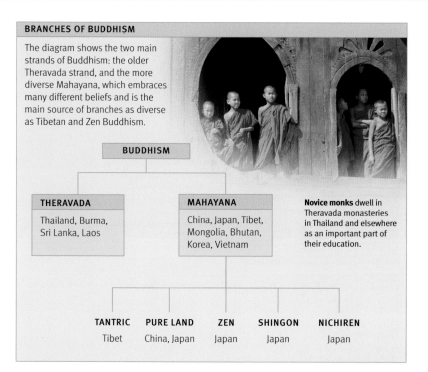

BUDDHISM

THERAVADA

Thailand, Burma, Sri Lanka, Laos

MAHAYANA

China, Japan, Tibet, Mongolia, Bhutan, Korea, Vietnam

Novice monks dwell in Theravada monasteries in Thailand and elsewhere as an important part of their education.

TANTRIC
Tibet

PURE LAND
China, Japan

ZEN
Japan

SHINGON
Japan

NICHIREN
Japan

THE SIKH GURUS

NO.	NAME	MAIN ACHIEVEMENTS
1	Guru Nanak (1469–1539)	Founder of Sikhism
2	Guru Angad (1504–1552)	Deviser of the Gurmukhi script
3	Guru Amar Das (1479–1574)	Introduced Sikh birth and funerary rituals
4	Guru Ram Das (1534–1581)	Founder of Amritsar
5	Guru Arjan (1563–1606)	Built the Golden Temple
6	Guru Hargobind (1595–1644)	Proclaimed the military role of the Sikh leader
7	Guru Har Rai (1630–1661)	Lived a simple life in a hill village
8	Guru Har Krishnan (1656–1664)	Succeeded his father, but died when still a boy
9	Guru Tegh Bahadur (1621–1675)	Founder of the Sikh center of Anandpur
10	Guru Gobind Singh (1666–1708)	Founder of the Khalsa

Guru Nanak appears with two companions—Bala, a Hindu, and Mardana, a Muslim— on a fresco in Amritsar, India.

BOOKS OF THE BIBLE

OLD TESTAMENT	BOOKS

Pentateuch

The first five books of the Bible, known to Christians as the Pentateuch, also make up the Jewish Torah. They describe the creation of the cosmos, the Fall of humankind, the ancestors of Israel, the captivity of the Jews in Egypt and their departure, or Exodus, and the giving of God's law to Moses.

Genesis
Exodus
Leviticus
Numbers
Deuteronomy

Ruth and her husband, Boaz, amid his wheat fields. The Book of Ruth highlights the value of compassion and kind conduct.

Historical books

These books tell the story of the Jewish people from the point at which they reach the Promised Land of Israel, through the settlement of Israel and the establishment of the monarchy, to the destruction of Israel and Judah by the empires of Assyria and Babylon, and the return of the Jews from exile in Babylonia.

Joshua
Judges
Ruth
1 Samuel
2 Samuel
1 Kings
2 Kings
1 Chronicles
2 Chronicles
Ezra
Nehemiah
Esther

Wisdom literature

Amongst the most poetic texts in the Bible, the wisdom books deal with a variety of different issues connected with human life and faith. Their texts embrace such subjects as suffering (in Job and Ecclesiastes), love (the Song of Songs), and everyday life (Proverbs). The Psalms are a series of hymns of praise and laments.

Job
Psalms
Proverbs
Ecclesiastes
Song of Songs

Prophets

The ancient prophets were the men who acted as God's spokesmen. Their sayings guided the people in all kinds of ways, from helping in everyday situations (such as finding lost farm animals) to making predictions about the future of the Jewish people. For Christians, many of their sayings look forward to the coming of Jesus.

Isaiah
Jeremiah
Lamentations
Ezekiel
Daniel
Hosea
Joel
Amos
Obadiah
Jonah
Micah
Nahum
Habakkuk
Zephaniah
Haggai
Zechariah
Malachi

The prophet Amos is often pictured blowing a horn because he likened the awesome power of God's will to a resounding trumpet call.

NEW TESTAMENT	BOOKS

Gospels

The four Gospels describe the birth, life, ministry, crucifixion, and resurrection of Jesus. The first three Gospels, Matthew, Mark, and Luke, share much material and are known as the Synoptic Gospels—Mark may have been the first to be written, and may have been used as a source by Matthew and Luke. John's Gospel is different from the others, placing more emphasis on the spiritual significance of Jesus's story.

Matthew
Mark
Luke
John

Acts

The Book of Acts tells how the Apostles responded to the resurrection of Jesus and how they carried on his ministry, in the process founding the Christian church. It describes the early Christians' various missionary journeys around the Mediterranean, most notably those of Peter, Philip, Barnabas, and Paul.

Acts

Epistles

The Epistles are a series a letters sent by early church leaders to Christians —both individuals and entire communities—in the Mediterranean world. They both helped the early Christian communities stay in touch with each other and allowed leaders to explain important points of teaching. Those written by St. Paul have been some of the most widely read of all Christian texts. The final book of the Bible, Revelation, describes visions of the heavens and the end of the world.

Romans
1 Corinthians
2 Corinthians
Galatians
Ephesians
Philippians
Colossians
1 Thessalonians
2 Thessalonians
1 Timothy
2 Timothy
Titus
Philemon
Hebrews
James
1 Peter
2 Peter
1 John
2 John
3 John
Jude
Revelation

Christianity came to the New World with European colonists and remains strong in countries such as Brazil, where this statue of Christ is located.

CHRISTIAN SAINTS

NAME	MAIN FEAST DAY	PATRONAGE
Andrew	November 30	Scotland, Russia
Anne	July 26	Brittany, Canada
Antony of Egypt	January 17	Monks
Augustine of Hippo	August 28	
Bartholomew	August 24	Tanners
Benedict of Nursia	July 11	Europe
Bernadette	April 16	
Catherine of Alexandria	November 25	
Cecilia	November 22	Musicians
Christopher	July 25	Travellers
Dominic	August 8	
Dunstan	May 19	Jewellers
Francis of Assisi	October 4	Conservation
George	April 23	England
Gregory the Great	September 3	
Ignatius of Loyola	July 31	Spiritual exercises and retreats
James the Great	July 25	Pilgrims
James the Less	May 3	
Jerome	September 30	Scholars
Joan of Arc	May 30	France
John the Apostle	December 27	Writers
John the Baptist	August 29	
Joseph	March 19	Fathers and families
Lucy	December 13	The blind
Mark	April 25	Secretaries
Mary, Blessed Virgin		Various
Matthew	May 14	Accountants
Patrick	March 17	Ireland
Paul	June 29	Greece, Malta
Peter	June 29	Popes
Philip	May 3	
Stephen	December 26	Bricklayers, deacons

John the Baptist

The death of St. Francis

NOTABLE POPES

For almost 2,000 years, from the time of St. Peter, the popes have led the Catholic Church. The early popes wielded great worldly power, influencing the fates of nations and rulers. Today, they see their role as spiritual leaders of the vast Catholic flock.

NAME	DATES OF PONTIFICATE	MAIN ACHIEVEMENTS
Leo I (the Great)	440–461CE	Promoted the doctrine of the Incarnation; made treaties with the Huns and Vandals to protect Rome; canonized.
Gregory I (the Great)	590–604CE	Reformed the administration, services, and ritual of the church; sent Augustine to convert the English; tried to end slavery; systematized chants used in church; canonized.
Gregory VII	1073–1085	Clashed with the Holy Roman Emperor, Henry IV, challenging the emperor's practice of appointing his own nominees to senior positions in the church.
Urban II	1088–1099	Launched the First Crusade, an attempt to overcome Muslim domination of the eastern Mediterranean that led to a string of regrettable wars between Christians and Muslims.
Innocent III	1198–1216	Repressed church abuses; encouraged the friars; built up both the spiritual and worldly power of papacy to its greatest extent.
Boniface VIII	1294–1303	Asserted the supreme power of the papacy, but his authority was challenged by the French king, Philip IV, who had him imprisoned; soon the papacy moved to Avignon.
Gregory XI	1370–1378	Freed the papacy from French political influence by moving it back to Rome—against the wishes of the French.
Martin V	1417–1431	Ended a period of division known as the Great Schism, during which rival popes had ruled from Rome, Avignon, and Pisa.
Julius II	1503–1513	Led political and military efforts to restore papal power in Italy; became an outstanding patron of the arts, employing both Raphael and Michelangelo.
Paul III	1534–1549	Began the Counter-Reformation, the movement opposing the reforms of the Protestants; excommunicated King Henry VIII of England; instituted the Jesuit order.
Pius IX	1846–1878	Undertook numerous reforms, in areas from relations with the Jews to church government, but lost political power, the Papal States being transferred to the new kingdom of Italy in 1870.
Pius X	1903–1914	Condemned modernism in theology, but upheld social reforms and reformed canon law; canonized.
John XXIII	1958–1963	Sought to promote unity between the various Christian churches and to modernize the Catholic Church, with mixed results.
John Paul II	1978–2005	Traveled and preached widely; defended the church in areas, such as communist countries, where it was threatened; fostered good relations with other churches.

NEW RELIGIOUS MOVEMENTS (FROM 20TH CENTURY)			
NAME	**FOUNDER AND DATE**	**AREA OF ORIGIN**	**ROOTS**
Nazareth Baptist Church	Isaiah Shembe, 1911	Africa	C
Iglesia ni Cristo	Felix Manalo, 1914	Philippines	C
Native American Church	1918	US	
Kimbanguism	Simon Kimbangu, 1921	Africa	C
Sufi Movement	Hazrat Inayat Khan, 1923	Holland	I
Reiyūkai	Kubo Kakutaro, 1924	Japan	B
Zion Christian Church	Engenas Barnabas Lekganyane, 1924	Africa	C
Cao Dai	Ngo Van Chieu, 1926	Vietnam	
Rastfarianism	Haile Selassie I, 1930	Africa/Caribbean	C
Seicho-No-le	Masaharu Taniguchi, 1930	Japan	
Soka Gakkai	Tsunesaburo Makiguchi, 1930	Japan	B
Nation of Islam	Fard Muhammad, 1931	US	I
Sekai Kyusiekyo (orig. Dai Nihon Kannonkai)	Mokichi Okada, 1935	Japan	
The Brahma Kumaris	Prajapita Brahma, 1936	Sindh, India (now Pakistan)	H
Shinnyoen	Shinjo Ito, 1936	Japan	B
Rissho Kōseikai	Nikkyo Niwano, 1938	Japan	B
Hao Hoa	Huynh Phu So, 1939	Vietnam	B
Kodo Kyodan	Okano Shodo, 1939	Japan	B
The Church of Shaiva Siddhanta	Gurudeva, 1949	Sri Lanka/ US	H
Satya Sai Baba Society	Satya Sai Baba, 1950	India	H
Church of Scientology	L. Ron Hubbard, 1954	US	
Family Federation for World Peace and Unification (Unification Ch.)	Sun Myung Moon, 1954 (as Unification Ch)	Korea	C
Transcendental Meditation	Maharishi Mahesh Yogi, 1957	India	H

NAME	FOUNDER AND DATE	AREA OF ORIGIN	ROOTS
Mahikari	Okada Kotama, 1959	Japan	Sh
International Society for Krishna Consciousness (ISKCON)	Abhay Charan De (Prabhupada), 1965	India	H
Osho	Rajneesh Chandra Mohan, 1966	India	B
Friends of the Western Buddhist Order (FWBO; originally WBO)	Dennis Lingwood (Sangharakshita), 1967	UK	B
The Family (Children of God)	David Brandt Berg, 1968 (as COG)	US	C
Bawa Muhaiyaddeen Fellowship	Bawa Muhaiyaddeen, 1971	US	I
Elan Vital (formerly Divine Light Mission)	Prem Pal Singh Rawat (Maharaji), 1971	India/US	
Santi Asoke Movement	Bodhirak, 1973	Thailand	B
Gush Emunim	Tzevi Yehudah Kook (Rav Kook), 1974	Israel	J
Dhammakaya Foundation	Luang Phaw Sot, 1977	Thailand	B
Falun Gong	Li Hongzhi, 1999	China	

Key: B=Buddhism C=Christianity H=Hinduism I=Islam J=Judaism Sh=Shinto

A member of ISKCON makes an offering at a Hare Krishna temple. ISKCON promotes devotion to the god Krisna and strict moral discipline as a route to salvation.

MAJOR WORLD FAITHS

NAME	PLACE, DATE	FOUNDER	GOD
Baha'i Faith	Tehran, Iran, 1863	Baha'u'llah	One God, who has been revealed through various religions
Buddhism	Northeastern India, *ca.*520BCE	Siddhartha Gautama, the Buddha	Nontheistic in Theravada tradition; polytheistic in Mahayana tradition
Cao Dai	Vietnam, 1926	Ngo Van Chieu	One God; also founders of other faiths (such as Buddhism, Daoism, Christianity) revered
Chinese traditional religion	Unknown, prehistoric	Indigenous	Many deities; twin forces of *yin* and *yang*
Christianity	Israel, *ca.*30CE	Jesus Christ	One God, in form of Holy Trinity of Father, Son, and Holy Spirit
Church of Christ (Scientist)	Massachusetts, 1879	Mary Baker Eddy	One God, no Holy Trinity
Church of Jesus Christ of Latter-Day Saints (Mormons)	New York, 1830	Joseph Smith	Three separate beings: God the Father; Jesus Christ the Son; the Holy Spirit

AFTERLIFE	TEXTS	ADHERENTS
Soul journeys toward or away from God	Writings of Baha'u'llah	5–7 million
Reincarnation; ultimate enlightenment	Pali canon, Mahayana sutras, etc.	360 million
Reincarnation; ultimate *nirvana* or Heaven	Cao Dai canon	4–6 million
Reincarnation or temporary hell; ultimate paradise	n/a	400 million
Eternal Heaven or Hell	Bible (Old and New Testaments)	2 billion
Heaven as a divine state of mind	Bible; Science and Health with Key to the Scriptures	Up to 400,000
Return to Spirit World; then Resurrection	Bible; Book of Mormon	12 million

Pope Benedict XVI celebrates the opening ceremony of Holy Mass for the XI Ordinary General Assembly of the Synod of Bishops. The Synod, which gathers Catholic bishops from around the world, meets once every three years, and discusses a topic selected by the pope.

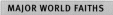

MAJOR WORLD FAITHS

NAME	PLACE, DATE	FOUNDER	GOD
Confucianism	China, 6th/5th centuries BCE	Confucius	n/a
Daoism	China, ca.550BCE	Laozi	Dao pervades everything; *yin* and *yang*
Falun Gong	China, 1992	Li Hongzhi	Many gods and spiritual beings
Family Federation for World Peace and Unification (formerly Unification Church)	South Korea, 1954	Sun Myung Moon	One God, often expressed as a dual being
Hinduism	India, prehistoric	Indigenous	Many deities, all manifestations of one supreme reality
Islam	Saudi Arabia, revealed in 7th century CE	n/a; Muhammad is Prophet	One God
Jainism	India, ca.550BCE	Mahavira	Many gods

At the Hindu Dussehra festival, an Indian woman makes an offering of lotus flowers at a statue of the river goddess Ganga. Dussehra celebrates the conquest of evil, especially by figures such as Rama and the goddess Durga.

AFTERLIFE	TEXTS	ADHERENTS
n/a	Confucian classics	5–6 million
Reversion to state of non-being	Daode jing; Zhuangzi	20 million
n/a	Writings of Master Li, including Zhuan Falun	10 million
Eternal	Sun Myung Moon, The Divine Principle	3 million (official figure)
Reincarnation; ultimate enlightenment	The Vedas, Upanishads, and Sanskrit epics	900 million
Paradise or Hell	The Qu'ran (scripture); Hadith (tradition)	1.3 billion
Reincarnation; ultimate liberation	Mahavira's teachings	4 million

MAJOR WORLD FAITHS

NAME	PLACE, DATE	FOUNDER	GOD
Judaism	Israel, ca.1300BCE	Abraham, Moses	One God
Rastafarianism	Jamaica, 1930s	Haile Selassie I	One, Jah, incarnate in Jesus and Haile Selassie
Church of Scientology	California, 1954	L. Ron Hubbard	n/a
Shinto	Japan, prehistoric	Indigenous	Many gods and spirits (kami)
Sikhism	Punjab, India, 1500CE	Guru Nanak	One God
Tenrikyo	Japan, 1838	Nakayama Miki	God the Parent
Zoroastrianism	Iran, 6th century BCE	Zoroaster	One God (Ahura Mazda) but dualism also embraced
Voodoo	West Africa, unknown	Indigenous	Many gods and spirits
Wicca	Britain, 1950s, but based on ancient beliefs	Gerald Gardner	Usually two: the Goddess and the God

Shinto priests, seen here taking part in a large ceremony at a shrine, are responsible for a range of rituals, including rites of birth, coming of age, and marriage (though not normally funerary rites), along with ceremonies marking calendar festivals.

AFTERLIFE	TEXTS	ADHERENTS
World to Come	Hebrew Bible; Talmud	14 million
In some cases	Holy Piby	1 million
Reincarnation	Dianetics, Scientology, and other writings of L. Ron Hubbard	
Some humans become *kami* after death	Kojiki, Nihon-gi	3–4 million
Reincarnation; ultimate merging with God	Adi Granth	23 million
n/a	Mikagurauta, Ofudesaki, Osashizu	1 million
Heaven or (temporary) Hell	Avesta	200,000
As spirit	n/a	8 million
Reincarnation; ultimate "Summerland"	n/a	1–3 million

FESTIVALS AND HOLY DAYS

These pages give the dates of some of the most important holy days and festivals in the major world religions. Several faiths use their own calendars, which vary from the Western or Gregorian calendar; in addition, some festivals, such as the Christian Easter, occur on different days in each year. The Western dates of festivals for one typical year, 2009, have therefore been given here.

JUDAISM

The Jewish calendar is lunisolar—there are 12 lunar months of 29 or 30 days each, and in some years an extra month is added to compensate for the difference between lunar and solar years. Therefore, the dates of Jewish holy days vary in relation to the Gregorian calendar.

WESTERN DATE	EVENT	HEBREW CALENDAR
March 10	Purim	Adar 14
April 9	Pesach (Passover)	Nisan 15–21 or 15–22
May 29	Shavuot (Pentecost)	Sivan 6–7
September 19	Rosh Hashanah (New Year)	Tishrei 1
September 28	Yom Kippur (Day of Atonement)	Tishrei 10
October 3	Sukkot (Tabernacles)	Tishrei 15–20
October 11	Simchat Torah (Rejoicing of the Law)	Tishrei 22 or 23
December 12	Hanukkah (Festival of Lights)	Kislev 25

CHRISTIANITY

Mary with Jesus

DATE AND/OR MONTH	EVENT
February/March/April	Lent (40 days)
April 10	Good Friday
April 12	Easter Sunday
May 21	Ascension
May 31	Pentecost (Whitsun)
November 29	Advent Sunday (Advent begins)
December 25	Christmas

ISLAM

Islamic holy days are celebrated on fixed dates in the Islamic calendar, which uses a lunar year about 11 days shorter than the solar year used in the Gregorian calendar. For this reason, Islamic holy days usually shift 11 days earlier in each Gregorian year. Dates in the Islamic calendar are also subject to local sightings of the new moon.

DATE AND/OR MONTH	EVENT	ISLAMIC CALENDAR
March 9/14	Mawlid an-Nabi (Birthday of the Prophet)	Rabi' Al-Awwal 12
July 19	Laylat al-Mi'raj (The Night Journey)	Rajab 27
August 22	Start of month of fasting	Ramadan
September 16	Laylat al-Qadr (Night of Descent of Qur'an)	Ramadan 27
September 21	'Id al-Fitr (Feast of Fast-breaking)	Shawwal 1
Dec 18–Jan 15	Month of the Pilgrimage	Dhu L-Hijjah
November 28	'Id al-Adha (Feast of Sacrifice)	Dhu L-Hijjah 10

HINDUISM

DATE AND/OR MONTH	EVENT
March/April	Holi
April 3	Ram Navami (Birthday of Rama)
July/August	Krisna Janamastami (Birthday of Krisna)
September	Ganesh Chaturthi (Celebration of Ganesh)
Sept 19–October 17	Navaratri or Durga Puja (Festival of the goddess Durga)
September 28	Dussehra (Celebration of the death of demon king Ravana)
October 17	Diwali (Festival of Lights)

BUDDHISM

DATE AND/OR MONTH	EVENT
May 9	Vesak (Birth, Enlightenment, and Death of the Buddha)
July onward	Vassa (Rainy season)
October/November	Kathina (Thanksgiving to monks)
October/November	Asalha Puja (Giving of the Buddha's First Sermon)

Reclining Buddha

SIKHISM

DATE AND/OR MONTH	EVENT
November 2	Birthday of Guru Nanak (alternate date 14 April)
November 24	Martyrdom of Guru Tegh Bahadur
January 5	Birthday of Guru Gobind Singh
March 11–13	Hola Mohalla (Sikh version of Holi)
April 13	Punjabi New Year
June 16	Martyrdom of Guru Arjan

The Guru Granth Sahib

GROWTH IN RELIGIONS

In spite of the critiques of religion put forward by scientists and atheists, the number of people professing some kind of religious belief is actually increasing worldwide. Christianity and Islam, because they are proselytizing religions (which seek to recruit new followers), and because they have been taken up widely in areas such as Africa and western Asia, are now espoused by more than half of the world's total population. Other faiths, such as Hinduism, have also expanded. Religions grow for all kinds of reasons—the missionary activities of their adherents, population increases, and the need to fill "belief

vacuums" that occur when primal or other local religions go into decline. The results of this growth vary widely. While many people in Africa left behind primal beliefs to embrace the many new Christian churches that have been founded there, in Europe dissatisfaction with Christianity and increased openness to ideas from the East has led to a modest growth in Buddhism and other Eastern religions. New religious movements, small in comparison with the older faiths, have also proliferated. Religion is proving adaptable to changing social needs.

This chart shows the approximate numbers of adherents to the largest faiths as percentages of the world's total population, along with those who have no religious affiliation. There is no way of assessing these figures precisely on a global scale, but the chart gives a broad idea of the relative sizes of the religions.

Christianity 32%

Other 2.4%

Judaism 0.25%

Sikhism 0.35%

Buddhism 5.5%

Chinese traditional 5.5%

Primal religions 5.5%

Islam 21%

Non-religious 15%

Hinduism 12.5%

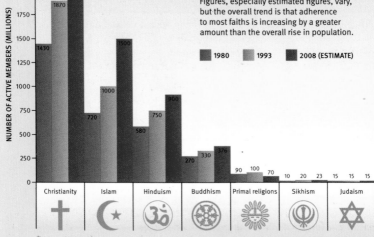

This chart shows the approximate numbers (in millions) of active members of the larger world religions over recent decades. Figures, especially estimated figures, vary, but the overall trend is that adherence to most faiths is increasing by a greater amount than the overall rise in population.

- 1980
- 1993
- 2008 (ESTIMATE)

NUMBER OF ACTIVE MEMBERS (MILLIONS)

Religion	1980	1993	2008 (EST.)
Christianity	1430	1870	2100
Islam	720	1000	1500
Hinduism	580	750	900
Buddhism	270	330	376
Primal religions	90	100	70
Sikhism	10	20	23
Judaism	15	15	15

GLOSSARY

Key
(**B**) Buddhism
(**C**) Christianity
(**D**) Daoism and other Chinese religions
(**H**) Hinduism
(**I**) Islam
(**J**) Judaism
(**Jn**) Jainism
(**S**) Sikhism
(**Sh**) Shinto
(**Z**) Zoroastrianism

ACTS, BOOK OF (**C**) Fifth book of the New Testament of the Bible, describing the first Christian church in Jerusalem and Palestine, the preaching of the Gospel to non-Jews, and the conversion and some of the missionary work of St. Paul.

ADI GRANTH (**S**) *See* Guru Granth Sahib.

ADUR (**Z**) The sacred fire that burns in Zoroastrian temples and holy places; also known as *atar*.

ADVENT (**C**) Period of approximately four weeks leading up to Christmas in the Christian calendar.

AHIMSA (**H**) (**B**) (**Jn**) Doctrine of non-violence of both thought and action.

AKHAND PATH (**S**) Complete and uninterrupted reading out loud of the Guru Granth Sahib.

ALLAH (**I**) The name of the One God.

AMRIT (**S**) Sweetened holy water used in religious ceremonies; the specific Sikh ceremony of initiation.

ANATTA (**B**) State of "no-self" or freedom from ego to which Buddhists aspire.

ANNUNCIATION (**C**) The announcement, made by the angel Gabriel to the Virgin Mary, that Mary was to be the mother of the Son of God.

ASKENAZIM (**J**) Jews who come from eastern and central Europe, and people descended from them who live in other parts of the world.

ASSUMPTION (**C**) Doctrine that affirms that when the Virgin Mary died both her body and soul were taken up to heaven.

ATAR (**Z**) *See* Adur.

ATMAN (**H**) The individual self.

AVATAR (**H**) Incarnation of a particular Hindu deity; especially the various incarnations of the god Visnu.

BAPTISM (**C**) The sacrament in which a person is admitted to the Christian church through a ritual involving the sprinkling of water or immersion in water.

BAR MITZVAH (**J**) Literally, "son of the commandment." The ceremony marking a Jewish boy's admission to the adult religious community; also the state of having reached religious adulthood. The equivalent for girls, celebrated in some Jewish congregations, is *bat mitzvah*.

BAT MITZVAH (**J**) *See* Bar Mitzvah.

BEATITUDES (**C**) Promises of blessing, particularly the series of declarations made by Jesus and recalled in the Gospel of St. Matthew beginning, "Blessed are the poor in spirit."

BIBLE (**C**) The collection of books that constitute the sacred text of Christianity. The Christian Bible is made up of the Old Testament, which includes the Jewish books of the law, Jewish history, and the prophets, and the New Testament, which deals with the life and work of Jesus and his followers. *See also* Hebrew Bible.

BODHISATTVA (**B**) Someone on the path to becoming a Buddha who puts off final enlightenment in order to help other people to reach the same state.

BRAHMAN (**H**) The supreme being. All other gods are aspects of Brahman.

BUDDHA (**B**) An enlightened being. All people are believed to have the potential to achieve this state.

CANONIZATION (**C**) The process by which the Christian church declares that a person is a saint.

CANTOR (J) Person who is trained to lead a prayer service in a synagogue.

CARDINAL (C) Senior priest in the Roman Catholic church who has been appointed by the pope as a member of the "College" that assists him in governing the church and that elects a successor when the pope dies.

CATHEDRAL (C) Christian church that is the headquarters of a bishop or archbishop, and contains his *cathedra* or throne.

CHAURI (S) Object like a whisk, waved over the Guru Granth Sahib as a mark of respect.

CHRIST (C) Literally, "anointed one;" title given to Jesus.

CONFIRMATION (C) Ritual in which those who have been baptized confirm their Christian faith. This ritual often involves those who have been baptized as infants and confirm their faith as adolescents or adults.

COVENANT (J) Agreement between God and the Jewish people identifying the Jews as the group chosen to play a special role in the relationship between God and humanity.

DAO (D) Path or way that an individual aims to follow; underlying way or pattern that governs the working of nature.

DARSHAN (H) Worship of a deity by means of viewing an image of the god or goddess.

DHARMA (H) The underlying path or pattern that characterizes the cosmos and the Earth. Also refers to the moral path that a specific person must follow.

DIASPORA (J) The dispersal of the Jewish population around the world, mainly as a result of persecution.

DIOCESE (C) The area under the spiritual leadership of a bishop.

EIGHTFOLD PATH (B) The path of disciplined living that Buddhists follow in the hope of breaking free of the cycle of death and rebirth. A diligent follower of the path aims to achieve correct understanding, intention (or thought), speech, conduct, occupation, effort, mindfulness, and concentration.

EUCHARIST (C) *See* Holy Communion.

GOSPELS (C) The four books of the New Testament of the Bible, attributed to the apostles Matthew, Mark, Luke, and John, which tell the story of Jesus's life and teachings. The term Gospel is also used to mean the content of Christian teaching.

GRACE (C) The power of God, which can enter into people, enabling them to do good or to achieve salvation.

GRANTHI (S) Official who takes care of the Guru Granth Sahib and the *gurdwara* in which it is housed. A granthi is also a skilled reader of the sacred book.

GURDWARA (S) Sikh temple; place where the Guru Granth Sahib is housed.

GURMUKHI (S) Script in which the Sikh sacred texts are written, said to have been devised by Guru Argand.

GURU (S) One of the ten founder-leaders of Sikhism.

GURU GRANTH SAHIB (S) The Sikh sacred book, also known as the Adi Granth.

HADITH (I) Traditional accounts of the deeds and teachings of the prophet Muhammad; the second source of Islamic law and moral guidance after the Qur'an.

HAGGADAH (J) Body of teaching of the early rabbis, containing legends, historical narratives, and ethical precepts.

HAJJ (I) Pilgrimage to Mecca. All Muslims hope to make this journey at some point in their lives, and the pilgrimage is the fourth of the Five Pillars of Islam.

HALAL (I) Conduct that is permitted; specifically, the permitted method of slaughtering livestock and the meat from such correctly slaughtered animals.

HASID (J) Member of a Jewish group founded in the 18th century which places a strong emphasis on mysticism.

HEBREW BIBLE (J) Collection of sacred writings that form the basis of Judaism, including the Torah, Prophets, and other sacred texts; the equivalent of the Old Testament in the Christian Bible.

HOLY COMMUNION (C) Rite involving the taking of wine and bread as the blood and body of Christ; known as Mass in Catholicism, Eucharist in the Anglican Church, and the Liturgy in the various Orthodox Churches.

HOLY TRINITY (C) The threefold God, consisting of the Father, Son, and Holy Spirit, three persons forming one godly being.

ICON (C) Sacred image, usually depicting Christ or one of the saints, used as a focus for devotion, especially in the Orthodox Churches.

IMAM (I) Leader of prayers in a mosque; or, one of the twelve great leaders of the Muslim community in the early period of the faith.

INCARNATION (C) Belief that in the person of Jesus Christ divine and human natures were made one.

ISRAEL (J) Eastern Mediterranean homeland of the Jewish people.

JINA (Jn) *See* Tirthankara.

JODO (B) *See* Pure Land.

KACCHA (S) Long shorts worn under other garments by Sikhs. One of the distinguishing "Five Ks" of Sikhism.

KAMI (Sh) Spirit or deity in Shinto religion. There are many thousands of *kami* in the Shinto pantheon.

KANGHA (S) Small comb worn in the hair by Sikhs. One of the distinguishing "Five Ks" of Sikhism.

KARA (S) Steel bangle worn by Sikhs on the right wrist. One of the distinguishing "Five Ks" of Sikhism.

KARMA (B) (H) The law of moral cause and effect that influences our rebirth after death.

KESH (S) Uncut hair. One of the distinguishing "Five Ks" of Sikhism.

KHALSA (S) The community of initiated Sikhs, founded by Guru Gobind Singh.

KHANDA (S) Two-edged sword of the kind used by Guru Gobind Singh in the ritual that marked the founding of the Khalsa; now a symbol of Sikhism.

KIRPAN (S) Sword worn by Sikhs. One of the distinguishing "Five Ks" of Sikhism.

KIRTAN (S) Hymn-singing that forms an important part of Sikh worship.

KOSHER (J) Term describing food that is fit to eat, according to Jewish dietary laws.

LAMA (B) Adept spiritual teacher in Tibetan Buddhism, specifically one who has undergone particular yogic or other training or one who is considered to be the reincarnation of a previous spiritual leader.

MANDALA (B) Sacred diagram, usually depicting the cosmos, used as a focus for meditation and in other rituals, especially in Tibetan Buddhism.

MASS (C) *See* Holy Communion.

MATSURI (Sh) Festival or ritual in Shinto. Many *matsuri* festivals feature public processions of shrine-bearing worshippers.

MIHRAB (I) Niche in the prayer hall of a mosque, which indicates the direction of Mecca and therefore the way people should face during prayers.

MINARET (I) Tower forming part of many mosques, from which the call to prayer is made.

MITZVAH (J) Commandment from God; specifically either one of the 10 principal commandments or one of the 613 instructions found in the Torah.

MOKSA (H) Release from the round of life, death, and rebirth.

MOOL MANTAR (S) Statement of Sikh belief in the Oneness of God, composed by Guru Nanak; also called the Mool Mantra.

MUEZZIN (I) Official who calls Muslims to prayer five times each day.

MULLAH (I) Islamic religious scholar, who may also preach and lead prayers in a mosque.

MURTI (H) Image or statue of a deity, seen as the dwelling-place or embodiment of the deity.

NABI (I) Prophet. A number of notable Jewish figures are considered prophets in Islam, as is Jesus; Muhammad is the last and greatest Islamic prophet.

NIRVANA (B) State of final liberation from the round of death and rebirth.

PARABLE (C) Story used to illustrate religious teaching, especially those used by Jesus, of which more than 30 are related in the Gospels.

PUJA (H) Worship.

PURE LAND (B) Paradise where, according to some forms of Buddhism, the souls of believers dwell after death; known in Japanese Buddhism as *Jodo*.

QI (D) The life-force or energy that animates things in the world according to traditional Chinese philosophy.

QUR'AN (I) The words of God, revealed to the Prophet Muhammad and later written down to form the sacred text of Islam.

RABBI (J) Teacher and spiritual leader of a Jewish community.

RAK'A (I) Sequence of movements made during prayers.

RAMADAN (I) Ninth month of the Islamic calendar; the month of fasting.

REFORMATION (C) Movement for the reform of the Christian church that began in the 16th century and led to the foundation of Protestant churches.

REFORM JUDAISM (J) Branch of Judaism that reinterprets the faith in the light of modern civilization.

SACRAMENTS (C) The solemn rites of Christianity. The Catholic and Orthodox churches recognize seven sacraments:

baptism, confirmation, Mass, penance, ordination, marriage, and unction (anointing with holy oil). Most Protestant churches recognize only baptism and the Eucharist as sacraments.

SADHU (H) Person who has dedicated their life to seeking God.

SALAT (I) Prayer; this is the second of the Five Pillars of Islam, and Muslims are expected to pray five times each day.

SAT GURU (S) The Sikh name for God; literally, "true Teacher."

SAWM (I) Fasting, especially during the month of Ramadan; the fourth of the Five Pillars of Islam.

SABBATH (J) The rest day of the Jewish week, lasting from sunset on Friday to sunset on Saturday.

SAMSARA (B) The cycle of life, death, and rebirth which marks existence for the majority of beings on Earth.

SANGHA (B) Order of Buddhist monks and nuns.

SEPHARDIM (J) Jews who come from Spain, Portugal, or North Africa, or their descendants.

SEVA (S) Service to others, one of the important principles of Sikhism.

SHAHADA (I) The Muslim profession of faith, translated into English as, "There is no god but God; Muhammad is the messenger of God." The *Shahada* is the first and most important of the Five Pillars of Islam.

SHARIA (I) The path to be followed in Muslim life and, therefore, Islamic law, based on the Qur'an and the Hadith.

SHI'I (I) One of the two main groups of Muslims, consisting of the people who believe that Muhammad's cousin 'Ali was his rightful successor as Caliph. *See also* Sunni.

STUPA (B) Architectural feature in the form of a bell-shaped mound containing relics of a Buddha or *bodhisattva*, often forming the main part of a temple.

SUFI (I) Member of one of a number of mystical Islamic groups, whose beliefs centre on a personal relationship with God. Associated with the ecstatic religious dances of the Dervishes.

SUNNI (I) One of the two main groups of Muslims, followers of those who supported an elected Caliphate. *See also* Shi'i.

SURA (I) Chapter of the Qur'an.

SUTRA (B) Collection of teachings, especially sayings attributed to the Buddha.

SYNOD (C) Formal meeting of church leaders, particularly bishops.

TALMUD (J) Text made up of a body of discussion and interpretation of the Torah, compiled by scholars and rabbis, and a source of ethical advice and instruction, especially to Orthodox Jews.

TANTRA (B) Text used in some kinds of Buddhism (mainly in Tibet) to help users to reach enlightenment, or practices based on such a text.

TIRTHANKARA (Jn) One of the 24 spiritual teachers or *Jinas* who have shown the way of the Jain faith.

TORAH (J) The first five books of the Hebrew Bible, seen as representing the teaching given by God to Moses on Mount Sinai.

TRIMURTI (H) Trio of principal Hindu gods—Brahma, Visnu, and Siva—or threefold image of them.

TRINITY (C) *See* Holy Trinity.

UMMA' (I) The Islamic community as a whole.

UPANISHADS (H) Sacred texts containing Hindu philosophical teachings.

VEDAS (H) Collections of hymns and other writings in praise of the Hindu deities.

YANG (D) One of the two over-riding principles in the cosmos, representing the male aspect of life; seen in terms of its interplay with *yin*.

YASASNA (Z) Ritual or worship in Zoroastrianism.

YHWH (J) The four letters representing the name of God in Judaism, said to be too holy to utter, but traditionally pronounced "Yahweh."

YIN (D) One of the two over-riding principles in the cosmos, representing the female aspect of life; seen in terms of its interplay with *yang*.

YOGA (H) Discipline, involving bodily exercises, mental work, and spiritual practices, designed to bring about *moksa*.

ZAKAT (I) The giving of alms in the form of a tax to help the poor; the third Pillar of Islam.

ZIONISM (J) Movement supporting the Jewish state of Israel. Zionism began in the 19th century to promote the foundation of a Jewish state.

ZURVAN (Z) Time; in some forms of Zoroastrianism, Zurvan is the primal essence of being, from which both the Wise Lord Ahura Mazda and the Hostile Spirit Angra Mainyu are said to derive.

INDEX

Page numbers in **bold** refer to main entries; numbers in *italics* refer to illustrations/captions.

ACKNOWLEDGMENTS

Author's acknowledgments
Philip Wilkinson would like to thank Zoë Brooks, John Brooks, Peter Ashley, Neil Philip, John Wilkinson, and James Wills for their support, and the team at cobalt id for their painstaking editing and design.

Publisher's acknowledgments
The publisher would like to thank Judy Barratt for her considered editorial input, Dr. Kim Bryan for proofreading, Dorothy Frame for indexing, and Charles Wills for co-ordinating Americanization.

Picture credits
The publisher would like to thank the following for their kind permission to reproduce their photographs:

(Key: a-above; b-below/bottom; c-center; f-far; l-left; r-right; t-top)

1 Corbis: Ajay Verma/Reuters (t). 2-3 iStockphoto.com: Gianluca Fabrizio (c). 4 Getty Images: John Henry Claude Wilson (c). 5 Corbis: Michele Falzone/JAI (c). 6-7 Getty Images: W.E. Garrett (c). 9 Corbis: Steve Raymer (t). iStockphoto.com: Wong Yuliang (c). Dorling Kindersley: Alan Hills © The British Museum (cb). 10-11 Getty Images: joSon (c). 10-35 iStockphoto.com: Elnur Amikishiyev (ftl/ftr). 12-13 iStockphoto.com: Simon Podgorsek (t). Alamy Images: Eddie Gerald (c). 14-15 Corbis: Antonio Dasiparu/epa (b). 15 Corbis: Reuters (tr). 16 Alamy Images: Interfoto Pressebildagentur (cb). 16-17 Getty Images: Martin Gray (t). 17 Alamy Images: ArkReligion.com (tr). 19 iStockphoto.com: Adivin (t). Alamy Images: Chris Willson (cb). 20 Alamy Images: ArkReligion.com (ct). 20-21 Getty Images: Martin Puddy (b). 22 Corbis: Nik Wheeler (bl). 23 Corbis: Summerfield Press (b). 24 Alamy Images: Sally and Richard Greenhill (b). 25 Corbis: Elder Neville/Corbis Sygma (tr). Getty Images: Stock Montage/Contributor (c). 26-27 Corbis: Dimitri Messinis/Pool/epa (b). 27 Corbis: Richard Hamilton Smith (cb). 28 Alamy Images: Photolocate (ct). Corbis: Abir Abdullah/epa (bl). 29 Getty Images: Bridgeman Art Library (t). 30 Corbis: Arte & Immagini srl (cr). Alamy Images: Israel images (bl). 31 Corbis: Sherwin Crasto/Reuters (b). 32 iStockphoto.com: Jeremy Edwards (b). 33 Getty Images: Keren Su (t). 36-37 Corbis: Bruno Morandi (b). 38-39 Alamy Images: World Pictures (b). 39 Dorling Kindersley: Ray Moller © Dorling Kindersley, Courtesy of the Powell-Cotton Museum, Kent (ct). 40-55 iStockphoto.com: Phil Scroggs (ftl/ftr). World Religions Photo Library: A.Humphery (ct). 41 Corbis: Kevin Fleming (b). 42-43 iStockphoto.com: Tony Sanchez-Espinosa (b). 43 Corbis: Daniel Lainé (tl). 44-45 Corbis: Bob Krist (c). 46 Corbis: Krause, Johansen/Archivo Iconografico, SA (c). 47 Corbis: Gallo Images (t). Alamy Images: Penny Tweedie (b). 48-49 Alamy Images: Images&Stories (b). 49 Getty Images: David Edwards (tr). 50 Alamy Images: Christine Osborne Pictures (t). Corbis: Mariana Bazo/Reuters (bl). 51 Dorling Kindersley: Lynton Gardiner © Dorling Kindersley, Courtesy of The American Museum of Natural History (t). Corbis: Anders Ryman (b). 52 Dorling Kindersley: Dave King © Dorling Kindersley, Courtesy of the Pitt Rivers Museum, University of Oxford (c). Corbis: Patrick Durand (b). 53 Alamy Images: Ian M L Jones (c). 54 Corbis: Bob Krist (b). 55 Alamy: Bill Bachman (tl). Corbis: Werner Forman (b). 56-57 iStockphoto.com: konradlew (t). Alamy Images: ImageState (b). 58-59 Alamy Images: Dennis Cox (b). 58-157 iStockphoto.com: Dean Turner (ftl/ftr). 59 Getty Images: Joseph Asarfati (tl). 60 Corbis: Richard T. Nowitz (c). 61 iStockphoto.com: Boris Katsman (t). 62 akg-images: Erich Lessing (t). 62-63 Corbis: Bojan Brecelj (b). 63 Alamy Images: Russell Kord (tl). 64 akg-images: Michael Teller (t). 65 Corbis: Richard T. Nowitz (t). Alamy Images: Mary Evans Picture Library (br). 66 akg-images: Erich Lessing (b). 67 Alamy Images: Eddie Gerald (t). Getty Images: AFP (c). 68 Corbis: Dr. John C. Trever, Ph. D. (tr). 68-69 Corbis: Philippe Lissac/Godong (b). 69 Alamy Images: Danita Delimont (t). 70-71 Getty Images: Kenneth Garrett (c). 72 The Bridgeman Art Library: Louvre, Paris, France (bl). 73 Corbis: Ted Spiegel (b). 74 Corbis: Richard T. Nowitz (b). 75 Alamy Images: Mike Abrahams (tl). Corbis: Richard T. Nowitz (br). 76 Alamy Images: Israel images (t). 77 iStockphoto.com: Chaim Danzinger (t). 77 Corbis: Fred de Noyelle/Godong (b). 78 Corbis: Robert Mulder/Godong (t). 79 Getty Images: Jewish School (t). Alamy Images: Danny Yanai (b). 80 iStockphoto.com: sterling_photo (c). Getty Images: Getty Images (bl). 81 Getty Images: Getty Images (cr). 82 Alamy Images: Terry Smith Images' Arkansas Picture Library (tr). Corbis: Silvia Morara (b).

83 Getty Images: Time & Life Pictures (br). 84 Alamy Images: Visual Arts Library (London) (c). 85 iStockphoto.com: Felix Möckel (t). 86 iStockphoto.com: Maurice Lee Choong Min (tr). 86-87 Getty Images: Leonardo da Vinci (b). 87 Dorling Kindersley: The British Museum (t). 88 Corbis: Bettmann (br). 89 Corbis: Phillipe Lissac/Godong (b). 90 Corbis: Christophe Boisvieux (t). Alamy Images: Interfoto Pressebildagentur (br). 91 Corbis: Arte & Immagini srl (b). 92-93 Corbis: National Gallery Collection; By kind permission of the Trustees of the National Gallery, London (b). 94 Alamy Images: Mary Evans Picture Library (t). 94-95 Alamy Images: Visual Arts Library (London) (b). 95 Corbis: Sucheta Das/Reuters (tr). 96 Alamy Images: Profimedia International s.r.o. (tr). The Bridgeman Art Library: Dreweatt Neate Fine Art Auctioneers, Newbury, Berks, UK (tr). 97 iStockphoto.com: Wolfgang Steiner (b). 98-99 Corbis: Angelo Benalcazar/Reuters (c). 100 iStockphoto.com: Nina Shannon (t). 101 Corbis: Philippe Lissac/Godong (tl). Alamy Images: Popperfoto (b). 102 Alamy Images: Peter Horree (t). Corbis: Phillipe Lissac/Godong (bl). 103 Corbis: Fine Art Photographic Library (b). 104 iStockphoto.com: Adeline Lim (t). Corbis: Vittoriano Rastelli (b). 105 Corbis: Andrea Jemolo (t). John Gillmoure (b). 106 Alamy Images: North Wind Picture Archives (c). 107 Getty Images: Vision (b). 108 Alamy: Visual Arts Library (London) (c). Corbis: Philippe Giraud/Goodlook (b). 109 Alamy Images: Bob Pardue (b). 110 Alamy Images: Mary Evans Picture Library (b). Konrad Zelazowski (b). 111 Alamy Images: J Marshall, Tribaleye Images (b). 112 Alamy Images: Jeff Greenberg (c). ClassicStock (b). 113 Alamy Images: North Wind Picture Archives (c). 114 Alamy Images: Robert Harding Picture Library Ltd (b). 115 Alamy Images: Oliver Benn (c). Corbis: Arne Hodalic (b). 116 Alamy Images: Tim Graham/TravelStockCollection, Homer Sykes (b). 117 Alamy Images: Sally and Richard Greenhill (c). Corbis: Reuters (b). 119 Alamy Images: Steve Skjold (b). 120 Alamy Images: Mary Evans Picture Library (c). 121 Alamy Images: dbimages (b). 122-123 Corbis: Brooks Kraft/Sygma (b). 123 Corbis: Ricardo Azoury (b). 124 Corbis: Jane Sweeney/Robert Harding World Imagery (b). 125 iStockphoto.com: Mary Ann Shmueli (t). 126 The Art Archive: Turkish and Islamic Art Museum Istanbul/HarperCollins Publishers (ct). Turkish and Islamic Art Museum Istanbul/Alfredo Dagli Orti (bl). 127 Alamy Images: Rolf Richardson (b). 128 Corbis: Werner Forman (c). 128-129 Corbis: Michele Falzone/JAI (b). 129 Alamy Images: Visual Arts Library (London) (c). 130 World Religions Photo Library: C.Osborne (c). 130-131 Alamy Images: Tengku Mohd Yusof (b). 132 World Religions Photo Library: C.Osborne (c). 132-133 Corbis: Faisal Mahmood/Reuters (b). 133 iStockphoto.com: Jodi Jacobson (b). 134 Alamy Images: World Religions Photo Library (b). 135 iStockphoto.com: Robert Churchill (t). 136 Corbis: Penny Tweedie (b). 137 World Religions Photo Library: C.Osborne (c). Corbis: Atlantide Phototravel (b). 138 Alamy Images: Charles O. Cecil (t). 139 Corbis: Kazuyoshi Nomachi (b). 140 Corbis: Danilo Krstanovic/Reuters (t). 141 Alamy Images: Gary Roebuck (tr). Sally and Richard Greenhill (b). 142-143 Corbis: Kazuyoshi Nomachi (c). 144 The Bridgeman Art Library: Private Collection, The Stapleton Collection (c). 145 Corbis: Kazuyoshi Nomachi (c). 146 The Art Archive: Topkapi Museum Istanbul/Gianni Dagli Orti (c). Corbis: Warren Clarke/epa (b). 147 Getty Images: Hulton Archive (c). 148 Alamy Images: Felipe Trueba (c). 149 Corbis: Paul Almasy (t). 150 iStockphoto.com: Graeme Gilmour (c). Corbis: Roger Wood (b). 151 Corbis: Reuters (t). 152 Alamy Images: F. Jack Jackson (c). 153 Alamy Images: Massimo Pizzotti (c). 154-155 Getty Images: AFP (b). 155 Corbis: Paul Almasy (t). 156 World Religions Photo Library: Paul Gapper (c). Getty Images: AFP (b). 156-157 Alamy Images: Dinodia Images (b). 158-159 iStockphoto.com: Robert Churchill (t). Alamy Images: Jeremy Horner (b). 160 Alamy Images: World Religions Photo Library (c). 160-161 Corbis: Robert Holmes (b). 160-232 iStockphoto.com: iStockphoto.com (ftl/ftr). 162 Alamy Images: ArkReligion.com (c). 163 Alamy Images: Wolfgang Kaehler (t). 164 Corbis: Robert Harding Picture Library Ltd (ct). Eye Ubiquitous (br). 165 Alamy Images: Simon Reddy (t). 166 The Bridgeman Art Library: Bristol City Museum and Art Gallery, UK (tr). 167 Alamy Images: John Warburton-Lee Photography (t). Corbis: Underwood & Underwood (t). 168 World Religions Photo Library: C.Osborne (ct). 169 iStockphoto.com: Nilesh Bhange (b). 170 Corbis: Francis G. Mayer (ct). Alamy Images: Dinodia Images (bl). 170-171 Corbis: Robert Maass (b). 172 Corbis: Christophe Boisvieux (b). 173 World Religions Photo Library: Louise B.Duran (b). 174 Corbis: Anders Ryman (ct). Corbis: Bob Krist (b). 175 Corbis: FAYAZ KABLI/Reuters (b). 176-177 Getty Images: Panoramic Images (c). 178 iStockphoto.com: Keith Molloy (t). Alamy Images: Dinodia Images (br). 179

Corbis: Alen MacWeeney (ct). Rafiqur Rahman/Reuters (b). 180 Alamy Images: Eddie Gerald (tr). 181 Corbis: Christophe Boisvieux (b). 182 Corbis: Alen MacWeeney (c). 183 iStockphoto.com: Micha Rosenwirth (t). 184 Corbis: Leonard de Selva (b). 185 Alamy Images: Maciej Wojtkowiak (tr). Dorling Kindersley: Steve Teague (b). 186 Alamy Images: dbimages (b). 187 Corbis: Tim Page (t). iStockphoto.com: Dušan Zidar (b). 188 akg-images: British Library (t). 188-189 Corbis: Jon Hicks/ Corbis (b). 189 Alamy Images: Maciej Wojtkowiak (t). 190 Alamy Images: Maciej Wojtkowiak (tr). iStockphoto.com: Kathy Konkle (b). 191 iStockphoto.com: Adrian Hillman (b). 192 World Religions Photo Library: G.B.Mukherji (b). 193 Corbis: Christine Kolisch (cr). 194 Alamy Images: Simon Attrill (t). 194-195 Alamy Images: Iain Masterton (b). 196 Corbis: Alison Wright (b). 196-197 Alamy Images: Fredrik Renander (b). 197 Dorling Kindersley: Steve Teague © Dorling Kindersley (ct). 198-199 Corbis: STR/epa (c). 200 Corbis: Rungroj Yongrit/epa (b). 201 Alamy Images: Chris Wong (tr). 202 Corbis: Lindsay Hebberd (ct). Catherine Karnow (t). 203 Alamy Images: Frederick Fearn (tr). 204 Alamy Images: Sherab (ct). 204-205 Alamy Images: D. Hurst (b). 205 iStockphoto.com: Fiona Mark (tr). 206 Corbis: Tim Page (br). 207 Alamy Images: Gianni Muratore (c). 208 Corbis: Munish Sharma/Reuters (c). 209 Alamy Images: ArkReligion.com (t). 210 Alamy Images: ArkReligion.com (c). 210-211 Alamy Images: Pakistan Images (b). 211 Corbis: Kapoor Baldev/Sygma (tr). Alamy Images: Interfoto Pressebildagentur (t). 214 Alamy Images: ArkReligion.com (ct). Corbis: Gunter Marx Photography (br). 215 Corbis: Michael Freeman (b). 216-217 Getty Images: Narinder Nanu AFP (t). 217 Alamy Images: World Religions Photo Library (c). 218 Corbis: Noshir Desai (cr). 218-219 Alamy Images: Indiapicture (b). 220-221 Alamy Images: Paul Doyle (c). 222-223 Corbis: Lindsay Hebberd (b). 223 Corbis: Ashley Cooper (tl). 224 Corbis: Manjunath Kiran/epa (c). 225 Alamy Images: Blaine Harrington III (b). 226-227 Corbis: Peter Guttman (b). 228 Corbis: Angelo Hornak (ct). Charles & Josette Lenars (br). 228-229 Corbis: Christophe Boisvieux (t). 230-231 Corbis: Gideon Mendel (b). 231 Corbis: Werner Forman (ct). 232 World Religions Photo Library: Louise B.Duran (bl). 233 Alamy Images: Dinodia Images (t). 234-235 iStockphoto. com: Arnold Lee (t). Corbis: David Ball (b). 236 Getty Images: Bridgeman (ct). 236-237 Corbis: Frank Lukasseck (b). 236-271 iStockphoto.com: Anne de Haas (ftl/ftr). 238 Alamy Images: Iain Masterton (c). 239 Alamy Images: Martin Norris (t). 241 Corbis: Bettmann (b). Mary Evans Picture Library: Mary Evans Picture Library (br). 242 Mary Evans Picture Library: Mary Evans Picture Library (b). 243 iStockphoto.com: Hector Joseph Lumang (t). 244 Mary Evans Picture Library: Mary Evans Picture Library (ct). 245 Alamy Images: dbimages (b). 246-247 Getty Images: DAJ (c). 248 Alamy Images: Expuesto, Nicolas Randall (b). 249 Corbis: Lowell Georgia (b). 250 Getty Images: Rex Butcher (b). 251 iStockphoto.com: Manuel Velasco (t). 252 Corbis: Liu Liqun (tr). 252-253 Corbis: Free Agents Limited (b). 253 Dorling Kindersley: Dorling Kindersley/Ashmolean Museum, Oxford (ct). 254 Corbis: Lordprice Collection (ct). iStockphoto.com: Orr Zahavi (br). 256-257 Corbis: Angelo Cavalli/zefa (b). 258-259 Alamy Images: David Noton Photography (b). 259 Corbis: Michel Setboun (tl). 260-261 Getty Images: AFP (b). 261 Alamy Images: David Seawell (tl). Mark Harwood (b). 262 Corbis: Yuriko Nakao/Reuters (c). 263 Corbis: David Higgs (t). 264 Alamy Images: Ei Katsumata (bl). 265 Alamy Images: SAV (tr). Corbis: Michael Freeman (b). 266 Alamy Images: The Photolibrary Wales (ct). Corbis: Michael S. Yamashita (b). 267 Alamy Images: blitzjp (t). 268-269 Corbis: Tibor Bognár (b). 269 Alamy Images: Jochen Tack (tl). 270 Corbis: Reuters (b). 271 Alamy Images: FilterEast (tl). iStockphoto.com: Japan Things (b). 272-273 iStockphoto.com: Manfred Konrad (t). Anna Ceglinska (b). 274-275 Corbis: Wilfried Krecichwost/zefa (b). 274-289 iStockphoto.com: Jess Wiberg (ftl/ftr). 275 Corbis: Christophe Boisvieux (tr). 276 iStockphoto. com: iStockphoto.com (t). Alamy Images: Artur Gora (b). 277 Alamy Images: Phillip Augustavo (t). World Religions Photo Library: Nick Dawson (b). 278 Tenrikyo Europe (tr). Corbis: Robert Holmes (b). 279 Alamy Images: Jon Arnold Images Ltd (c). 280 Alamy Images: PCL (tr). iStockphoto.com: Joy Powers (b). 281 Corbis: Régis Bossu/Sygma (b). 282-283 Getty Images: Shaul Schwarz (t). 284 Corbis: Underwood & Underwood (t). iStockphoto.com: Lucian (b). 285 Getty Images: AFP (b). 286 iStockphoto.com: Baloncici (ct). 286-287 Alamy Images: Robert Harding Picture Library Ltd (b). 287 Alamy Images: Bildarchiv Monheim GmbH (tl). 288 Corbis: Bettmann (t). Alamy Images: Everynight Images (b). 289 Corbis: Rainer Holz/zefa (c). 290-291 Alamy Images: Rachael Bowes (t). Corbis: John Heseltine (b).

292-293 Corbis: Blaine Harrington III (b). 292-317 iStockphoto. com: iStockphoto.com (ftl/ftr). 293 Corbis: Leonard de Selva (ct). 294 Alamy Images: Visual Arts Library (London) (bl). 295 Alamy Images: Vova Pomortzeff (tr). Visual Arts Library (London) (bl). 296 Alamy Images: The Print Collector (tr). Corbis: Images.com (cl). 297 Alamy Images: Rough Guides (tr). 298 Corbis: Ali Meyer (ct). Alamy Images: Visual Arts Library (London) (cb). 299 Corbis: Alinari Archives (br). 300 Alamy Images: Photolocate (cb). 301 Alamy Images: Peter Barritt (b). 303 Corbis: Araldo de Luca (tr). iStockphoto.com: iStockphoto.com (b). 304 The Bridgeman Art Library: Edinburgh University Library, Scotland, With kind permission of the University of Edinburgh (cr). 305 The Bridgeman Art Library: Archives Charmet (b). 306 Alamy Images: ArkReligion.com (t). 307 Alamy Images: Peter Horree (b). 308 World Religions Photo Library: Louise B.Duran (cb). 309 World Religions Photo Library: Louise B.Duran (ct). Claire Stout (cb). 310 Corbis: Leonard de Selva (b). iStockphoto.com: Joris Van Ostaeyen (tl). 312 Bridgeman: Archives Charmet (br). 313 iStockphoto.com: Gautier Willaume (tl). akg-images: Visioars (br). 314 Corbis: Ron Chapple Stock (tl). Zeng Nian (br). 315 The Bridgeman Art Library: The Bridgeman Art Library (br). 316 Corbis: Asian Art & Archaeology, Inc. (tr). 317 Alamy Images: Tibor Bognar (bc). 318-319 Alamy Images: wael hamdan (t). Corbis: Olivier Martel (b). 320 Corbis: Araldo de Luca (b). 320-352 iStockphoto.com: iStockphoto.com (ftl/ftr). 321 akg-images: akg-images (t). Alamy Images: Visual Arts Library (London) (br). 322 Alamy Images: World Pictures (b). 323 iStockphoto.com: btrenkel (tr). Alamy Images: ArkReligion.com (b). 324 The Bridgeman Art Library: Dahesh Museum of Art (tl). Alamy Images: Visual Arts Library (London) (bl). 325 Alamy Images: camhi franck (br). 328 Alamy Images: Visual Arts Library (London) (tr). The Print Collector (b). 329 World Religions Photo Library: C.Osborne (b). 330-331 Corbis: Gianni Giansanti (b). 332-333 Corbis: Jayanta Shaw/Reuters (b). 334-335 Corbis: Kimimasa Mayama/epa (b). 336 Dorling Kindersley: Kim Sayer/ Dorling Kindersley © Dorling Kindersley, Hepworth Estate (cr). 337 Dorling Kindersley: Gary Ombler ©Dorling Kindersley, Courtesy of the Central London Ghurdwara (b).

Every effort has been made to trace the copyright holders. The publisher apologizes for any unintentional omission and would be pleased, in such cases, to place an acknowledgment in future editions of this book.

All other images © Dorling Kindersley
For further information see: www.dkimages.com